FUN AT HOME

with *Dian Thomas*

CRAFTS

KIDS

Holidays

Cooking

ideas

Publisher: Dian Thomas

Editors: Shannon M. Harmon
                      Dianne T. King

Art Director: DeeAnn Thaxton
Senior Illustrator: Greg Thurber
Illustrators: Janie Anderson
                      Deneice Liljenquist
                      DeeAnn Thaxton

Publishing Director: Greg Thurber

Designer: Richard Haight

Selected Titles: Gerry Bloomberg

Published by: The Dian Thomas Company
                      P.O. Box 171107
                      Holladay, Utah 84117

Copyright: 1993 The Dian Thomas
                      Company

Library of Congress Cataloging
and Publishing Information:

Thomas, Dian
     Fun at Home with Dian Thomas

ISBN: 0-9621257-9-2

NOTICE: The information in this book is true
and complete to the best of our knowledge. All
recommendations are made without guarantees
on the part of the author/publisher. The author/
publisher disclaims all liability in connection
with the use of this information.

Printed in the U.S.A.

Printing 10 9 8 7 6 5 4 3

Table of Contents

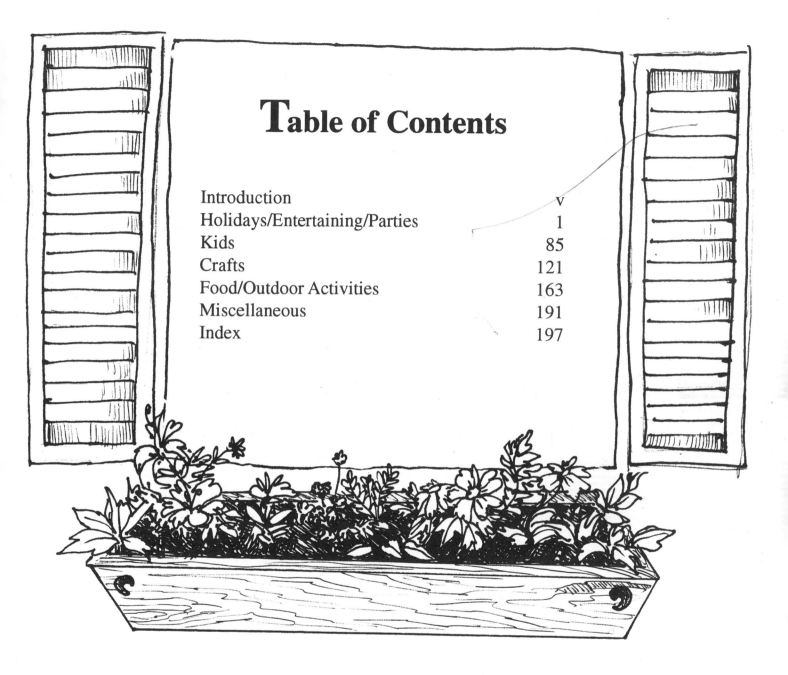

Dedicated to:

All my friends, the
viewers, who
for the past four
years have watched,
tried, and shared
my ideas.

Fun At Home

WITH

Dian Thomas

Introduction

Look inside and find a treasure trove of easy, inexpensive ideas, all of which have been shown over the past few years on the "Home" show and featured in many of the show's weekly newsletters. These do-it-yourself-or-with-your-children projects and recipes are great for families and friends to work on together.

You'll find a little of everything and something to please everyone—from wardrobe enhancers to birdhouses, from improvised outdoor camping equipment to pet dragons, and from holiday menus to edible ties.

As always, I encourage my readers, my friends, to use these ideas as springboards to their own creations. Adapt—and improve upon—any of what follows to come up with your own unique treasures and treasured times with those you love.

Holidays, Parties and Entertainment

New Year's Eve Extra-Ordinary Ideas

Take the Christmas ornaments off your tree and replace them with balloons. Before you blow up the balloons, place a small piece of paper with a New Year's wish written on it in each balloon, or fold dollar bills to put inside. Blow up the balloons and tie to the tree with ribbon, being very careful not to pop the balloons. Finish decorating the tree with confetti. At the end of the evening, pop the balloons and claim the wishes/money inside.

■ New Year's Time Capsule

Here are a few suggestions for your capsule: photos, newspaper articles, baseball cards, lists of your favorite things (foods, movies, TV shows, etc.), a list of goals, a lock of hair. Place items inside a pantyhose container. Decorate the outside by drawing faces on with permanent markers and gluing on yarn hair. Put inside a wide-mouth glass jar. On the outside of your jar write "Do Not Open until 1999" (or whatever year you decide to open it). Bury it in the backyard or hide in the basement or attic.

■ New Year's Party Invitations

For a unique New Year's party invitation, buy an inexpensive mask (or cut your own out of black poster paper). Cut a piece of cardstock the same size as the mask. Glue along the top of mask so it can be opened like a card. On the outside front, draw eyes on so they show through the mask eyeholes. On the back write information about the party.

■ Mirrored Ball Like the One Dropped On New Year's Eve

Use a large styrofoam ball or a basketball. Glue 1-inch mirror pieces all over, making sure to apply glue to both mirror and ball. Insert a hook into top to hang. Glue glitter between mirrors.

■ Decorated New Year's Mask

Pop out the lenses of a pair of inexpensive sunglasses. Cut out poster paper designs and glue on the front of the glasses; decorate with sequins, feathers, lace, etc.

■ New Year's Noisemakers

Use a clean, empty two-liter pop bottle filled with small buttons, bells, or dry beans to make a fun noisemaker. Decorate the outside of each pop bottle with felt, lace, buttons, and bows. Shake, using the bottle neck as the handle.

For another kind of noisemaker, put a few dry beans or small rocks in the end of a pop can. Tape the hole shut. Cut a piece of wrapping paper twice as wide as the circumference of the can. Roll the can up in the paper and tie both ends with ribbon.

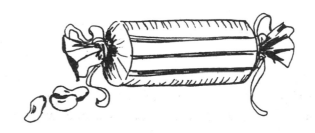

Hearts Are Forever

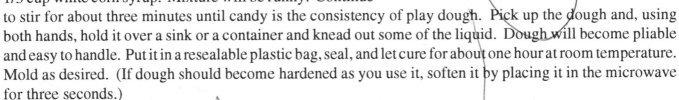

■ Chocolate Clay Valentines

▲ Basic Recipe:

Place 10 ounces of any color chocolate candy melts (with confectionary coating) in an oven-proof dish. Melt in a 150-degree oven for 20-25 minutes. Remove from oven. Stir in 1/3 cup white corn syrup. Mixture will be runny. Continue to stir for about three minutes until candy is the consistency of play dough. Pick up the dough and, using both hands, hold it over a sink or a container and knead out some of the liquid. Dough will become pliable and easy to handle. Put it in a resealable plastic bag, seal, and let cure for about one hour at room temperature. Mold as desired. (If dough should become hardened as you use it, soften it by placing it in the microwave for three seconds.)

Candy melts for use in the recipe are available at candy and confectionary counters in about 20 colors. Measure quantities in the recipe carefully. Do not double or quadruple the recipe. It is too difficult to knead larger batches.

◆ Variations:

● **Rose Bouquet**: Pinch off about 1/10 of the candy dough and roll it to a thickness of about 1/4". Use a small round cutter to cut out circles. Thin one side of each circle by pressing it with your palm on the counter. Use fingers and hands to shape the rose petals by overlapping the thick edges and furling out the thin edges of the circles. Wrap petals around each other to shape roses and rosebuds of desired sizes. Use skewers for stems. Bunch together in vases and tie with ribbons to make bouquets.

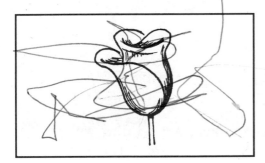

● **Corsages**: Follow directions for roses above. Assemble roses and rosebuds into a corsage and decorate with bows and hearts.

● **Heart Bouquet**: Roll dough to about 1/4" thickness. Cut with heart-shaped cookie cutters. If desired, different sizes and colors can be used. Place on wooden dowels and assemble 12 in a vase for a valentine bouquet. Tie with velvet bows.

● **Heart-Face Suckers**: Follow directions for heart bouquet above. Place on popsicle sticks instead of skewers. Decorate as desired. Wrap bunches of suckers in cellophane or plastic wrap. Tie with ribbon.

● **Teddy Bear Mold**: Use a small teddy bear mold that has been brushed with oil. Press chocolate dough into the mold. Invert. Add eyes and nose. Small candy hearts can be pressed into the tummies of the bears. Box and label "You make my life bearable."

● **"Peas Be My Valentine"**: Mold pale green chocolate dough into five small round balls by pinching off pieces of dough and rolling them between palms of hands. Shape a "pod" from darker green dough. Put molded peas into pod and place in a box. Attach label.

● **"I Love You a Bunch"**: Mold purple chocolate dough into marble shapes by rolling pieces between palms of hands. Stack together to resemble bunches of grapes. Place in a box and label.

● **"If You Carrot All for Me, You'll Be My Valentine"**: Mold orange chocolate dough into a carrot shape. Place in a box and label.

● **Hot Lips**: Shape red chocolate dough into lip shapes. Place two sugar cubes soaked in lemon extract and place in lips to resemble teeth. Just before serving, light the sugar cubes. You'll have flaming lips. You can place on top of vanilla ice cream.

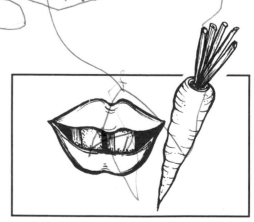

Valentine Projects for Kids

Here are some nifty Valentine projects especially for kids.

■ Toilet Tissue Cats

▲ *To make, you'll need*: One toilet tissue roll (per feline), pink toilet tissue, black puff paint or magic marker, cheek blush or red puff paint, brown or black posterboard or cardstock (for ears, paws, and tail), scissors, hot glue gun, yarn, bow, toothpick, small foil or paper heart shape, and small Valentine candies.

▼ *Directions*: With puff paint or marker, sponge or paint cat or lion face on tissue roll. Gently sponge on cat's cheeks with blush or puff paint and other facial features with black puff paint or marker. From posterboard or cardstock, cut out ears, tail, and paws, making sure posterboard paws cover bottom hole of tissue roll, and glue to roll. Top with yarn "fur" and bow. Fill roll's center with candy hearts, kisses, or other small Valentine candies. Glue a foil or paper heart with love message ("You're purr-fect" or "No lion—I love you") to a toothpick and push toothpick into top of tissue roll, or glue message in front.

■ Child's Peek-a-Boo Valentine

▲ *To make, you'll need*: Newspaper, scissors, red or pink posterboard, enough lace to trim outside edge of cut-out heart, hot glue gun, and puff paint (dark color of your choice).

▼ *Directions*: Make large heart from newspaper and use as pattern to cut heart shape from posterboard. (Make sure heart is big enough so that a hole large enough for your child's face can be cut from center.) Cut hole in middle for child's face. Decorate with hearts and cupids; glue lace around outer edge. Using puff paint, write "Be My Valentine." Variation: Make a smaller heart shape and cut out circle in middle. Place child's school or other recent photograph in the circle; decorate.

■ Valentine Lei

▲ To make, you'll need: Plastic wrap, small Valentine cookies or candies, and red or pink ribbon.

▼ Directions: Tear off a sheet of plastic wrap as long as you want your lei/necklace to be, plus six inches. Place candy/cookies face down and centered across the wrap, leaving three extra inches at each end. Fold top portion of wrap over sweets, then the bottom portion up. Scrunch wrap between pieces and tie with ribbon so that you have alternating goodies and bows. Knot both ends. Secure ends around neck with ribbon.

■ Heart-Shaped Cupcakes

Prepare cake batter. Line a muffin tin with paper baking cups. Place marble or small ball of aluminum foil in each cup between the paper liner and muffin tin. This makes a heart-shaped "mold" in which to bake cupcakes. Pour in batter and bake as usual. Don't fill cups too full or you'll lose the heart-shaped effect of the cupcake. Frost with a complementary flavor of icing and decorate with Valentine candies.

■ Super Kiss

▲ To make, you'll need: 1/4 c. margarine or butter, 1 10-oz. package marshmallows (about 50) or 4 c. miniature marshmallows, and 5 c. crispy rice cereal or chocolate crispy rice cereal.

▼ Directions: Melt margarine or butter in large saucepan over low heat. Add marshmallows and stir until completely melted. Stirring constantly, cook 3 minutes longer over low heat. Remove from heat. Add cereal and stir until well coated. Cool slightly but not completely. Butter your fingers. Press warm mixture into large, buttered funnels. When cool, unmold from funnel and wrap in plastic. Makes 2 to 4 large kisses.

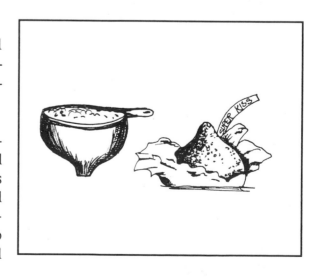

8

All-Occasion Messages

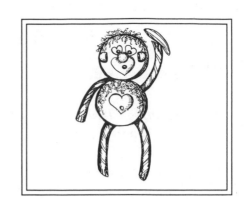

Perhaps no other day in the year was created more for fun—and whimsy—than Valentine's Day. But you can surprise your sweetie with one of these easy "I-made-it-myself" expressions of love on any day of the year.

■ SnoBall Caterpillar Cake

Arrange Hostess® SnoBall snack cakes to form body of caterpillar. Attach red or black licorice sticks to side of each snack cake for legs. Use two gumdrops for eyes and two pipe cleaners topped with gumdrops for antennae. For a birthday, just add a candle to each snack cake. This is wonderful for last-minute surprise parties.

■ Every Bunny Needs Some Bunny to Love

Snow bunnies aren't just on the slopes. Using a pink or white SnoBall snack cake as the head, attach small black gumdrop eyes and a small red gumdrop nose to the face with toothpick halves. For the mouth and whiskers, use red string licorice. The two ears can be cut from pink poster or construction paper and pushed into the top of the bunny head.

■ No Lion, I Love You!

The lion's head is a pink or white SnoBall snack cake; its mane is made of stick pretzels which fan out in all directions from the cake base. Also use stick pretzels for the whiskers. For the eyes use a small green gumdrop cut in half; add small purple candy "irises." The mouth is a 2"-3" piece of red string licorice. For the nose, cut off the flat end of a large red gumdrop. Cut the remaining piece in half vertically for the ears, and secure all gumdrop facial features to the SnoBall with toothpicks.

■ My Heart Beats for You

This drum is silent—but so easy to make. Using a Hostess® Ding Dong snack cake, pipe large connecting "x's" around the circumference with white frosting. For the drumsticks, use two pretzel sticks with a gumdrop stuck on one end of each.

■ Don't Forget I Love You

This elephant is an excellent "I Love You" reminder. Use a pink or white SnoBall snack cake for the body. The trunk is a 3-4" piece of red stick licorice, and the tail, attached to the opposite side of the cake, is a 4" piece of red string licorice. Using frosting to attach facial features, use two red hots candies for the eyes and place at the far right of the cake so the elephant appears to be "in profile." Cut a large orange gumdrop in half and use one piece for an ear (place in center of SnoBall). Two orange gumdrop feet attached to the bottom of the SnoBall with toothpicks complete the elephant.

■ Quit Clowning Around! Be My Friend!

This clown's head is a pink or white SnoBall snack cake, and his clown's hat is an inverted sugar cone (cone can be filled with candy, a small toy, or even jewelry). To make the face, use a black gumdrop cut in half vertically for the eyes; add purple candies to make "irises." The nose is a large red gumdrop, and the mouth is a 3" piece of red string licorice. Top the cupcake with toasted coconut "hair" (using frosting as glue). Invert the cone, decorated with heart candies, onto the SnoBall head and top cone with a large pink gumdrop.

■ A Squeeze and a Kiss

This squeeze and a kiss is almost as good as the real thing. Hang a note around a plastic squeeze-it container of Kool Aid® that reads "Here's a squeeze and a kiss." However, don't write the word "kiss"; instead, let a real Hershey's® Kiss stand for the word.

■ You Are Dino-mite!

To make a dinosaur to go with this special message, use a Hostess® Twinkies® cake for the body. Place candy corns along the top of the Twinkie to form the dinosaur's spine. Use small candies for the eyes and four small gumdrops attached to toothpicks in each to secure to the bottom of Twinkie for the legs..

■ You're Purr-fect for Me!

This all-occasion cat is a variation of the SnoBall bunny (p.9). For the eyes, use heart-shaped candies and for the nose, a small red gumdrop. The small triangular cat's ears are cut from strawberry fruit leather (or they can also be cut from pink poster or construction paper).

Green Food for St. Patrick's Day

Next St. Patrick's Day, when everyone's Irish again, use these green food ideas to get into the spirit of things.

● **Magic Green Milk**: Pour 2-3 drops of green food coloring (for 6-8 ounce glasses) in clear milk glasses. When the children come in to eat, pour their milk in the glasses. It will swirl green—like magic.

● **Microwave Meatloaf—With an Irish Touch**: Make up, but don't bake, your favorite meatloaf recipe, doughnut shape, in a microwave-safe pie tin. Place microwave-safe custard cup in the "hole" space in the middle of the meatloaf. Cook in microwave. (A 1 1/2-pound meatloaf takes about 9 minutes.) Turn dish 1/4 turn every three minutes during cooking time. Allow two to three minutes' standing time at the end of the cooking time. Remove from the microwave. Cook one package of frozen peas. Just before serving, remove the custard cup from the middle of the meatloaf. Pour the hot peas in the center.

● **Green Potatoes**: Stir green food coloring in milk you add to potatoes before mashing.

● **Shamrock Pizza**: Make your favorite pizza crust. Shape a shamrock on a large pizza or baking sheet with three circular pizzas and one thin, rectangular one (as stem). Raise edges of pizza to contain filling. You can flavor each part of the shamrock differently: pepperoni, another sausage, ham and pineapple, and the stem mushroom.

● **Green Bread**: Ask your baker to color some bread green for you. Or, if you bake your own bread, add green food coloring to the liquid ingredients. Make the dough bright, as it tends to bake to a lighter color.

● **Pear Shamrock Salad**: Make a lime jello salad. Arrange pear halves in a shamrock shape on top of the salad. Three pear halves will form the shamrock, with the small ends of the pears toward the center of the shamrock shape. Cut a thin slice the length of a pear half to place as stem of the shamrock.

Or, use the pears without the jello salad, coloring them green by pouring green food coloring into the syrup of the pears and letting them sit in the refrigerator overnight in the colored syrup. Arrange them on cottage cheese or lettuce leaves and form the shamrock shape. Or, arrange the pears in a glass dish and top with lime sherbet.

St. Patrick's Day Fun

Here are some St. Patrick's Day projects that will delight even the littlest leprechaun.

■ Shamrock Bread Loaf

▲ *To make, you'll need*: Any bread dough recipe; green food coloring; 1"-wide strips of brown paper, well buttered (you can use brown grocery bags, but not the recycled type); florist pins; and 1" green ribbon.

▼ *Directions*: Make the bread dough, adding plenty of green food coloring to the liquid (it will lighten as other ingredients are added). Using enough dough for one loaf of bread, mold it into a smooth, round ball. Place one strip of paper around loaf, crossing the ends over and attaching to top; center with a pin. Place the second strip of paper around loaf in the same manner crosswise to the first, creating four quarters. Allow dough to rise until double, then bake according to your recipe. After bread has cooled, remove paper strips and replace with ribbon and bow.

■ Leprechaun

▲ *To make, you'll need*: Green apple, tangerine, dimensional craft paint, green and flesh-colored felt, glue, toothpicks, orange yarn craft hair, small black felt doll's hat (from craft store), and narrow green ribbon.

▼ *Directions*: With paint, make eyes and mouth on tangerine. Cut arm strip and hands according to diagram, adjusted to fit size of apple. Glue hands to each end of arm. Turn apple upside down, place arm across apple, and attach with a toothpick inserted partway at center top. Carefully place tangerine on other end of toothpick. Make a circle of craft hair slightly smaller than diameter of tangerine and attach with glue or pins to form beard and hair. Decorate hat band with ribbon and place hat on tangerine over hair. Keep in place with straight pins.

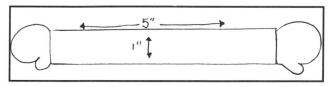

■ A Rainbow and Pot of Gold Centerpiece

▲ *To make, you'll need*: Styrofoam wreath form cut in half; aluminum foil; variety of rainbow-colored fruits such as blueberries, apple halves, strawberries, orange slices, pineapple, and grapes; toothpicks; gold foil-covered chocolate coins; small pot; dry ice chunks; and warm water. Completely cover styrofoam with foil. Using toothpicks, attach fruit in rows, completely covering form, to resemble a rainbow. Place one end of rainbow in pot filled with dry ice. (Caution: Use gloves to handle the ice; do not let children play with it.) Spread coins around pot or under rainbow and add a few leprechauns. Pour a little warm water over the ice.

Easter Party Favors

Start a month before next Easter, and you'll be ahead of the group with personalized ideas for children's parties, baskets for members of the family, and hand-decorated eggs.

■ Easter Personalized: Inside and Out

These can be a snap if the kids themselves are involved in making some of the decorations. If the eggs for the traditional Easter egg hunt are color-coded, the older children will not gather up all the goodies before the younger children have a chance to find some. Simply divide the number of eggs into equal groups. Assign one batch of eggs to each age group. For example, one batch of eggs can be dyed blue and assigned to nine- and ten-year-olds; another batch can be dyed orange and assigned to five- and six-year-olds, etc. Simply hide the eggs designated for older children in more difficult places than those designated for younger children. That way each child gets an equal chance to find some of the Easter eggs.

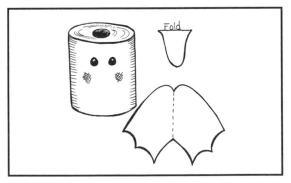

● **Easter bunny baskets from rolls of toilet tissue**: Easy, fun Easter baskets can be made using a roll of toilet tissue. Use a magic marker to draw a face on the roll of paper. Eyes are easy to do if you think of them as two printed capital "D's" turned on their sides. Use black to outline the eyes, add three curved lines to the outside of the eyes for eyelashes, and paint blue pupils inside the eyes. Two black dots can be a nose. The mouth is simple if you think of it as two capital "U's" joined together. If you want cheeks, draw or paint them on with red or pink magic markers, make-up, or crayons.

A duck's beak and a pair of feet can be cut from orange construction paper. Cut out the shapes and glue them into place on the roll of paper. Feet for bunnies (with three toes) and bunny ears can be cut from pink or blue construction paper. Use a sponge to outline them with dabs of white paint to create the appearance of fur. To place the ears on the bunny baskets, spread the paper with your thumb and forefinger and push the ears into the opening and then let the paper snap back into place.

Decorate the baskets by putting small flowers or pom-poms on the heads of the animal baskets. It's fun to put a miniature hat on a duck basket intended for a little boy. Most important of all, to complete the basket, put artificial grass in the opening in the roll of the toilet paper and push Easter eggs down into the grass.

● **Surprise Easter Eggs**: Choose a number of small items as gifts for a girl or a boy. Assemble the items on, inside of, and around each other. The bundle created is the beginning of an egg. Make the egg by wrapping crepe paper streamers around the gifts, shaping the egg as the streamers are wrapped around and around. When the egg is the size you want it to be, secure it by wrapping ribbon, rickrack, or yarn around the egg and tying or tacking them in place with a bit of glue. Kids of all ages love unwrapping the eggs and finding the surprises inside.

● ●

How About a Giant Easter Egg!

Anyone can get or give regular-size eggs during the Easter season, but a huge one, stuffed with goodies?

■ **Giant Easter Egg**

▲ *To make, you'll need*: 1 9" sturdy balloon (the kind that can be filled with helium works best); 12" wide, regular-weight aluminum foil (about 36 feet); colored foil (available at craft stores); clear tape; sharp scissors; glue; and goodies for inside the egg such as Easter grass, small stuffed animals, or small toys.

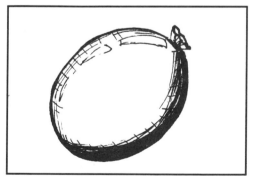

▼ *Directions*: Inflate the balloon, tying a knot at the end. Tear the aluminum foil into 3-foot-long strips. Place the balloon, blowing spout up, on a piece of foil. Gently form the foil around the balloon. Continue with the rest of the foil, fully covering the entire balloon and molding it into an egg shape until it feels firm and solid. Let the air out of the balloon by poking a pin through the foil. Carefully cut a door-shaped opening on one side with sharp, pointed scissors. Fold open and remove the balloon, then fill the cavity with the surprises. Close the door and seal tightly with tape. Finish the egg by covering it with several sheets of the colored foil. Secure loose edges with glue and decorate with ribbons or flowers as desired. This same technique could be used on any size balloon—just make sure the balloons are sturdy ones. Helpful hint: a 25-inch balloon required a 75-foot roll of heavy-duty foil and a 250-foot roll of regular foil.

14

Excitement for Easter

If you start saving your hard-boiled eggs two weeks before Easter next year, you'll be able to make an Easter egg tree topped off with Easter lights (by Celebration Lights, about $12.99 in most stores).

■ Easter Tree

▲ *To make each tree, you'll need*: 1 tree branch (it may be any size, but the more smaller branches it has, the more places there will be for hanging ornaments), plaster of paris, 1 bowl or plastic container (the size will depend on how tall the tree branch is), 1 basket (slightly larger than the bowl), Easter grass, popped popcorn, tiny silk flowers, and hot glue gun.

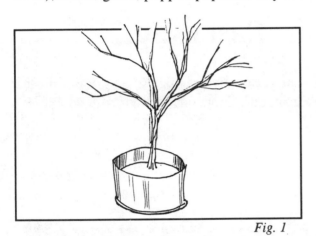

Fig. 1

▼ *Directions*: Mix the plaster in the bowl according to package directions. Insert the tree branch and let it harden. Place the bowl inside the basket and cover it with the grass. Using the glue gun, attach the popcorn and the flowers on the branch as though it were just blooming (Fig. 1).

▲ *To make each hatching chick ornament, you'll need*: 1 real egg, 2 yellow pom-poms (1" for the body and 1/2" for the head), 2 wiggly craft eyes (1/8" to 1/4"), scrap of orange felt cut in 3/8" triangle, 4" of narrow yellow ribbon, and hot glue gun.

Fig. 2

▼ *Directions*: Break the egg in the normal manner. Remove the contents, wash, and allow both pieces to dry thoroughly. Glue the two pom-poms together. Attach the eyes and the triangle of felt for the beak to the smaller pom-pom. Set the completed chick inside the larger egg half. Glue the ends of the ribbon on opposite sides inside the egg to form a handle. Glue the two halves of the egg together on one side. Leave the egg open slightly, allowing the chick to peek out as though it were just hatching (Fig. 2).

◆ *Tip*: If you do not have any craft eyes, a simplified version can be made by using a round paper hole punch and black construction paper.

You've Never Seen Easter/Spring Baskets Like These!

If you're tired of the same old Easter/spring baskets year after year, here are two new grand twists on the subject.

■ Chocolate Easter Basket

You can make this attractive basket with a balloon.

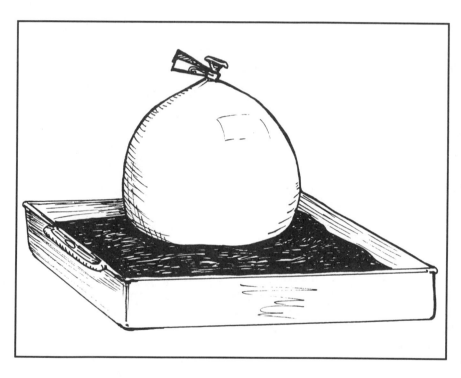

▲ *To make, you'll need*: Balloon (large, good quality), about 1/4 pound chocolate coating compound (also called summer coating, pastel coating, confectioner's coating, almond bar, this chocolate does not require the delicate handling of regular dipping chocolate), "bulldog" clip (or other clip that will hold the balloon closed without tearing), and waxed paper.

▼ *Directions*: Cover a large cookie sheet with waxed paper. Blow up the balloon until the top takes the shape and size you want for your basket. (Caution: don't blow the balloon up to its usual capacity, or it will pop easily when you place it in the chocolate.) Don't tie the end of the balloon closed. Twist the end tightly, then secure the end with a clip.

Melt the chocolate coating in a large container in the oven on the lowest setting (140-150 degrees), checking and stirring often. Or you may choose to melt it in the top of a double boiler, with the water in the lower pan hot but not boiling. (If you choose the latter method, be sure not to spill or splatter water into the chocolate.) Stir the chocolate often as it melts.

Next, dip the balloon carefully in the chocolate. (The melted chocolate should be warm, but not hot, to keep the balloon from popping.) Dip until enough of the balloon is covered to form the basket shape you want. Let excess chocolate drip off, then place the dipped balloon on the waxed paper-covered cookie sheet.

Place the balloon/basket with cookie sheet in the refrigerator until the chocolate is hardened and cool to the touch (about 12-15 minutes, or until hard).

To remove the balloon from the basket, hold the twisted end of the balloon closed with one hand and remove the clip with your other hand. Slowly release the air, a little at a time, from the balloon. The balloon should pull away from the basket as it deflates. (You may have to jiggle the balloon gently away from the bottom of the basket.)

Store your completed basket in a cool, dry place until time to serve. Fill it with green-dyed coconut "grass" (see below), then nest candy eggs, chicks, bunnies, etc., in the completed basket.

■ Coconut "Grass"

To color coconut, place coconut in a canning or mayonnaise jar with a good lid. Drop in two or three drops of food coloring. Close the jar tightly, then shake until the coconut is colored. (If the color is too bright, add more coconut and shake again. If it is too light, add more food coloring and shake.) Spread the coconut out on waxed paper or plastic wrap to dry before using it.

■ Easter Basket with Real Grass

The real grass in this basket provides a bright, spring-green background to decorative eggs and/or silk flowers.

▲ *To make, you'll need*: A medium-sized decorative basket, heavy clear plastic (such as a thick drop cloth—not plastic wrap), charcoal, potting soil or plant starter, vermiculite, and fast germinating seed (wheat, alfalfa, radish—can be bought in health food or seed stores).

▼ *Directions*: Cut the plastic large enough to line the inside of your basket with at least four to five inches excess all the way around. Pour in enough charcoal on top of plastic liner to cover the bottom of the basket. Fill the basket to within one inch of the top with a mixture of potting soil (or plant starter) and vermiculite. Sprinkle the surface generously with seed, then cover with a thin sprinkling of potting soil or plant starter. Water well, making sure all seeds are wet. Pull the excess plastic over the top of your planted soil to cover and preserve moisture. Place the basket in a warm, sunny place. In two to three days, your grass should begin to appear. Within a week to ten days, you can nest decorated eggs or arrange silk flowers in the grass. Depending on the seed you use, the grass makes a tangy, nutritious addition to sandwiches or salads as well.

■ Egg Animals

Transform ordinary eggs into appealing bunnies and chicks with eggs (dyed or undyed), markers, construction paper, and posterboard scraps.

▲ *To make, you'll need*: Hard-boiled eggs or whole eggshells with egg blown out of them. You'll want a white, undyed egg for a bunny, eggs dyed yellow for chicks.

▼ *Directions*: Enlarge the patterns above so that the feet measure 2" to 2 1/2" long. Trace the pattern on white posterboard (for bunny) or yellow or orange posterboard (for chick), then cut out feet. Cut bunny ears from white construction paper, the chick's beak from yellow or orange, and chick's crest from red or orange construction paper. Use a hot glue gun or craft glue to attach the eggs, larger side down, to the feet, and the construction paper details to the eggs. Use marking pens to draw features on the eggs.

You may want to add a pom-pom or cotton-ball tail to the bunny and a feather tail to the chick.

An Easter Basket Full of Fun Ideas

For your kids, with your kids: a bunch of Easter ideas easier to make than pulling a rabbit out of a hat.

■ Easter Necklace

Tear off a piece of plastic wrap the length you want your necklace to be, plus 4". Begin placing items (Easter candies, small toys, tiny baskets) along the edge of the wrap, 2" in and 1" from top at 2" intervals. Fold the 1" overlap down over items and roll them toward you until items are entirely wrapped. Tie off ends and between each item with pastel ribbon. Use pieces of ribbon at ends to tie necklace.

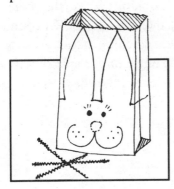

■ Paper Bag Easter Bunny Basket

Lay a lunch-sized paper bag flat out in front of you. Starting halfway up the bag, draw a horizontal line 1/2" in from side into center of bag. With pencil, draw a pair of rabbit ears that extend from midpoint of bag to top. Cut out ears' front and back, leaving them intact. Decorate with bunny face. Finish with small pink pom-pom nose and colored pipe-cleaner whiskers. Open up bag, insert quart-sized milk carton with top half cut off, and fill with Easter grass and candy.

■ Cello-Veggies

Onion: Cut a 5" x 5" square of clear cellophane and place light-colored candies in middle. Bring up all sides and insert three pieces of green Creative Twist cut into 6" lengths. Secure with clear tape to hold twist in place and cut off overlapping cellophane. For roots, use excelsior or a piece of raffia cut in narrow strips and glued in place.

Radish: Made like Easter necklace, only using a 3" x 3" piece of red cellophane. Roll up candy in cellophane and tape edges to hold closed. Tape top together; leave bottom scrunched to resemble roots. Fill with red jelly beans or red hots. For radish top, use green Creative Twist.

Beet: Follow directions for radish, only use purple cellophane and tape around bottom; clip leftover cellophane at bottom to resemble roots. Fill with candy, small toys, or trinkets.

Felt Carrot: Cut orange felt into two identical carrot shapes. Glue or sew edges together and fill with candy. For curly carrot top, overstuff with Easter grass.

◼ Spoon Bunnies

With pastel puff paints or permanent magic marker, draw eyes and mouth on rounded side of pastel-colored plastic spoon. With pink or red marker (or puff paints), dabble on cheeks. Let dry. Tie three strands of 1 1/2" heavy black thread together in middle and glue above mouth for whiskers. Above threads, glue small pink pom-pom for nose. Cut ears out of felt the same color as spoon and glue smaller "ears" of pink felt on pastel-colored ears. Glue ears to back of spoon. Place a round sucker in spoon and tie in place around neck with a piece of ribbon. On the sucker stick, glue a small white pom-pom for the tail.

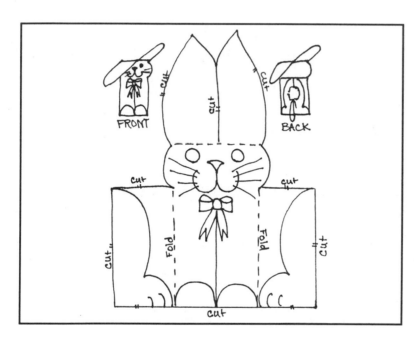

◼ Whirly Bunny

Enlarge or shrink pattern as desired and place on 8 1/2" x 11" piece of pastel-colored paper. Fold on dotted lines and cut out where indicated. Draw in bunny features with pen or marker. Bend one rabbit ear forward and one back (in opposite directions so they act as "propellers"); fold as indicated along sides. Fasten sides together in back with paper clip and glue a cotton-ball tail on backside. Hold bunny high and drop; it will flutter slowly to the floor.

Uncle Sam Wall Hanging

Here's a version of Uncle Sam to make as a wall hanging following the popular patriotic theme.

▲ **To make, you'll need**: Paper to enlarge pattern, white yarn, batting, 1 plastic curtain ring, red embroidery floss, 1 peach-colored 1/2" pom-pom, 2 18mm flat black eyes or buttons, powdered blush, small American flag, glue gun, sewing machine, 1 1/2 yards white eyelet 1" wide, 1/2 yard red ribbon 1" wide, and pieces of felt in the following colors and sizes: (1 each) 12" x 6" black, 18" x 12" white, and (2 each) 36" x 36" blue, 18" x 12" peach.

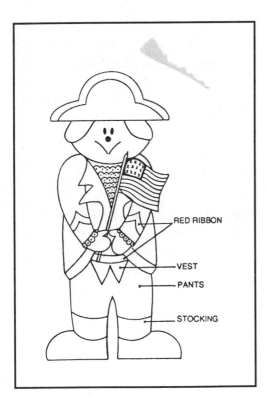

▼ **Directions**: Use the picture as a basic placement guide for the various pattern pieces. Unless otherwise indicated, you may either sew or glue pieces together. If it requires sewing, use a 1/4" seam allowance.

1. Enlarge patterns and cut out of felt according to pattern layout.

2. Glue the eyelet in layers on the white dickey, then glue the dickey on the body.

3. Glue pants, stockings, and shoes on the body.

4. Glue a piece of ribbon at waistline across body and vest.

5. With decorated piece on top, sew the two body pieces together, leaving the neck open. Stuff lightly, then sew neck closed.

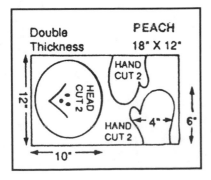

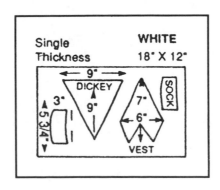

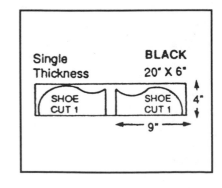

6. Using a double thickness, sew the two lapels. Glue in place on top of the body, covering the raw edges of the dickey, vest, and pants.

7. Again using a double thickness, sew the two arms together, leaving the wrists open. Lightly stuff and then sew closed. Glue pieces of red ribbon to sleeves, turning edges under the back.

8. Sew the hands together, leaving the wrists open. Lightly stuff, then sew closed. Glue pieces of eyelet to wrist edge with the scalloped edges toward the fingers. Overlap the arm on the hand and glue in place. Glue finished arms to body.

9. Sew the face together, leaving top open. Stuff lightly and sew closed. Embroider a V-shaped mouth using the red floss. Glue the nose pom-pom and eyes in place. Brush cheeks with pink powder from your makeup kit.

10. Wrap white yarn around a 15" book or piece of cardboard 30 times. Slip off and, bunching it close together, sew at each end. Glue one end of the yarn to the center top of the head, drape it down one cheek, and glue the other end at center back of the head. Repeat entire step for the other side of the head.

11. For the hat, glue one of the blue pieces to the red piece, with bottom edges even. Repeat with the other two pieces. Starting 2 1/2" in from bottom edge, sew the two hat sections together, ending up 2 1/2" in on the opposite side. Lightly stuff the top of the hat and place the head in the opening. Glue the hat down over the hair and head. Sew the curtain ring onto the back of the head for hanging.

12. Glue the head to the body, overlapping about 4".

13. Place the flag in the hands, glue in place, and Uncle Sam is ready to hang on your door or wall.

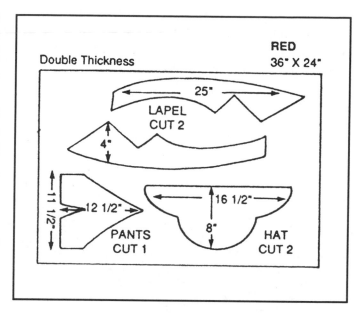

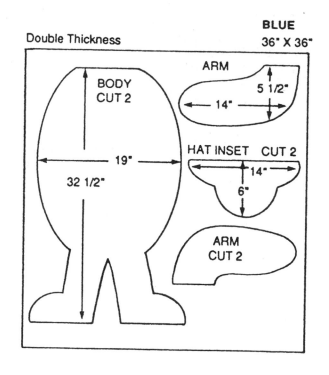

Wave the Flag Proudly

America's national holidays that allow us to wave our flag proudly start on Memorial Day in May, sparkle on the Fourth of July, and continue through November with Veterans' Day; and every four years, there's our presidential election. Here are some good ideas for a Yankee Doodle party, including dessert.

■ Tissue Paper Uncle Sam

▲ *To make, you'll need*: 3 rolls white tissue paper, 1 roll pink tissue paper, blue and pink poster paper, blue felt, cotton balls, black and red puff paints, pink paint, small sponge, red masking tape, hot glue gun, small American flag, and small foil stars.

▼ *Directions*: Cut out two feet from blue poster paper. Glue to underside of roll of white tissue paper, allowing them to protrude. Using red masking tape, place vertical strips around the roll 1" to 1 1/2" apart. Make the torso from a second roll of tissue paper. Cut out arms from blue poster paper and hands from pink. Glue flag to one hand. Cut jacket out of blue felt. Use foil stars for jacket buttons. Hot glue jacket to tissue roll, then hot glue this roll to the first roll. To make the face, use the pink roll of tissue. Sponge paint cheeks with pink paint. Create eyes from black puff paint and mouth from red. Generously glue on cotton balls for hair and beard and use several for eyebrows. Glue head to torso. Fourth roll forms hat. Place strips 1" to 1 1/2" apart. The bottom third of the roll carries the hatband, made from a blue felt strip. Carefully cut out three stars in the front of the hatband, which will allow tissue to show through. For the brim, glue a round piece of blue poster paper (cut 2" larger than the circumference of the tissue roll) to the top of the head. On top of the poster paper, glue "hat" to complete your Uncle Sam.

◆ *Betsy Ross Variation*: Three rolls of tissue paper form skirt, bodice, and head. After attaching feet to the first roll, gather red fabric (the same width as tissue roll is high and 2 1/2 times the circumference of the roll) around top and glue in place. For bodice, crisscross red lace up and over the top of the roll to give the illusion of shoulders. Arms and hands are the same as Uncle Sam's, but Betsy holds a small flag sticker in a tiny embroidery hoop. For her head, paint face like Uncle Sam's and attach curly craft hair. Her cap is a round piece of muslin, gathered and stuffed with cotton. Glue lace around top edge of tissue roll and glue muslin cap onto lace.

■ Lifesavers® Firecrackers

▲ *To make, you'll need*: 1 package Lifesavers, red masking tape, small foil stars, and 7"-8" silver pipe cleaner.

▼ *Directions*: Cover roll of Lifesavers (except for the ends) with red tape and randomly glue on foil stars. Insert the pipe cleaner into the Lifesavers' holes, leaving at least 2" of the pipe cleaner "wick" exposed. Glue two foil stars together back to back at tip of wick.

■ Really Rock-It
(Fourth of July Rocket)

▲ *To make, you'll need*: 12" pieces of 1" PVC pipe, 6 1/2" of 3/4" predrilled wooden dowel, 3" x 4" wooden base, round piece of leather, screws, tape, stars or holiday stickers, 1" cork, 10" length of metallic string, and large metallic confetti (optional).

▼ *Directions*: Paint wooden base and predrill hole for screw. Screw predrilled dowel into base. Cut a piece of leather into a 1" round and screw or tack into top of dowel piece. Decorate PVC pipe with tape strips, stars, flag stickers, etc. Using cork for top of the rocket, thread string through the cork, knot end, and tape other end to PVC pipe. (Leave 6" to 7" of string to "catch" the cork as it pops off the end.) Pull up the pipe and push it down and the cork will pop off, creating a rocket effect. For a colorful explosion, pour metallic confetti into the PVC pipe beforehand.

■ Uncle Sam Necklace

▲ *To make, you'll need*: 1 wooden old-fashioned clothespeg (clothespin with wire spring will not work) with hole drilled completely through just below head; 2 blue barrel beads; 2 white round beads; 2 red flower beads (that resemble red sparklers); glue; 1 yard narrow ribbon or cord; needle; red, white, blue, skin-colored, and black acrylic paints; 1 small black plastic hat (small enough to sit atop clothespeg "head"); and cotton balls.

▼ *Directions*: Paint "legs" of clothespeg white. Paint middle part blue and head part a skin color. Using black, paint up 1/2" on the legs to form shoes or boots. Paint or draw on red stripes over the white area to form striped pants. Paint the face: pink dots for cheeks, black dots for eyes, and red smile. Hair and beard are cotton balls; glue onto back of head. Secure small black plastic craft hat to head. Arms are made by threading blue barrel beads onto ribbon or cord; hands are small white beads and red flower bead "sparklers."

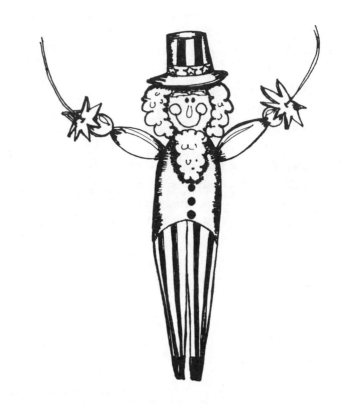

■ Banana Firecracker Dessert

For each serving, place 2 to 3 scoops of ice cream in a sundae dish. Cover with strawberries. Using a banana as straight (not curved) as possible, cut off bottom. Stand banana in the center of ice cream mound to hold banana upright. Trim off top of banana as level as possible. Pour a few drops of lemon extract onto a sugar cube. Place it on top of the banana and light for a flaming banana firecracker. (Be sure to extinguish before eating!)

Optional: Use thin licorice strips twisted around the banana and secured with small toothpick pieces.

New Twists on Patriotic Decorations and Desserts

If you're tired of the same patriotic sparklers and decorations, try one of these to light up your Fourth.

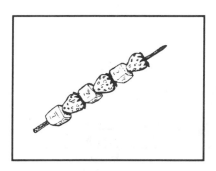

● **Edible sparklers** (to be used in combination with firecrackers for the table): Using long bamboo skewers, alternate each with strawberries and angel food cake. Attach a long party candle to the top by placing it between the fruit and top with blue ribbon. Pierce 10-12 of the skewers, now turned into strawberry shortcake on a stick, into the top half of a watermelon, along with several genuine sparklers. Place melon in a large cake pan and surround with dry ice.

● **Firecracker for the table**: Using one-pound coffee cans, cut out one-inch-thick styrofoam to the shape of the can with the open edge. Push to bottom of coffee can and position a candle in the middle of the styrofoam. Drop small pieces of dry ice into each can.

Now add hot water to each can and pan holding the watermelon. Light firecrackers and sparklers. When the candles burn down on the edible sparklers, add whipped cream to each skewer, and you've got your own small celebration.

● **Festive serving bowls**: Here's a new and unique use for the "Uncle Sam" party hat: Turn upside down and place a fruit or vegetable bowl inside and use as a serving container. Use a smaller "Uncle Sam" hat for a dip.

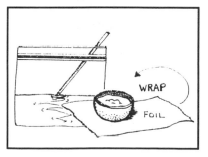

● **Cake in orange cups**: While sitting around your backyard campfire later that evening, bake a cake in the coals. Cut 12 to 18 12" squares of heavy-duty foil; set aside. Cut 6 to 8 oranges in half and scoop out orange fruit and pulp. Leave peel intact as a baking cup. Prepare cake according to package directions. Fill each orange peel 2/3 full with prepared cake batter. Place one filled orange in center of foil piece. Bring foil together at top and twist to make airtight. Place in coals for 15 to 20 minutes. You then place leftover orange fruit in a heavy resealable plastic bag, squeeze fruit, open the top, put in a straw, and you have fresh orange juice.

Costume Parties: Not Just for Halloween

Here's a trick for making costumes that look good enough to eat.

● To look like one of the "**California Raisins**," use sprayed foam rubber supported high across the shoulders with a hole cut in the middle for the child's face. Use a felt-tip marker to draw a face for the raisin in the center. Wear a pair of white gloves and dark glasses—and start dancing.

● Since raisins come from grapes, the next logical costume is a **bunch of grapes**. Blow up about 30 dark red balloons, tying a knot at the ends. Using safety pins, attach the tip of the balloons to a pair of tights. Wear a green hat or get a piece of green styrofoam for the stem.

● You might dress up as a **box of french fries**. Take two pieces of posterboard (or use a large cardboard box, painted red, with the bottom cut out) to hang from your shoulders to serve as the box of fries. Use pieces of soft foam for the fries, paint them, and glue them to the inside back, sides and front of box.

● Go Japanese in a **sushi costume**. To make the rice, glue styrofoam packing "peanuts" around the neck and on the sleeves of a white sweatshirt that fits your child. To make the seaweed, cut a piece of green canvas that can be wrapped around your child front to back. The canvas should be fitted from under the arms to below the knees. Fasten it with Velcro or safety pins. Cut foam in the shape of a slice of avocado and a piece of crab meat. Spray paint the avocado shape green and the crab shape red. Fit the shapes into the canvas so they appear out the top of the costume, behind the child's head, and glue them into place. To find packing peanuts, go to a packing/moving store or a variety store. To find canvas, go to an army surplus store or camping supplies store. To find foam, go to a foam supply store or packing/moving store.

Make Your Own Costumes

As I've said, costume parties are any-time-of-year affairs. And for what the costumes cost to buy, it's a good thing. You can whip together the hottest rage for considerably less.

■ Batman

▲ *To make, you'll need*: Black sweatsuit (desired size), 1 1/2 yards black tricot, small piece of heavyweight pellon, sponge, yellow acrylic paint, black thread, and needle.

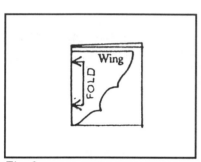
Fig. 1

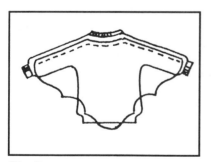
Fig. 2

▼ *Directions*: Lay sweatshirt flat, arms extended. Measure length from wrist to wrist: the width of wingspan. Fold black tricot in half crosswise. With a light-colored pencil, draw a straight line beginning at fold and extending toward selvage edges. (Line should be 1/2 of wrist to wrist measurement.) Draw wing scallops (see Fig. 1). Cut out wings. Pin to shirt. Handstitch wings to back of sweatshirt (follow dotted line of Fig. 2).

For bat emblem on front and back of shirt, draw a bat shape on sponge. Cut out. Dip sponge in yellow acrylic paint and push onto front of sweatshirt. Let dry. Stencil back of shirt.

Headpiece: Lay large piece of paper on table. Have person you are making costume for lay head sideways on paper. Outline profile from nose to base of head. Draw straight line across bottom. Make extension long enough to use for tying on headpiece (Fig. 3). These are side pieces. Using this pattern, cut two pieces from black tricot, 4" wide strip of black tricot for center piece, and four bat ears. (Also cut two of heavyweight pellon.) Stitch ears, right sides together, trim seams, then turn right side out. Press flat. Pin ears to side pieces where ears should be (Fig. 4). Stitch in place. With right sides together, stitch one side piece to center piece. Repeat process with other side piece. Turn right side out. Cut holes in headpiece for eyes. Tie headpiece on with extensions.

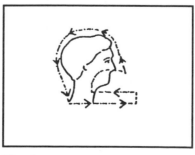
Fig. 3

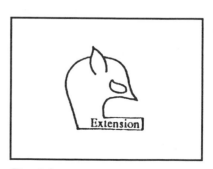
Fig. 4

■ Ghostbuster

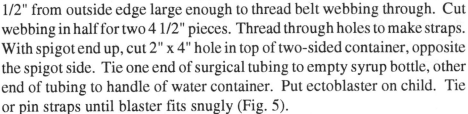

▲ **To make, you'll need**: Sweatsuit (desired color, size), two-gallon plastic water container with spigot and handle (two-sided), surgical tubing (2 1/2"), three yards 1"-wide belt webbing, empty syrup bottle, heavyweight pellon, and white Velcro.

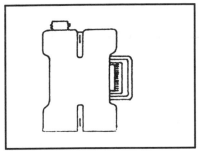

Fig. 5

● **Ectoblaster**: Cut holes in center divider of plastic water container approximately 1/2" from outside edge large enough to thread belt webbing through. Cut webbing in half for two 4 1/2" pieces. Thread through holes to make straps. With spigot end up, cut 2" x 4" hole in top of two-sided container, opposite the spigot side. Tie one end of surgical tubing to empty syrup bottle, other end of tubing to handle of water container. Put ectoblaster on child. Tie or pin straps until blaster fits snugly (Fig. 5).

Fig. 6

● **Arm badge/shirt emblem**: Cut two 3 1/2" circles from pellon. Draw Ghostbuster symbol on both circles; color with permanent marker. Attach to pellon strips for armband or attach to sweatsuit (Fig. 6).

■ Super Mario

▲ *To make, you'll need*: Blue sweatpants; red sweatshirt; 1/2 yard blue material to match pants; purchased false nose; white gloves; painter's cap (spray painted red); red, white, yellow, and black felt; 1/2 yard brown fake fur; brown yarn; batting; 1 piece cardboard 3" x 12"; 2 circles 1 1/2" in diameter for the buttons; glue gun, masking tape; and double-sided tape.

▼ *Directions*: Cut a half circle 2 1/2" in diameter out of the white felt. Cut a 1 1/2" block letter "M" out of the red felt. Glue the "M" to the half circle, then glue that to the front of the cap. To make the hair, wrap brown yarn around the width of the cardboard, packing it fairly close. Put the cardboard next to your sewing machine and as you slowly slide the yarn off the cardboard, stitch down the center of the yarn leaving a 1 1/2" fringe on each side. Continue wrapping and sewing until you have a piece long enough to go around the cap. Glue the sewn part on the fringe to the edge of the painter's cap. Cut the ears out of brown fur; sew with right sides together. Turn, then glue to either side of cap. Cut the bib out of the blue material. Sew straps and bib with right sides together; turn and press. Sew straps to bib top. To make buttons, cut two 2 1/2" circles from the yellow felt. Put a small piece of batting in the center. Place the cardboard circle on top, then pull the felt up and over to the back side and glue, easing felt around cardboard. Glue to bib.

You can sew the bib to the sweatpants or, if long enough, simply tuck it in. To make the tail, sew a 4" x 18" piece of fur into a tube with one end closed. Gently stuff with batting. To make the striped tail, use the masking tape and mark 2" apart. Spray the exposed fur with black spray paint. When dry, remove tape and sew tail to pants. Cut eyebrows and mustache out of black felt. Attach to face with small pieces of double-sided tape.

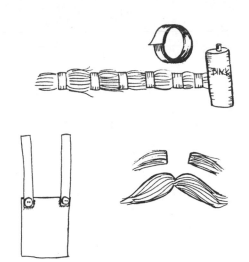

■ Dancing Flower

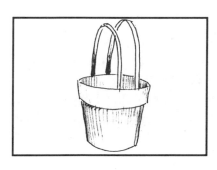

▲ *To make, you'll need*: Large plastic flowerpot (big enough for the child to stand in) with the bottom removed and four holes drilled in the rim—two in front and two in back, 1" foam insulation board, green long-sleeved leotard and green tights, green felt, oversized sunglasses, elastic, 2 yards 3"-wide ribbon tied into a bow, spray paint, glitter, decorative colored tape, electric knife, and men's suspenders or soft cotton rope.

▼ *Directions*: Trace the flower and guitar on the foam board. Cut out with an electric knife. Spray paint them and decorate with the tape and glitter as you choose. Cut four leaves (each about the length of the child's arm) out of the green felt. Draw the veins on the leaves with a magic marker. Sew a leaf on each arm of the leotard at the shoulder and wrist area. Sew one end of each of the other two leaves at the waist (giving a skirt-like effect). Sew the bow to the neck of the leotard. Cut the ear pieces off the sunglasses leaving about 1 1/2". Carefully center the glasses and poke the side pieces through the foam board. Cut a piece of elastic large enough to go around the back of the head, then tie it to the sunglasses to hold the flower on the face. Pull the ends of the suspenders (or pieces of rope) through the holes in the pot and tie securely. This will hold the pot up about waist height to make it easier for walking.

◆ *Note*: The patterns are approximate sizes. Adjust them to fit the person for whom you are making the costume. Many fun costume ideas are also available in pattern books.

Costumes Aren't Just For Halloween

Here are some wonderful costume ideas that will make any holiday party special and fun. After all, if you show up dressed as a black widow spider with tentacle arms to grab the nearest "victim," or as a Christmas tree all lit up, or as a hamburger ready for a bite, who wouldn't love it!

■ Black Widow Spider

▲ *To make, you'll need*: Black sweatsuit, black stocking cap and gloves, 2 pairs of black tights, black garbage bag, small backpack with black straps, quilt batting or newspaper, 2 pieces of black twill tape or string, 2 large orange pom-poms, 2 wiggly craft eyes, red felt or fabric, Glo-it® paint, glue, and tape.

▼ *Directions*: With the batting or newspaper, softly stuff the backpack and the legs of the tights only. Place the body of the tights into the backpack, allowing two legs to extend on either side. Securely attach with tape. Cover the backpack with the garbage bag, taping together on the underside. Cut a "chest size" hourglass shape of red felt and paint around the outside with the Glo-it paint so that the child can be more easily seen in the dark. Baste the hourglass shape onto the front of the sweatshirt. Glue the pom-poms onto the front of the hat, then glue the eyes to the pom-poms. To make the spider legs move, tie one end of the string 2" from the end of the lowest leg. Leaving about 10" between the legs, wrap and tie the string around the second leg. After the child is dressed in the sweatsuit and backpack, tie the string around the child's wrist, again leaving about 10" between. As the child moves his or her arms, the legs will move as well.

■ Special for Halloween or Autumn, a Pumpkin

▲ *To make, you'll need*: Colored or Halloween garbage bag, packing tape, stuffing material (newspapers, pillows, etc.), green felt, safety pins, elastic, and fall leaves (optional).

▼ *Directions*: Cut bottom of garbage leaf bag open. Reinforce by taping cut edge with packing tape. Turn top edge of bag down 2 inches. Tape with packing tape to make a casing. Cut a slit in casing, reinforcing with tape. Pull drawstring through hole. Cut arm holes on sides of bag; reinforce. Turn bag inside out and upside down. Tape on person around tops of legs, gathering as you go. Turn bag up, put arms in holes, and tighten drawstring. Stuff. Leaves are cut out of green felt and attached to shoulders with safety pins. Hat can be made of green felt glued into a cylinder shape. Attach elastic to bottom of sides to go under chin, or hot glue fall leaves to a headband for another type of hat.

■ Sandwich Board Technique

You can make costumes using sweatsuits and foam. To make a chocolate chip cookie, a hamburger, or a Christmas tree, the same steps are used in all three. Cut the foam with an electric kitchen knife, spray paint, and attach shoulder straps with glue or by making small holes (about 1 1/2" from the edge), threading the strap through, and tying. Always reinforce the straps with extra tape on the underside to prevent them from tearing through.

▲ *For the cookie, you'll need* 2 circles of 1/2" foam (adjust the size to fit the child), golden-brown and dark-brown spray paint, 1 1/2"-wide cotton webbing for straps, brown stocking cap, and sweatsuit.

▼ *Directions*: Spray the circles with golden-brown paint. When it is dry, spray small dots with the dark-brown paint to represent the chocolate chips. Attach the shoulder straps and the costume is finished.

▲ *For the hamburger, you'll need*: Brown sweatsuit; 2 circles of 2" foam for the bun, 1 square of 1/2" foam for the cheese, 1 circle of 1/2" foam for the tomato, and 1 roughly cut circle of 1/2" foam for the lettuce; glue or contact cement; and spray paint in golden-brown for the bun, red for the tomato, yellow for the cheese, and green for the lettuce.

▼ *Directions*: Paint each piece of foam and let dry thoroughly. If you want to make a sesame bun, paint small dots of lighter brown paint on one of the brown pieces of foam. (To give dimension to the pieces and to make them look more realistic, vary the intensity of the paint, making some areas darker or lighter than others.) Glue the lettuce, tomato, and cheese to the inside of the bun, allowing edges to hang over. Attach the shoulder straps and your walking hamburger is all ready.

▲ *For the Christmas tree, you'll need*: Green sweatsuit, 2 pieces of 3" foam, 1 piece of 1/2" foam for the star (which goes around the face) and the ornaments, green spray paint and other colors as desired for the star and ornaments, battery-operated Christmas lights, a fanny pack, and glue or contact cement. You may also use a small garland, plastic candy canes, or other decorations.

▼ *Directions*: Draw the tree design on the foam, then cut with the electric knife. Soften the edges and sculpt the tree by angling the knife on its side. Cut narrow, elongated slits in the body of the tree (do not cut all the way through) to add dimension. Make a large star, cutting out a hole in the center just large enough for the face. Cut round balls or bells for the ornaments. Spray paint all the pieces. Attach the ornaments to the tree with the contact cement. Make small holes in the foam and insert the lights, running the wires on the back side to hide them. Attach the shoulder straps. Carry the battery pack for the lights in the fanny pack, and you'll really glow in the dark.

A Different Kind of Makeup

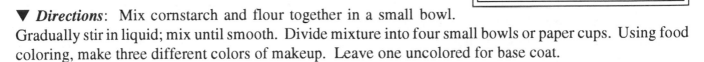

You can raid your kitchen cabinets for safe, inexpensive ingredients for this "recipe" for Halloween makeup for kids (but you can use it too).

■ Basic Recipe

▲ *To make, you'll need*: 3 tablespoons cornstarch, 1 tablespoon flour, 3/4 cup white corn syrup, 1/4 cup water, and food coloring.

▼ *Directions*: Mix cornstarch and flour together in a small bowl. Gradually stir in liquid; mix until smooth. Divide mixture into four small bowls or paper cups. Using food coloring, make three different colors of makeup. Leave one uncolored for base coat.

To apply: Using two-ply facial tissue, separate ply so you only use one ply at a time. Tear single ply into 2" strips. (Have a good supply ready so you can apply them quickly.) Dip a small paintbrush into uncolored base makeup and begin applying makeup to forehead. Put tissue strips over base coat and paint again. Repeat process until you have a base coat on all facial areas you want covered. Avoid using near eyes. Let dry 15-30 minutes, then begin applying colored makeup to desired areas. Tip: Use several coats of colored makeup to intensify color.

■ Variations

● **Wolfman**: For a furry effect, brush base coat on face and quickly apply strips of long-pile fake fur to areas. You can also do your hands for furry wolfman paws.

● **Big Bird**: Brush base coat around outside of face and attach feathers.

● **Dinosaur**: Apply untinted makeup to face; cover with tissue strips. Press crispy rice cereal onto wet makeup and let dry. After first coat has dried completely, apply second layer of tissues over crispy rice cereal. Let dry. Apply colored makeup for final touch and a great "reptile" effect.

■ To Remove Makeup

Splash face with warm water and begin peeling makeup off. Rinse face again with warm water and pat dry. You may wish to use a moisturizer afterward if face feels dry. Caution: Dispose of makeup and tissue in garbage can, not down the drain.

Ghoulish Guises

Next Halloween when you want to decorate your outside for all the visiting ghosts, refer to these inexpensive ideas, and you'll have the scariest yard in the neighborhood.

■ Lamppost Witch

▲ *To make, you'll need*: Large plastic pickle jug (for head), rope (for hair), witch's hat, old clothing, cape, pair of cotton garden gloves, old shoes, and newspaper (for stuffing).

▼ *Directions*: Cut top off plastic pickle jug to slip over top of lamppost. With permanent marker draw face on jar. Cut different lengths of rope for hair. Tape or glue to top of pickle jug. For shaggy effect, separate plies by untwisting and pulling apart. Slip shirt or dress down over lamppost top and tie at neckline to post. Stuff with newspaper. Stuff cotton garden gloves with newspaper and safety pin to bottom of sleeves for hands. Place shoes on ground underneath the skirt or dress with only toes showing. (To keep shoes from "walking away" during the night, place duct tape around heels and attach to bottom of lamppost.) Tie a witch's cape around "shoulders" to post; top with witch's hat. To "haunt" your yard, place cassette recorder underneath witch's dress and put in your favorite "ghoul tunes."

■ Coat Hanger Bats

▲ *To make, you'll need*: Wire coat hangers, black plastic garbage bags, self-stick reflective tape, polyester stuffing (or newspaper for stuffing), and black electrical tape.

▼ *Directions*: Lay black garbage bag on flat surface. Bend wire coat hanger to resemble bat wings (see Fig. 1). Place wire hanger on garbage bag; using black electrical tape, tape hanger to garbage bag, excluding hanger hook. Cut garbage bag around edge of hanger. To form body and head, cut a strip from the black garbage bag that measures approximately 6" x 12". Fold in half lengthwise and tape in back to form a tube. Gather one end of tube and wind tape around to close. With polyester stuffing or newspaper, make a ball about the size of a small fist. Insert in tube; wind tape to form body. Make another ball of stuffing or newspaper and insert in tube. Wind tape around ball, forming head. Cut ears from portion of the garbage bag left over from gathering (see Fig. 2). Add features (eyes, fangs, wing detail) by cutting pieces from the self-stick reflective tape. Tape body and head portion to the wings (wire hanger). Wrap black electrical tape around hook part of wire hanger and the "bat" is finished. Note: One large black garbage bag will make four bats.

Fig. 1

Fig. 2

◼ Ironing Board Ghost

Stand an ironing board up with rounded end up (this will be the head). Drape a white sheet over the ironing board, forming a "ghost." Cut eyes, nose, and mouth from black felt and tape or pin to sheet where the "face" should be.

◼ Garbage Bag Spider

For body: Crumple up newspaper and fill black garbage bag until almost full. Gather up top of bag and tie it shut (use black string or electrical tape). For legs: Cut another black garbage bag into eight strips. Roll one sheet of newspaper and then roll up in one end of the strip of the black bag. Tape shut with black electrical tape. Roll up another sheet of newspaper and roll up in other end of same strip. Tape shut with electrical tape. Continue this process until you have eight legs for the spider. Attach legs to the spider by taping them to the top of the body of spider. Cut spider eyes from orange reflective tape and place on the "body" of the spider where the "face" should be. Cut the excess garbage bag left at the top of the spider (when you gathered the top of the body and taped it shut) in strips for "hair" or use a colorful wig to give the spider more color and personality.

· ·

Halloween Haunted House

Anyone can carve faces in pumpkins—but you can also carve a haunted house, complete with broccoli shrubbery, palm trees, and potato cars, and you can also make ghosts from suckers.

◼ Jack-O-Lantern House

▲ *To make, you'll need*: A large pumpkin with at least one side that is fairly wide and flat, sharp knife, and ice cream scoop. (Optional: If you wish to make a pattern for the floor and windows, you will need paper, pencil, ruler, and pins.)

▼ **Directions**: Begin by cutting off the top of the pumpkin at an angle so that the lid will fit securely when replaced. (If, as you are cutting, you put a small notch on the back of the lid, it will always be easy to put on right.) Use the ice cream scoop to clean the seeds and membranes from the inside. Near the middle and slightly up from the bottom, carefully cut out a rectangle for the door. Cut two squares, one on each side of the door, for the windows. (If you wish to use a pattern, pin it on the pumpkin and cut around it.) Be sure to remove the door and each of the windows in whole pieces. By carefully trimming the inside, narrow the windows and door pieces to about 1/2" thickness. Cut and remove the individual window panes as indicated in the picture. Replace the windows in the pumpkin, allowing them to jut out ever so slightly. Position the door on the pumpkin as though it were just being opened.

■ Setting the Scene

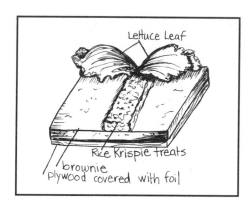

▲ **You will need**: One 2' x 2' x 1/2" piece of plywood covered with aluminum foil (adjust size of board to coordinate with the size of your pumpkin), two or three packages of brownie mix, one or two recipes of marshmallow Rice Krispie® treats, broccoli, leaf lettuce, top and bottom from a fresh pineapple, one parship or large white radish, round toothpicks, potato, carrots, small tree branch, marshmallow, Kleenex®, string or yarn, dry ice, and one 1-lb. size coffee can or a size that will fit in your pumpkin.

▼ **Assembly**: Place the pumpkin on the board. Bake the brownie mixes (spread very thin) and cool. Cut in pieces to form the ground around the house. Use the Rice Krispie treats to form a road, path, and stairs leading to the house. Use the broccoli and lettuce leaves for shrubbery. To make the tree, stick a toothpick into the bottom of the pineapple, then stick the other end of the toothpick into the thicker end of the parsnip; in the same manner, attach the top of the pineapple to the thin end of the parsnip. You could also use a small tree branch attached with a screw or nail from the underside of the board and hang ghosts made from marshmallows covered with white Kleenex and tied with string to the neck area. Carve a car from the potato, using carrots for wheels. To make the Halloween picture complete, place the coffee can in the bottom of the pumpkin. Fill it halfway with hot water and then add dry ice.

■ Ghost Suckers

▲ **To make, you'll need**: Round suckers (Tootsie Roll Pops® work very well), white Kleenex® or napkins, string or yarn, and fine-point felt-tip pen.

▼ **Directions**: Place the center of the opened Kleenex on top of the sucker (leave the wrapper on). Pull the Kleenex over the sucker, completely covering it. Gather it in at the point where the sucker stick meets the candy. Tie it tightly at that point with the string to create the ghost's head and body. Draw the face on with the marker.

Autumn Party Ideas with Tricks and Treats

You can start your Halloween party with a neat trick: just put dry ice in your garbage disposal, and you have a Halloween volcano.* And now for the treats: make an entire Halloween dinner in a pumpkin. With pumpkins available all autumn, you also can cook this unusual meal after Halloween—just leave off the painted face.

*More detailed instructions are on page 62.

■ Dinner in a Pumpkin

1 small to medium pumpkin
1 onion, chopped
2 tbsps. vegetable oil
1 1/2-2 lbs. ground beef
2 tbsps. soy sauce
2 tbsps. brown sugar
1 4 oz. can sliced mushrooms, drained
1 can cream of chicken soup (undiluted)
1 1/2 cups cooked rice
1 8-oz. can sliced water chestnuts

Cut off top of pumpkin and clean out seeds. Paint a face on pumpkin. In skillet saute onions in oil until tender. Add meat and brown; drain. Add soy sauce, brown sugar, mushrooms, and soup. Simmer ten minutes. Add cooked rice and water chestnuts. Spoon mixture into pumpkin. Put pumpkin on baking sheet. Bake one hour at 350 degrees, until pumpkin is tender. Serve scooped-out pumpkin as a vegetable.

■ Pumpkin Tip

When cutting out the top of the pumpkin, put a notch in it. You'll have an easy fit when placing it back on.

■ More Spooky Desserts

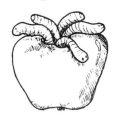

1. To make baked apples with worms, just scoop out the center of Delicious apples, fill with Red Hots® candy, bake at 350 degrees for 35-40 minutes, and top with Gummi Worms®.

2. Another treat certain to be popular with the kids is a spider cake. Start with a white frosted cake and, using chocolate frosting in a resealable plastic bag, draw concentric circles on the cake. Using a toothpick, draw lines through the circles to make a spider web. Make a spider out of two chocolate donuts with pipe cleaners for legs and place spider on the web.

3. The scariest cake has been saved for last. Using a sheet cake with chocolate icing, make a ghost shape with white frosting. Put two empty eggshell halves where the eyes would be, place a sugar cube in each shell, and pour lemon extract over the cubes. Mom or Dad can light the sugar cubes for a flaming ghost.

Turkey Tips

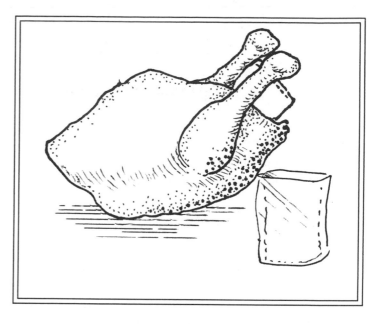

Double stuff the turkey for variety. If guests or family members prefer different kinds of stuffing, double stuff the turkey. Stuff neck cavity with one kind of dressing and tail/back cavity with a different kind. You might fill one cavity with celery stuffing and the other with oyster stuffing.

■ Unstuff the Turkey Instantly

Unstuffing the turkey is a cinch with this technique. The key is a cheesecloth bag put in the turkey to hold the stuffing. To make bag, cut a piece of cheesecloth large enough to cover inside of turkey cavity with several inches extra. This will probably be a 20" to 25" square. Stitch cloth to form a two-sided bag. Tuck bag into turkey with unstitched edges poking out. Spoon dressing into bag until cavity is loosely filled. Fold bag closed and tuck edges up into cavity. Secure bag by folding drumsticks under wire holder or thick skin that holds legs together.

After turkey is cooked, open stuffing bag and spoon out a little dressing. Grasp outside edges of the bag firmly and pull out of turkey (dressing and all). No dressing will be left in turkey. Empty dressing into dish and serve.

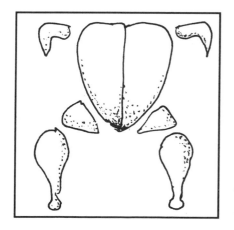

■ Carving Tip

Just out of the oven with juices dripping, the turkey looks and smells wonderful. To graciously serve it from platter to plate, try these carving techniques. 1. Remove the drumstick and thigh by pressing leg away from body. Joint connecting leg to backbone may snap free. If it doesn't use a sharp knife and cut leg from backbone. Cut dark meat completely from bone structure by following body contour carefully with a knife. 2. Cut drumsticks and thighs apart by cutting through joint. Place thighs on separate plate. It's easy to cut meat if you tilt drumstick to a convenient angle and slice toward plate. 3. To slice thigh meat, hold piece firmly on the plate with a fork. Cut even slices parallel to the bone. 4. Remove half the breast at a time by cutting along the breastbone and rib cage with a sharp knife. Lift meat away from the bone. 5. Place a half breast on a cutting surface and slice evenly against grain of the meat. Repeat with second half of the breast when additional slices are needed. End result is a beautifully carved turkey.

■ Two for One

Cook two smaller turkeys instead of one big one. They cook faster, and you can serve one whole and one sliced.

38

Thanksgiving Centerpieces

Kids can get pretty impatient waiting for the turkey on Thanksgiving Day, so here are some great ways to keep them busy while you're getting ready.

■ Pilgrim and Indian Centerpieces

▲ *To make, you'll need*: Butternut squash (slice a small piece off the bottom to make it stand upright), white felt, narrow ribbon and braid, acrylic puff paints, craft doll hair, black pilgrim hat (from craft store), and glue.

▼ *Directions*:

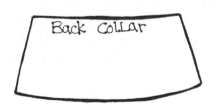

1. With puff paint, draw on eyes and mouth. For Indian, add small dots of paint around neck for beads. Dry thoroughly.

2. Glue on hair. For Indian, braid craft hair and glue two braids to a narrow piece of decorative ribbon or braid. Wrap braids around head, then glue or pin in back. Add small feathers if you like.

3. Adapt patterns (front and back collar for man, cap and apron for woman) to fit size of your squash. Cut pieces from white felt. Make pleats in corners of cap to shape and fold back 1/4" for brim. Glue on cap, apron, and collars. Make belt from narrow piece of ribbon. Glue in place. Using puff paint, add a gold belt buckle. Add a small bow at woman's neck.

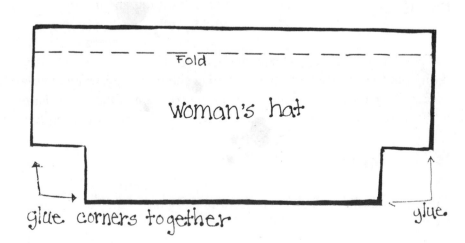

■ Turkey from a Pumpkin

▲ *To make, you'll need*: A pumpkin, sweet potato or yam, raisins, apple, frozen bread dough, bamboo skewers, 5" piece of 1/4" dowel, and toothpicks or pins.

▼ *Directions*: 1. Allow dough to thaw, then roll into 1/4"-thick rectangle. Cut into 2"-wide strips of varying lengths (longest ones being about 9", depending on the size of the pumpkin). Make diagonal snips 3/4" long and 1" apart on both sides of strips. Place on cookie sheet and follow package instructions for baking. (To add color, sprinkle seasoning salt on before baking.)

2. Using diagram, carve a turkey head from yam. Attach raisin eyes and small pieces of apple for beak and wattle with toothpicks. To attach head to pumpkin, sharpen both ends of dowel with a pencil sharpener. Insert one end in pumpkin and other in yam.

3. Tail feathers are added by inserting skewers 1" into pumpkin, then carefully sliding cooked breadsticks onto skewers. Make 2 or 3 rows with shorter feathers in front. Hang a small bow made from paper twist around neck and a pilgrim hat on its head, and your turkey is complete.

■ Mayflower Squash

▲ *To make, you'll need*: A large banana squash, posterboard (cut into three 4" x 3", two 5" x 4", and one 6" x 5" rectangles), and 1/4" dowels (two 11" and one 14").

▼ *Directions*: 1. Carve squash as in drawing and remove the top piece. Scoop out all seeds and membrane. 2. Punch holes in opposite sides of boards and insert them on dowels. Insert dowels in squash. (Add a small flag made from colored paper at top of each dowel if you wish.) Fill boat with "dipping" vegetables and you have a wonderful relish tray for your centerpiece.

To make ship more realistic, you will also need: Blue cellophane, small clear plastic cups, dry ice, and hot water. Scrunch cellophane around squash, hiding the cups in folds 4 or 5 inches apart. Place small chunks of dry ice (please handle with gloves and don't allow children to play with it) in each cup. At serving time, pour hot water on the ice, and your Mayflower is magically at sea.

■ Leftover Magic

Make a fun leftover turkey sandwich using a large hard roll or soup bun (or use leftover bread dough to make your own buns). Make tail feathers from cherry tomatoes, olives, pineapple, cheese chunks, etc., skewered on fancy toothpicks. Add a turkey head made from posterboard and a few condiments, and your turkey sandwich is ready.

Last-Minute Thanksgiving Centerpieces

■ Autumn Basket

▲ *To make, you'll need*: Ornamental corn (size and amount will depend on the size of basket you use), basket or box, autumn leaves, Spanish moss, and hot glue gun.

▼ *Directions*: Carefully remove and save the husks from the corn. If the husks are too brittle, soak in water for a short time. Cautiously cut kernels from one side of each ear of corn, making one flat side. Arrange the corn, flat side down (alternating bottom and top of each piece for better fit) around the outside of the basket/box. You may do it horizontally or vertically, depending on the size of the basket as well as the size of the corn. Hot glue each side as you complete the arrangement. After the corn is glued on, use the husks, leaves, and moss to fill in any open spaces and to cover the handle if the basket has one. Fill basket with an autumn floral arrangement.

■ Turkey Centerpiece

▲ *To make, you'll need*: 1 6" styrofoam ball; 1 piece of 1"-thick sheet styrofoam; paper twist, opened and flattened; craft wiggly eyes; any combination of wheat, cattails, autumn leaves, feathers, or silk flowers; hot glue gun; and large pins.

▼ *Directions*: Make a silhouette pattern about 6" high of a turkey head. Trace it on the sheet of styrofoam and cut out (an electric knife works very well). Cut off and discard 1/3 of the foam ball. Using the paper twist, cover the turkey head and the body. Glue or carefully pin the two pieces together. Glue on the eyes. Make a wattle from the paper twist and glue in place. Make the tail feathers from a combination of the wheat, etc., sticking the stems into the foam ball or gluing them in place.

■ Turkey Napkin Holder

▲ *To make, you'll need*: One surgical glove, scraps of felt, rock salt, craft glue, and napkins.

▼ *Directions*: Fill the surgical glove with the rock salt. Tie end closed with a twist tie or a knot. Using the scrap felt, cut out eyes and wattle. Glue in place on the glove thumb. Using the opened napkins, weave them in between the fingers of the glove to form the tail. Place the dinner napkin in between the neck (thumb) and the tail (fingers) of the turkey.

41

New Ideas for Thanksgiving

Here are some around-the-world ideas for Thanksgiving. Take a favorite ethnic dish and make it better by adding leftover turkey. From Italy there's turkey a la spaghetti—just add turkey to the spaghetti after you've put the sauce on. From China, stir fry vegetables in oil, add cooked turkey, heat, and you have turkey stir fry. From Mexico, roll sauce and turkey in a tortilla and you've made a turkey enchilada. From the United States, shred the turkey, add barbecue sauce, heat, serve on a bun, and you have turkey barbecue.

● **A favorite** leftover idea is to take the small ornamental Indian corn ears, butter them, place them in a paper bag and put into the microwave on high for two minutes—and it's popcorn.

● **For leftover gravy**, pour any leftovers into a muffin tin, freeze, and store the frozen rounds in plastic bags—the result is serving-size portions. You can do the same thing with leftover stuffing. Just scoop the stuffing with an ice cream scoop and store in plastic bags in the freezer.

● **For lumps in your gravy**, put gravy in the blender.

● **To hold off youngsters' hunger** while they're waiting for the big feast:

● **Cranberry Slush**

1 12-oz. pkg. fresh cranberries
Juice of 3 lemons
2 cups sugar
1 tsp. grated orange peel
1 qt. cold water

Make it ahead and store it in the freezer so you don't have to throw out your cooking schedule.

In a saucepan, boil cranberries, sugar, and 2 cups water until berries pop. Process in blender until smooth. Add lemon juice, 2 cups cold water, and orange peel. Freeze in container. Remove from freezer about 1 hour before serving. This light refreshing slush makes about 10 cups.

Have a Berry Merry Christmas

Cranberries, one of only three native American fruits, are the perfect addition to holiday food and decorations. With recipes that will enhance any holiday buffet, we've certainly gone beyond the string-em-up roping we've all been hung up on.

■ Cranberry Meatballs—Perfect for Buffets

1 lb. lean ground beef
1/4 cup tomato catsup
1/2 cup dried bread crumbs
1 tsp. salt
1 tbsp. Worcestershire sauce
1 egg, slightly beaten
1 can cranberry sauce
1 tbsp. lemon juice
1/3 cup brown sugar

Combine first six ingredients and mix well. Roll into meatballs and place on a cookie sheet. Bake for 15-20 minutes at 350 degrees. Combine remaining three ingredients and heat. Place the meatballs in a crockpot or chafing dish. Pour the sauce over the meatballs and simmer for about 30 minutes.

■ Cranberry-Pecan Stuffing—A Special Variation on the Classic

6 cups whole-wheat bread crumbs
1/2 cup sugar
1/2 cup water
2 cups fresh cranberries
1 cup chopped onion
1 cup diced celery
1 cup (2 sticks) butter
1/2 cup orange juice
1/2 tsp. allspice
1 cup chopped pecans
2 large eggs, slightly beaten
Salt and freshly ground black pepper

Spread the bread cubes in an even layer on a baking sheet and toast in 300-degree oven until well browned, about 10-15 minutes. Remove from the oven and set aside. While the bread is toasting, put the sugar and water in a medium saucepan and bring to a boil, stirring to dissolve the sugar. Boil about 5 minutes, until it becomes syrupy. Add the cranberries to the saucepan and let them simmer until the first few berries begin to pop, about 5 minutes. Remove from heat immediately and let the berries set in the syrup for 5 minutes. With a slotted spoon, remove the cranberries to a large mixing bowl, draining off the syrup. Saute the onion and celery in the butter until crisp-tender, about 7-10 minutes. Add to the mixing bowl. Add the toasted bread cubes and the remaining ingredients to the mixing bowl and toss lightly to combine. Taste and correct the seasoning with salt and pepper.

■ Cranberry Pineapple Smoothie Base

1 cup light corn syrup
1 can whole-berry cranberry sauce
1 8-oz. can crushed pineapple, undrained

In blender combine all ingredients; process until smooth. Store covered in refrigerator for up to one week.

■ Cranberry Pineapple Smoothie Beverage—A Healthful Snack

2 cups cranberry pineapple smoothie base
1 large banana
4 cups ice cubes

Prepare cranberry pineapple smoothie base. In blender, combine two cups smoothie base and banana; process until smooth. With blender running, add ice cubes, several at a time. Process until thick and smooth.

■ Cranberry Breakfast Ring—Makes a Holiday Breakfast Special

2 (1/4-oz.) packages dry yeast
3 1/2-4 1/2 cups flour
1/2 cup sugar
1 tsp. salt
1 cup milk
1/4 cup water
1/2 cup butter or margarine
2 eggs, beaten
1 tsp. lemon rind, grated
3/4 cup sugar
1 cup walnuts, chopped
2 tsps. cinnamon
1/2 cup butter or margarine, melted
Frosting (recipe below)

In a large bowl, combine yeast, flour, sugar, and salt. Set aside. In a saucepan, combine milk, water, and butter. Heat until warm. Add to dry ingredients and beat until smooth. Add eggs and 1 1/4 c. flour, beating again until mixed. Stir in remaining flour and lemon rind. Cover and refrigerate until ready to shape rings. To make rings, turn dough onto floured board and divide in half. Roll one half into a 14" x 7" rectangle. Spread half of cranberry orange sauce over dough. Combine sugar, nuts, and cinnamon. Sprinkle half of mixture over dough. Drizzle with 1/4 c. melted butter. Beginning with one long side, roll up dough and seal edges. With seam edge down, place dough in a circle on a greased baking sheet. Press ends together to seal. Cut slits two-thirds of the way through ring at 1-inch intervals. Repeat process with remaining half of dough. Cover rings and let rise in a warm place until double in size (about 1 hour). Bake in a preheated 375-degree oven 20 to 25 minutes or until done. Bread is done when you thump the ring and it makes a hollow sound, not a thud. Frost if desired. Makes two rings.

■ Frosting

1 cup confectioner's sugar
2 tbsps. warm milk
1/2 tsp. vanilla

Mix all ingredients until smooth; drizzle over rings.

The Ultimate Gingerbread House

A lot of amazing gingerbread houses were checked before this one was designed that anyone can make.

■ *Suggested candies and cookies to use for the decorations*:

Red and green M&Ms® or jelly beans—fence
Peanut brittle—paths
Wafer cookies—shutters and doors
Necco® candy wafers—roof
Lifesavers®—windows
Candy canes, large and small—decorations
Starlight® mints—decorations
Oreo® cookies—paths
Lorna Doones®—shutters and doors
Triscuits®—roof
Orange sticks—paths
Gumdrops—trees

Put all of the candies, separated, into muffin tins so they are easy to see and use.

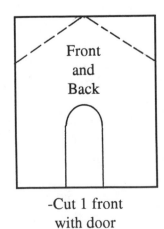

Front and Back

-Cut 1 front with door
-Cut 1 back without door

This pattern needs to be enlarged

Sides

Cut 2

Roof

Cut 2

"Glue" any combination you choose onto your gingerbread house with royal frosting. The most important ingredient is your imagination!

45

■ Gingerbread—the creative cookie

2 3/4 cups sifted flour
1 tsp. ginger
1 egg
1 tsp. cinnamon
1/3 cup brown sugar (packed)
1/2 tsp. salt
2/3 cup molasses
3 tsps. baking powder
1/8 tsp. cloves
1/2 cup oil

Mix thoroughly and chill several hours or overnight. Roll dough on an oiled piece of foil the size of the baking pan you are using. Place dough on baking pan by turning foil over and then peeling the foil off. Bake at 300 degrees for 20-30 minutes. Place pattern on hot gingerbread and cut immediately with a sharp knife. Lift pieces out carefully and cool on cake racks. The gingerbread should be very hard when cool. (If necessary, the pieces can be returned to the cookie sheet and baked for 5-10 minutes longer.) Assemble the house with royal frosting and add candies and cookies of your choice to decorate.

■ Royal Frosting

3 egg whites
1/2 tsp. cream of tartar
1-lb. box powdered sugar (about 4 cups)

Beat the egg whites until stiff peaks form. Add the cream of tartar. Beat in the powdered sugar until stiff. (It should hold a sharp line when cut through with a knife.) Put in an airtight container and store in the refrigerator. Remove the frosting you are using to decorate and keep the rest tightly covered.

Up on the Rooftop and Down on the Lawn

If you've always wanted to put Santa and his reindeer up on the roof, here's how—plus a lot of safety tips for you. When you're finished on the roof, come down to the lawn to make easy holiday sculptures.

■ Outdoor Decorating

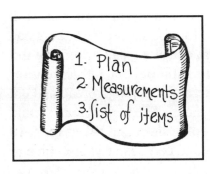

1. Go for a ride in your town to get ideas. "Borrow from the best and leave the rest."

2. Make a drawing of your home and yard. Sketch in ideas using colored pencils; it's easier to make changes on paper!

3. Make a list of needed items—outdoor and indoor lights, spotlights, garlands, cutouts, extension cords, remote controls, etc.

4. Take accurate measurements of your home—no need to buy more than necessary. Locate outside sources of electricity. You may be able to plug your lights in directly or you may need to buy light socket adapters. Decide what type of clips you will need to hang your lights—shingle clips, gutter clips, or ones specifically for use on brick.

5. Invite friends and relatives over for a "decorating the house" party and have fun together.

■ "Safety First" When Decorating

Only buy lights that have the UL seal. Make sure that any extension cords you need are designed for use outside and that they can handle the wattage you intend to use. Read the instructions on the box. Do not use more lights than are suggested for one socket, never use indoor lights outside, and never plug indoor and outdoor lights together. If you live in windprone areas but want to put up cutout decorations, a good way to anchor them is with large bags of sand (often available at lumber stores). Seal the sand in plastic bags for weather protection. You may also need to anchor your cutouts with wire to a chimney if putting them on your roof.

■ Artificial Christmas Topiary Deer

▲ *To make, you'll need*: #10 electrician's wire*, florist's wire, 1 wire tomato cage, pliers, wire cutters, artificial evergreen garland (you may use discarded artificial tree or even live branches), and tiny Christmas tree lights.

*Amounts will depend on the size of the tomato cage you use.

▼ *Directions*:

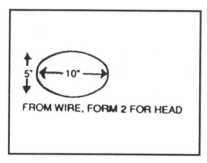

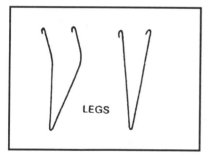

Using the wire cutters and pliers, form two ovals from the wire, each about 10" long and 5" wide. Put one inside the other, lengthwise, at right angles, and wire the ends firmly together at the two crossing points. About 1/3 of the way from one end, make another circle of wire around the combined ovals (see illustration). This forms the head of the deer. Using the pliers, bend the three prongs (the part that would stick into the ground) of the cage at a 45-degree angle to the rest of the cage, forming the deer's neck. Attach the head by placing it over the tomato cage prongs and wiring securely into place. From the electrician's wire (or coat hangers or the prongs from a broken tomato cage), form the four legs (see illustration). Attach the hooks on the cage and wire securely.

Now that the frame is made, wrap it with the tree lights. Start with the end of the lights at the head (you can put a red bulb at the point for a nose) and work around and down so that the plug end finishes on a leg.

The final step is to put on the greenery. Wire two pieces of garland (with several smaller branches on each) on the small circle at the head for the antlers. Using larger pieces, cover the rest of the deer, wiring securely as you go. When you are finished, you may wish to add a bow around the neck, pinecones for eyes, or a red ball ornament for the nose. Variations: Using the same technique, you can create other animals, such as a teddy bear. By using artificial snow or white garland, you can even create a polar bear.

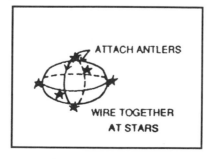

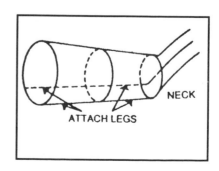

Christmas Decorating Ideas

■ Personalized Christmas Stockings

Choose a theme. If someone's a golfer, cut a golf club-shaped stocking out of felt. Tennis racquets and baseball bats are other possibilities.

Trace the item on two squares of same-colored felt, lay one square on top of the other, and cut out your shape. Sew together, leaving room for the opening to stuff the stockings by using Velcro. Sew on added decorations and trim. If you were making a tennis racquet stocking, you might use thin strips of white felt for the strings.

■ Crystal-Like Ice Candles

▲ *To make each candle, you'll need*: 1 tea candle, 1 gallon-size ice cream bucket (or any plastic container that has straight sides), water, and freezer (or very cold weather).

▼ *Directions*: Fill the ice cream bucket with water and set outside (or in freezer) to freeze. You will find that the sides and bottom are the first to freeze. Just before the water is completely frozen, pour out the water (or scrape out, if somewhat slushy). This will leave a hole in the center of the ice block. Turn the container upside down and allow the ice the slip out (you may need to put a warm damp cloth over it for a moment to loosen it). Turn it right side up again, placing the candle in the hole. Line your steps or sidewalk with the "crystal" candle holders and light the candles for a beautiful entrance. If the temperature stays below freezing, these candle holders will last for several days; just add new candles as necessary.

Santa and Reindeer

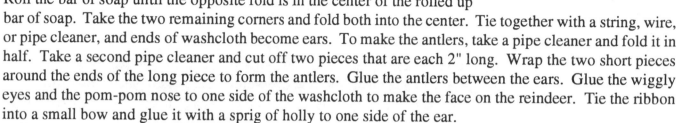

Here's a reindeer centerpiece that you can make from washcloths and bars of soap.

▲ *To make, you'll need*: one brown washcloth, one hand-size bar of soap, one 1/2" red pom-pom, two brown pipe cleaners, two 1/2" oblong wiggly eyes, piece of ribbon to tie bow, sprig of holly, and a piece of wire.

▼ *Directions*: Fold a corner of the washcloth over the bar of soap. Fold the opposite corner toward the soap so it comes to the center of the washcloth. Roll the bar of soap until the opposite fold is in the center of the rolled up bar of soap. Take the two remaining corners and fold both into the center. Tie together with a string, wire, or pipe cleaner, and ends of washcloth become ears. To make the antlers, take a pipe cleaner and fold it in half. Take a second pipe cleaner and cut off two pieces that are each 2" long. Wrap the two short pieces around the ends of the long piece to form the antlers. Glue the antlers between the ears. Glue the wiggly eyes and the pom-pom nose to one side of the washcloth to make the face on the reindeer. Tie the ribbon into a small bow and glue it with a sprig of holly to one side of the ear.

▼ *Steps for making reindeer*:

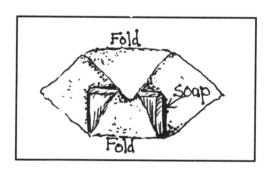
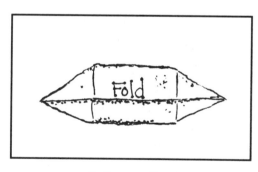

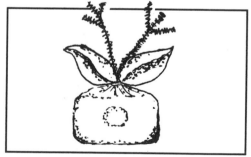

◆ *Variation*:You can make a Santa with the same basic directions as the reindeer except: * Use a 1/4" pink pom-pom for the nose and 1/2" round wiggly eyes. * When you pull the points together and secure them, make a Santa hat out of a felt triangle and use curly chenille for the fur on the edge. Pull it down over the "points" and glue in place. * Use a strip of curly angel hair for the beard.

I've Really Done It This Time!

Perhaps you're a person who can look at anything and see another use for it. But foam sealant, ordinarily used for filling in walls or insulation, as artificial snow for Christmas decorations? That's right, and it looks great.

▲ *To make, you'll need*: Waxed paper, expanding foam sealant (available at most hardware stores), rubber gloves (if they do not come with the sealant), pine boughs, wreath or Christmas tree, white flat spray paint, Christmas ornaments of your choice, toothpicks, and glue.

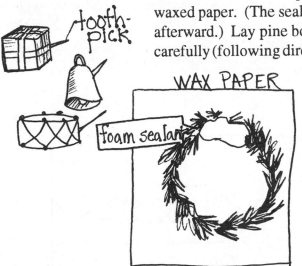

▼ *Directions*: Centerpiece Assembly—Cover all work surfaces thoroughly with waxed paper. (The sealant sticks to everything, but waxed paper can be peeled off afterward.) Lay pine boughs or wreaths on the waxed paper. Wearing the gloves, carefully (following directions on the can) spray the foam on the boughs. (It expands four to five times its original size.) Make the foam heavier at the beginning of the branch and lighter at the tips. Spray one time only, unless you need to fill in a missed area. Allow the foam to harden for about eight hours. (Hint: Some foam has a yellowish tinge. If this is the case, when the foam is thoroughly dry, spray with the white flat paint. You may also wish to purchase "snowflakes" at a craft store. Spray or paint glue on the foam and sprinkle with the flakes.) Glue the toothpicks to the bottom of the ornaments. When dry, arrange the ornaments on the bough and stick the picks into the foam to hold in place.

◆ **Variations**

You may wish to spray your whole Christmas tree with the foam. Since the foam is very light, but indestructible, it works very well. Just remember to make the "snow" heavier closer closer to the trunk and lighter at the ends of the branches so that it looks realistic.

EXTRA● EXTRA ● EXTRA ● EXTRA

■ **To Preserve Family Memories, Use Pictures**

Don't just paste your pictures into a photo album. Use one or more of these creative ways to display them.

❏ Make a collage of school pictures, showing how your child has gotten older with each passing year.

❏ Put an appropriate-sized picture inside a decorative jar for a photo display. Decorate the top with fabric and ribbon.

❏ To send a thank-you note for a gift, add a picture of yourself with the gift.

❏ If your children come home with items that they've made for you and with pictures taken of them in activities, have them make a treasure box, decorating the outside with Contact paper. Make them responsible for saving all memories in the box. Every so often, you and your children can sort through the box and separate the things into envelopes or projects.

❏ A special kind of box is a heritage box. Cover the outside with a collage of family shots, made by photocopying pictures and cutting them out and grouping them together. Make a family tree chart for the box's top. Inside, in order, file letters, life accounts, oral histories, group photos in protective paper, etc.

❏ Make a family Christmas ornament every year by taking a sturdy paper board, covering it with holiday wrapping paper, and gluing a family grouping to it.

Don't Throw Out Those Christmas Cards

Peek boxes. They're exactly what they imply. Special, my-very-own scenes in a box that children can make. All you need are some old Christmas cards and leftover gift boxes.

▲ *To make, you'll need*: Lots of old Christmas cards, a leftover gift box (5"-6" deep works best), scissors, spray paint, glue or tape, and toothpicks or light wire.

▼ *Directions*:

Fig. 1

Begin the project by letting the kids help you separate the cards into categories: children, animals, buildings, etc. Look at the cards and decide on a theme for your peek box. It could be centered around the outside with snow and ice or the inside with a fireplace and holiday fare.

Cut the box to form the base for your scene. This can be done by cutting one side out of the box until you are even with the bottom, but leave a 1" lip on each side for stability. If you want to replace the lid, you will need to cut a three-sided flap in the lid that can be lifted up to let some light in. Spray paint the inside and outside of the box or cover it with wrapping paper (see Fig. 1).

To prepare the cards, cut out the individual figures or buildings, leaving a 1/2" tab at the bottom that can be folded back under to make a support to glue to the box, allowing the figures to stand. If there isn't enough space to leave a tab, one can be made by cutting out a piece of leftover card into a narrow strip and gluing it to the back of the figure. Extend it far enough beyond the figure to fold back and form a tab. If you have a picture that is very slender or if the paper doesn't have enough body to stand up, you can give them extra support by gluing a toothpick or some wire to the back of the figure.

Now the real fun and creativity begin. You are going to start putting the final scene together. Start gluing at the back and work forward to the opening. You can glue some of the pictures on the back and sides of the box and then continue with the ones that are free-standing so you have a three-dimensional look (see Fig. 2).

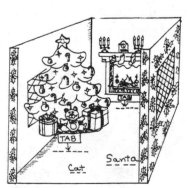

Fig. 2

If you want to make it even more fun, turn it into a puppet stage. Glue the bottoms of two boxes the same size together. Cut one end from each box (as described above) so that the openings are facing the opposite direction. An example scene would be an outdoor scenario with pine trees, ice, and snow all around. You can also cut an opening in the bottom of the boxes where they are glued together to make an ice skating pond. Make a skating puppet by gluing a popsicle stick to the back of a penguin and holding it up through the hole to skate. The space cut out for the ice pond can be lined with a short string of tree lights that are hooked up to a battery. This adds sparkle and fun to your peek box.

For the Child in All of Us

These gift and decorating ideas for the kids will keep them busy.

■ Pop Can Ornament

▲ *To make, you'll need*: One soda pop can, fabric craft paints, scraps of felt, pipe cleaners, and glue.

▼ *Directions*: Crush each pop can by squeezing in the middle first and then smashing the ends together by stepping on the can (the opening becomes the mouth). Spray paint the can any color, but spray the top portion a flesh color. Using craft paints, add eyes and lashes and outline opening for mouth. Add miniature pom-pom for nose. Allow paint to dry thoroughly. Add antlers from pipe cleaners and ears from felt. Make Mr. and Mrs. Santa, Christmas carolers, and angels by substituting hair for pipe cleaners and felt hat for ears.

■ Santa Express Train

▲ *To make, you'll need*: Two-inch-thick foam, electric knife, and fabric craft paints.

▼ *Directions*: Draw the shapes of train cars on foam; cut out the shapes using electric knife. Paint each car as you like after outlining each section in black.

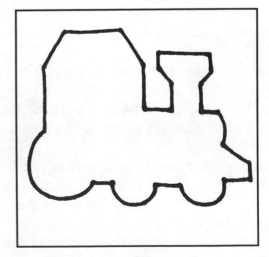

■ Gift Boxes from Recycled Egg Cartons

▲ *To make, you'll need*: Egg cartons, small black plastic craft hats, fabric craft paints, and glue.

▼ *Directions*: Stack two egg carton bottoms together (cut away sides facing). Glue a hat onto each egg section and then add snowman faces and buttons on each for snowmen by the dozen. Tie the cartons together with ribbon.

■ Gift Sacks

These can be made by recycling brown paper bags. Use your imagination, construction paper, cotton balls, ribbons, etc., to create a whole "sack village" plus Santa and his reindeer. Your child can help you using his or her hands and acrylic paints. Put a little paint on a paper plate, place the child's hands in the paint, and press onto paper sack. Allow handprints to dry, cut them out, and glue carefully on the top of another paper bag to create antlers. Using paints, paint on faces; use miniature pink pompoms for the noses (Rudolph will get a large red pom-pom). For Santa, glue white cotton balls around his painted face for hair and beard. For houses, cut out shapes of doors and windows from other colored paper bags and outline with craft paints; glue on outside of bag. Add an additional piece of paper folded over the top of bag for the roof; add stickers to decorate. Punch holes at the top of the sack and thread with ribbon to tie closed.

■ Reindeer Antlers

▲ *To make, you'll need*: Half-inch-thick foam, electric knife, brown spray paint, glitter, and craft paint.

▼ *Directions*: Draw a circle about 2" larger than your face, adding antlers to the top. Cut the middle from the circle, leaving a 2" edge. Spray paint both sides brown and let dry. Add holly leaves and other decorations and wear like a hat.

Holiday Centerpieces

These will solve your problem of what to put in the middle of the dinner table, buffet table, or mantel this year.

■ A Fruit Centerpiece

Get a wooden board and place nails in the board as spikes. Buy some apples and oranges. Core apples and peel oranges and cut bigger holes in them. Stick fruit on the spikes. Place tapered candles in apples, votive or scented candles in the oranges. Arrange with evergreens and colorful ribbon for Christmas.

■ A Snowman Centerpiece

The snowman can be made in any size; here are instructions for one 12" high. You will need: 1/2 cup margarine, 16-oz. package miniature marshmallows, 20 cups popped popcorn, black top hat made from construction paper, and candy or nuts for buttons. To make: melt margarine and marshmallows in saucepan and pour over popcorn. Spray hands with vegetable oil. Form popcorn into three balls—small, medium, and large. To secure the balls on top of each other, form a well in the top of each ball and a bump on the bottom of the ball that will sit on top of it. They fit together like a jigsaw puzzle. Decorate with top hat and candy/nuts for face and buttons.

■ Reindeer for the Buffet Table

Make reindeer using candy canes and black pipe cleaners as antlers. Buy a small Santa and sled; connect to reindeer with ribbon. Take a large piece of styrofoam and put reindeer down each side. In the middle of the styrofoam, hollow a trough. Place dishes in trough in which you have put hot water. Wearing gloves, put in pieces of dry ice to create the effect of a sleigh drifting through snow.

Gift Decorations

Here's a grab-bag of gift-giving ideas for the holiday season.

■ Hanging Gingerbread Men

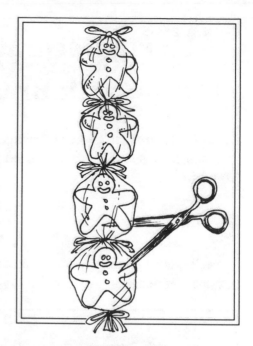

String together some gingerbread men as a tasty farewell treat for visitors. To make the string, roll out 10-12 feet of plastic wrap. Place decorated gingerbread men face down lengthwise about 2 inches apart along the wrap. Fold wrap in from both sides, overlapping it to cover gingerbread men. Use colorful red and green Christmas ribbons to tie a secure bow around the wrap between each gingerbread man. Top the string with a large, full bow. Hang your colorful string of gingerbread men beside the front door.* As holiday guests leave, snip off a gingerbread treat for them to munch on their way.

■ Christmas Tree and Present Box

A great gift for friends or relatives who might not have a Christmas tree is to include a tree with the gifts.

Obtain a shoe box, dress box, or coat box. If box has a separate lid, use a wide piece of tape to make a hinge so lid opens only one way. You may wish to wrap the top and bottom individually with Christmas wrapping before you hinge the top.

Cut a Christmas tree shape from green construction paper or draw one on paper. Make tree just large enough to fit into top of box and paste it inside of lid. Decorate the Christmas tree with little colored paper ornaments. When box opens, tree stands upright with presents at its base.

■ Tin-Can Card Holder

Make your Christmas cards easy to read with this handy holder. Cut both ends from a tall, narrow can. Potato chip cans work well. Secure red or green yarn to the inside of can with masking or filament tape. Wind yarn up and down inside and outside of can until yarn completely covers it. Strips of yarn should be close together. Secure end of yarn to inside of can with another piece of tape.

Slip Christmas card under one strip of yarn so yarn holds it to can along fold of card. Card hangs open and makes it easy to read special mesages all through the holidays.

* Tie length of matching ribbon to a small or child-size pair of scissors and attach to wrap.

Party Decorations and Fun with Bread Clay

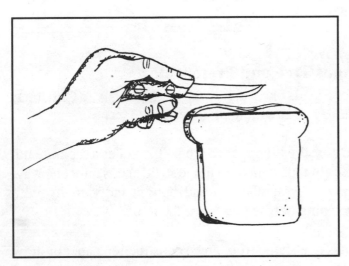

From Easter to birthdays to Christmas, these "clay" animals and scenes guarantee oohs and aahs. You need bread, eggs, and imagination from your kids as they do the work.

■ Basic Clay Recipe

Ingredients: 8 slices day-old bread (or 8 slices fresh bread that has been set out on the counter to dry slightly) and 1/2 cup white craft glue.

▼ Directions

Cut crusts off bread. Break bread into small pieces in a large bowl. Add glue a little at a time, combining the bread pieces and the glue by kneading with the hands until a smooth, clay-like mixture is formed. The kneading process may take 15 or 20 minutes. Once it is smooth and pliable (like modeling clay), set it aside. Wash your hands and apply hand lotion so bread dough clay won't stick to your hands as you mold it and apply it to the eggs.

■ Hard-Cooked Eggs

Select smooth, dry, white eggs that are not cracked or chipped. Place eggs in an enamel, stainless steel, or glass pan. Do not stack eggs on top of one another. Do not overcrowd the single layer of eggs in the pan. Cover eggs completely with cold water. Leave the pan uncovered. Heat on medium or medium-low until very tiny bubbles can be seen rising from the heat; drain and immediately flush eggs with cold water so that their temperature is immediately lowered. Let eggs dry. Handle dry eggs with clean, dry hands.

◆ *Note*: If you prefer, the bread dough clay can be molded around wooden eggs instead of hard-cooked eggs.

■ Painting

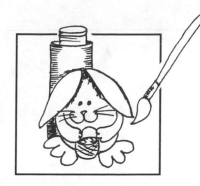

Let the egg and clay models set overnight to dry. Then use a small brush to paint with acrylic paint.

▼ *Suggestions for molding clay animals and other figures:*

● **Turtle**: Pinch off a piece of bread dough clay big enough to flatten into a turtle shape that is about 3" x 5" x 3/4" thick. Shape feet and head on the turtle. Use a toothpick to make holes for eyes in the head. Press and glue a hard-cooked egg into the center of the flat turtle shape for a body. Let the turtle dry overnight. Paint the egg to resemble a turtle shell.

● **Duck**: Shape duck feet from the bread dough clay. Set a hard-cooked egg on top of the feet to form the duck's body. Glue the egg in place. Pinch off some dough and shape it into wings. Glue them to the egg. Shape a head and bill. Glue them in place. Let dry overnight. Paint.

● **Bear**: Use a hard-cooked egg for the tummy. Set and glue it onto shaped bear feet. Add body parts (ears, head, paws) shaped from pieces of bread dough clay. Glue the pieces in place. Let dry. Paint face and details.

● **Goldilocks and the Three Bears in a Basket**: Make Goldilocks' face from a hard-cooked or a wooden egg. Glue pieces of yellow yarn to the egg for hair or mold hair from bread dough clay. When dry, paint the face and other details as desired. Place Goldilocks in a small doll furniture bed and cover with a piece of fabric to resemble a quilt or blanket. Put the bed, Goldilocks, and other dolls in an Easter basket. Add three egg bears.

● **Penguin Basket**: Use a hard-cooked or wooden egg for the body. Mold pieces of bread dough clay into feet. Press the egg onto the feet. Glue in place. Add back, flippers, and penguin head molded from pieces of clay and glued into place on the egg. Let dry. Paint. Set finished penguins on a mirror that has been placed in an Easter basket. Surround the mirror with cotton batting so that it resembles ice and snow.

● **Dinosaur Basket**: Use hard-cooked or wooden eggs for the body. Add body parts, shaping a head, back, and tail to resemble a dinosaur of your choice. Glue the parts to the egg and let them dry overnight. Paint. Set a variety of dinosaurs in an Easter basket that has been partially filled with natural-colored artificial or dry grass. Add dinosaurs and dinosaur eggs. For dinosaur eggs, use eggs that have accidentally cracked in cooking or handling, or purposely crack any hard-cooked egg. The egg should be cracked all over. Dip the cracked, cooked egg in a mixture of powdered grape punch mixed in 2 cups of water. Remove from punch. Peel the egg. The dark punch will leave vein-like markings on the egg. This will resemble the markings on a dinosaur egg. Place several dinosaur eggs and dinosaurs in an Easter basket or use them for a fun centerpiece.

A Western Round-up Birthday Party for Kids

As a theme for birthday parties for little kids, think "western" and let 'er rip!

■ Cactus Decoration

For this attractive stand-up "cactus" complete with spines, you'll need: foam core (posterboard with foam sandwiched in the middle) at least 4' high, green poster paint, pink tissue paper, toothpicks, craft knife, and sponge brush.

To assemble, draw a large cactus shape (4' or larger on the foam core cardboard). Cut out carefully with a craft knife. Use sponge brush to streak green paint vertically on cactus. Cut circle, 6" in diameter, out of pink tissue paper. Pinch and gather paper at the center of circle to form a flower. Attach it at top of cactus. Stick toothpicks into foam core around the edges of your "cactus" and at intervals throughout figure to form spines. (You may need to glue the toothpicks if they do not stick into the foam securely.)

Cut triangle about 1 1/2"-2" tall from the scraps of foam core cardboard and attach to cactus back so it will stand alone. You can also brace the figure with large rocks.

■ Paper Bag Cowboy Vests

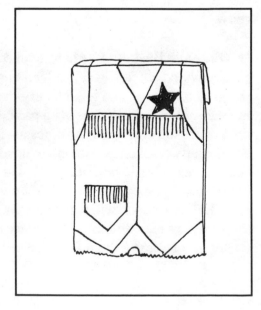

Each young guest can decorate his or her vest with markers. To make each vest, cut the bottom from a large paper bag. Cut bag open vertically at glued seam. (Cut off remaining part of the seam.) Lay bag flat. Fold each side to meet in the center like a vest. Cut out neck, large armholes, and rounded edges at bottom of each side in front. Glue shoulder seams. Cut parallel slits all around bottom and around rounded edges of vest's front-bottom to form fringe. Draw a star-shaped sheriff's badge on one side of the vest.

■ Cow Milking Game

Children will enjoy milking this cow. You'll need a 2' x 3' sheet of foam core or plywood, rubber glove, markers, and a picture of a cow (from a coloring book) to serve as a pattern. You can use an opaque projector (libraries or churches have these) to enlarge the cow's picture to poster size. Draw cow to fill foam core. (Do not draw udder.) Use markers to outline, put in details, and color cow. Use a craft knife to slit along leg and back abdomen where the udder would be. Slip rubber glove into slit. Attach it on back. To prepare cow for milking, fill the glove with liquid. Close the top of glove. (Tie end opposite fingers in a secure knot, or close it with rubber band or bag tie.) Punch a small hole at end of each finger, then allow children to "milk" the glove-uddered cow.

■ Roping the Steer

A variation on the traditional ring toss game, you'll need heavy cardboard, posterboard, foam core or plywood, a 3' length of furring strip, wooden stick or broom handle with a point filed on the end, heavy wire or coat hanger, and some heavy rope.

Reproduce a long-horned steer's head on the cardboard or posterboard. Make sure that the horns protrude 5-6" from the head. Cut out the head with a craft knife. Draw in the steer's features with markers. Mount head on strip so that head stands upright for an indoor game. Place the stick end into a container filled with rocks, or three or four inches into lawn for an outdoor game.

For lariat circle, bend heavy wire or coat hanger wire into a 6"-diameter circle. Push wire into a length of rope, weaving rope so that wire is covered. Secure wire; glue rope so that the circle is complete and no sharp ends of wire protrude.

To play the game, children stand 2-3' from the steer's head, then toss the wire/rope circle over steer's horns.

Dry Ice Delectables

Dry ice needs to be handled with caution, as it is about 70 degrees below zero. Always use gloves to handle it—you can get burned badly. Do not allow children to handle dry ice. A hammer is useful to break the large pieces into smaller ones.

■ "Smoking" Centerpieces Add Party Atmosphere

Choose any size waterproof container. Empty ice cream buckets covered with Contact paper, for example, work very well. Put pieces of dry ice in the container and pour hot water on it. If ice does not smoke enough, add a little more water. A number of containers placed around a room will create a "foggy" atmosphere for parties and dances.

■ Fire-Breathing Dragon

Obtain two 18-ounce and two 36-ounce empty oatmeal boxes. Remove the lids. Spray paint two yards of cream-colored Contact paper with bright green fluorescent paint. Also spray paint the bottoms of all four boxes. Cut a curve in one of the large boxes so that the dragon's body will appear curved when put together. Cover all the boxes with the green Contact paper. Hold the boxes together with bands of 1 1/2"-wide dark green plastic tape. Cut two 3" x 5" V-shapes from the open end of the last small box so that the dragon's mouth is formed. Glue two pieces of wide yellow rickrack in the dragon's mouth for teeth. Place tufts of gold yarn on the back of the box for hair. Glue two large green pom-poms in front of the hair for eyeballs. Use large wiggly eyes or black buttons glued to the pom-poms for pupils. Cut two teardrop-shaped nostrils from bright pink felt and glue them to the "nose" above the mouth. Glue the small box onto the front of the large box to make the head. Cut two dragon wings from posterboard and spray paint them green. Attach them to the large boxes with the green plastic tape.

Decorate the dragon with bright pink freckles made by cutting circles from pink felt and gluing them on the cheeks and on the body of the dragon. Use a piece of dark red felt to make a "forked" tongue. Glue it in the open mouth so that it hangs over the lower lip. Make a small cylinder from a 3"-wide piece of posterboard. Glue a large green pom-pom to one end of the cylinder. Decorate it with pink circles cut from felt. Tape it in place to make the dragon's tail.

Put some small pieces of dry ice in a custard cup. Place the cup in the mouth of the dragon. Pour some hot water on the ice. You will have a fire-breathing dragon. The custard cup will hold enough dry ice to "breathe fire" for five minutes.

■ Puff the Magic Lion

Empty an 18-ounce oatmeal box. Cut out the bottom of the box. Cover the box with gold Contact paper. Cut the top off a #16 balloon. Discard the end that would be used to blow the balloon up. Stretch the other end of the balloon over the open end of the box and tape it in place. Use the lid of the box to make the lion's face. Cover the top of the lid with a circle cut from gold felt and glue to the lid. Cut a small circle, about 1 to 1 1/2" in diameter, from the center of the lid to make the lion's mouth. Glue a strip of brown fringe about 1" wide around the lid to form the lion's mane. Cut ears from gold felt and "cheeks" from pink felt. Glue them in place. Use a small brown pom-pom for a nose and attach small wiggly eyes. Cut jagged teeth from white felt and circle the mouth with a piece of red yarn. Glue a small red bow under the lion's "chin."

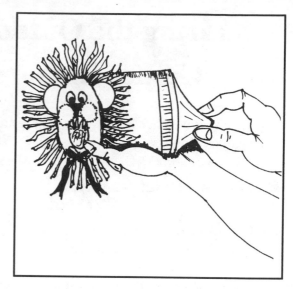

Pieces of dry ice placed inside the lion will form a gas that can be expelled in small "puffs" by holding the lion box in one hand and grasping the center of the balloon piece between the thumb and finger of the other hand and stretching and releasing the balloon in a pumping motion. The puffs of cold air will blow out candles on a birthday cake, etc.

■ Birthday Cake Volcano

Bake a chocolate or dark-colored cake in a bundt cake pan. Decorate with frosting, cherries, pieces of green gumdrops, and animal crackers. Place a small paper cup in the center of the cake. Fill the cup with pieces of dry ice. If it is a birthday cake, light the candles. Pour some hot water on the dry ice, causing the volcano to steam and smoke.

■ Old Faithful Geyser

Turn on the hot water faucet in the kitchen sink. When it is running, place chunks of dry ice in the garbage disposal. Move the faucet to side of the sink that has the disposal in it and hit the switch. Old Faithful will erupt.

Bring the Outdoor Games Indoors

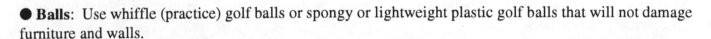

When winter weather keeps your kids inside, bring outdoor games indoors.

■ Indoor Miniature Golf

Set up this game in your living room or family room to provide fun for the whole family.

● **Putters**: Each putter requires one 3" length of 1" dowel and a 30" length of 1/2" dowel. You'll need to drill a hole in the middle of the 1" dowel piece to fit the 1/2" dowel. Insert the longer dowel into the hole in the wider, short piece. Glue to secure, then paint if you wish.

● **Balls**: Use whiffle (practice) golf balls or spongy or lightweight plastic golf balls that will not damage furniture and walls.

● **Traps and Obstacles**: Let your imagination go in setting up your course. Tin cans with both ends cut out (and painted, if you wish) and lengths of large PVC pipe or dryer vent tubing make challenging, fun tunnels. Use towels draped on the carpet or smoothed on the floor for sand traps or "ponds" (use a blue towel). Small pillows and throw rugs or pieces of carpet can outline and provide barriers and textured "greens." Weighted milk cartons or plastic two-liter pop bottles provide obstacles to putters. Boards, cardboard boxes, or lengths of posterboard can be set up as bridges or ramps.

● **Holes**: Cut little doors in the sides of a cardboard box, or cut a hole in a rug sample. Make a cardboard ramp up into a shallow box with a hole cut in its top surface.

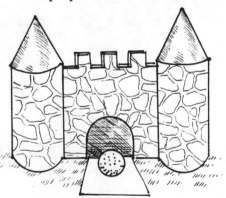

● **Construct a "Castle"**: Cut tower and crenellation outlines in the top edge of a cardboard box. Cut a trap door or entrance door into one side of the box for the "hole." If you wish, cut the entrance two to three inches up the side of the box, then place a board or cardboard ramp across a towel "moat" to lead to the castle entrance.

● **"Monster Mouth" Holes**: One-gallon plastic milk cartons make amusing monster mouths. Cut a hole near the bottom of the carton in a mouth shape, and complete with teeth or fang obstacles, if you wish. Use paint, glue on construction paper, or felt eyes and other features to complete the monster face. Place a rock, piece of wood, or other object in the carton to weigh it down during play.

■ Horseshoes

Horseshoes adapt well to indoor play. You'll need a cardboard cereal box, a cardboard tube (one that might come with paper towels, waxed paper, or foil, for instance), and posterboard or cardboard. Place the empty cereal box on its side, taping the once-opened end of the box closed. Trace the circular end of the cardboard tube in the middle of the horizontal top of the cereal box. Cut along the inside of the traced circle. Set the cardboard tube upright in the cut-out circle. The tube should sit snugly. Tape it in place, then paint or cover the tube and box to decorate, if you wish.

Next, cut horseshoe shapes from posterboard or cardboard. Make sure they're large enough to fit around the cardboard tube. You may want to weight the horseshoes with paper clips—one on each end and one in the center. Children can toss the cardboard horseshoes to "ring" the cardboard tube.

■ Hopscotch

This game takes a minimum of equipment and preparation. Using masking tape, outline a hopscotch diagram on your game room or family room carpet or vinyl floor. Children can use coins, keys, or other small, flat, throwable items as hopscotch markers.

A Real Block Party

■ **Here's what a real block party is, at least where toys are concerned.**

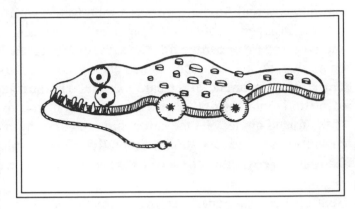

You can buy inexpensive wood scraps from craft stores, lumberyards, frame shops, construction shops, etc., and use them to assemble fun toys and other items. Many companies package assorted sizes and shapes of wood pieces. Some have them packaged and on sale for five to seven dollars. Toothpicks, wooden clothespins, popsicle sticks, and tongue depressors are other readily available "wood pieces" that are useful in making a variety of crafts. Simply add some paint, glue, nails, buttons, yarn, rope, ingenuity, and imagination, and the result can be fun and fascinating for people of all ages. Here are some suggestions to get you started:

Lion: Start with a block of wood from a 2 x 4 as a basic shape. Space four dowels cut the same length on the block and glue them in place for legs. Another 2 x 4 block glued on top of the dowels forms the body. If you drill a hole in it, yarn or untwined rope can be glued in place for a tail. A circle of wood makes a head. Glue tongue depressors or popsicle sticks around the circle, sunflower fashion, to form the lion's mane. Make a face from a smaller circle. Use buttons, pom-poms, etc., for eyes and nose or paint the features on the face. Glue the circle face on top of the mane. If your bag of wood scraps contains four small wheels, nail them to the 2 x 4 base and the toy will roll, or a child can pull it with an attached rope or string.

Bunny: Use a large circle of wood for the body. Glue tongue depressors on a smaller circle and fasten in place for the head. Yarn can be glued around the edges of circles to "outline" the ears, etc. Toothpicks make good whiskers on bunnies, lions, and other animals. Other household scraps of wood or textiles can be used to decorate, or paint the bunny and the other animals.

Giraffe: Use four wooden clothespins for legs, a block of wood for the body, a dowel for the neck, and a small block of wood for the head. Tear off irregular circles of masking tape and place on the giraffe, then spray paint. Then tear off the tape; the painted and unpainted areas will give the simulation of spots. Use yarn pieces for the giraffe's tail and mane.

Lily Pad: Use a block of wood for the pond. Paint it blue. Use round wood pieces for the lilies. Paint them green. Add miniature fish, blossoms, etc., to the pond.

Alligator: Use a 2 x 4 block for the body. Cut end of a smaller block at angle and nail or glue in place to resemble an open mouth. Add button eyes. Paint or trim with wide rickrack or other fabric scraps. Add wheels if you wish.

Party Favors

Use Polaroid® pictures in these special "frames" as gifts for your guests.

■ Basic Directions

● **Choose a Pattern**: Ideas can come from logos, advertisements, cookie cutters, letterheads, original drawings, children's paint books, a picture, etc.

In choosing the pattern, remember two things: 1. The silhouette or the outside lines of the pattern will become the shape of the finished frame. The silhouette lines of the pattern, therefore, need to be pleasing to the eye and fairly simple. 2. The pattern should contain an inside outline of a simple geometric shape (a square, a circle, a rectangle, an oval, etc.). For example, an outline of a teddy bear or another small figure holding a sign, or a basketball hoop with a basketball poised over it would be a good choice, because the sign and/or the basketball provide a geometric shape that can become a cut-out area that reveals or "frames" the picture. If the chosen pattern contains no geometric outline, look for an area within the pattern where one can be drawn or sketched in by hand. The geometric shape should enclose a 3" x 3" space, which is the size of a Polaroid picture.

● **Sizing the Pattern**: Once the pattern is chosen, you may need to enlarge it or reduce it in overall size. Frames can be any size you choose. Enlarging or reducing the pattern is simple to do by using a copy machine, an opaque projector, graph paper, or paper marked by measured squares.

● **Cutting the Frame**: Use soft pine wood that is 1/2-3/4" thick. Trace the outline of the pattern onto the wood and cut around the basic shape with a miter saw. Trace the opening for the picture and cut it out with a skill saw. If you wish, take the pattern to a lumberyard, a hardware store, or a carpenter. They will do the cutting for you.

● **Painting the Frame**: * Use a water-based acrylic paint in colors to complement your room's decor. * Apply a white (or other color) base coat on the face of the cut-out frame by using a 1" or 2" sponge brush. * Thin down colored acrylic paint just a little. * Dip a toothbrush into the paint. Holding the frame perpendicular to the counter at about eye level, fleck the paint off the toothbrush by flipping the end of the brush with the thumb. The paint will "splatter" in small flecks. Hold the brush 6-8" from the frame. Use two colors of paint for the flecking process, but fleck them on separately. Black and red are a nice contrast for white, but any colors that harmonize and contrast with each other will work well. Paint the edges and back of the frame with black paint, using a #10 brush. Screen printing or stenciling may be done on the frame.

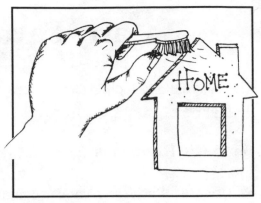

● **Finally**: Attach a sawtooth metal hook to the back of the frame for hanging.

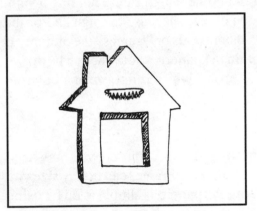

◆ **Home Frame**: Use a pattern of the silhouette of a house that has been enlarged to about 5" x 7". Cut out a 3" x 3" square window in the center of the house so that a picture can be placed in back of it. Use the pattern to cut the wood frame. Paint with a white base coat. Fleck with black and then red paint. Outline the sides of the frame with black paint. Cover the back with black paint and attach a metal hanger. When frame is dry, place a favorite picture in the window.

"Construction" Party

A fun way to top off a house construction or remodeling project is with a "construction party." Hot dogs and corn are always picnic staples, but serving them on paint rollers makes it a bit different. Put condiments in clean, unused paint cans and paint brushes to dab them with—and use paint roller pans to hold the corn—not the usual accompaniments. Here are some more ideas.

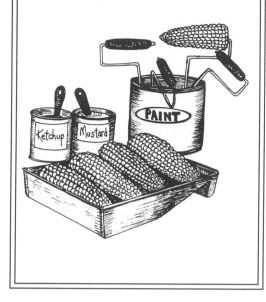

■ Tool Box of Chocolates

For a unique and different dessert suggestion while entertaining guests in a new home, take a regular tool box and fill it with chocolates in the shapes of tools. To do: Melt one cup of summer coating chocolate in the microwave on high for five minutes. Get plastic chocolate molds in the shape of hammers, wrenches, and other tools. Spoon the chocolate carefully into each mold and refrigerate for at least 10 minutes. Chocolates, if completely cool, will pop out of the molds easily.

■ Brick Centerpieces

For a stylish and appropriate centerpiece, use your leftover bricks. First clean them off and tie a ribbon around center in a floral bow. Top off by gluing silk or dried flowers to center of ribbon.

■ Hard-Hat Serving Dishes

A new look for serving fresh fruits can be captured by painting the outside of hard hats to look like a fruit of your choice. First put two coats of white gesso paint on the outside of several hats and then use an acrylic paint to decorate them (acrylic paint doesn't stick well to plastic, but it adheres to the gesso). For example, you might paint one hat using the colors dark green, light green, and white to create the look of a watermelon. Then paint the brim bright red with black spots for seeds. You can also paint a cantaloupe, grapes, a strawberry, and an orange.

To display, use a flat board covered with paint seal. Then paint the appropriate leaves or vines where the particular fruit (hat) would sit. To hold it upright, hammer nails in a circle in which the hat is then placed.

To serve, line the inside of the hat with aluminum foil and fill with fresh fruit.

Get Set to Blow

Do you wish you could decorate your big summer wing-ding with the balloon extravaganza that you see in the magazines? Here's how it's done.

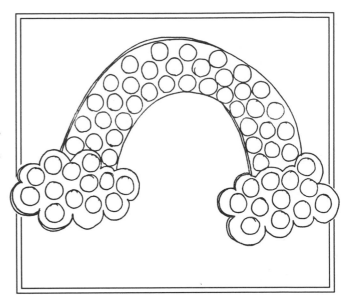

● Rainbow

Using either foam core or heavy cardboard, draw outline of rainbow and clouds in desired size. Cut out with X-Acto knife. Paint cloud area white and rainbow desired colors. Make rainbow strips wide enough to accommodate long, rainbow-colored, thin balloons. Blow up balloons and tie ends. Using an ice pick or other sharp object, poke holes through cardboard on both ends of rainbow strips. Insert tied ends of balloons through holes. Tie additional knot in end of balloon to secure to cardboard or foam core. To keep long balloons arched on cardboard/core, apply double-stick tape to cardboard/core, then stick balloons on. Poke holes randomly in clouds. Blow up several round, white balloons (different sizes) and insert ends through holes. Tie knot to secure. Display as desired.

● Grapes

Follow the same general procedures, only cut cardboard/foam core in shape of a grape cluster. Spray paint cardboard/core with purple paint. Blow up several purple balloons in a variety of sizes; attach to cardboard/core. Blow up about four green balloons for leaves; attach to top of grape cluster. Use green curling ribbon tied to leaves to give "vine" effect.

● Arch

This decoration requires helium-filled balloons. You can buy or rent a tank of helium; you are charged only for the amount of helium you use.

Choose four colors of same-size balloons for your arch. Using balloons in two colors, fill with helium and tie ends, then hook balloons together with paper clips. Fill remaining two colors of balloons with helium, tie ends, then hook together. Join the two sets of balloons by twisting pairs together, making a cluster of four balloons. To form arch, use strong nylon filament line (heavy fishing line) to attach clusters of balloons. To make assembling arch easier, tie nylon line to chair while adding balloon clusters. Unroll more line as needed until arch is desired size.

To give arch a spiral effect, attach first cluster of balloons by wrapping one of the colored balloons around nylon line. After completing another cluster of four balloons, attach to line by wrapping a second color of balloon around line. Continue making clusters and alternating colors of balloons wrapped around line until arch is desired size.

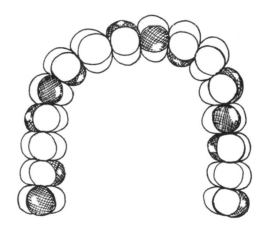

Alternate arch: A simpler version can be made by attaching colored, helium-filled balloons to strong nylon line one at a time. Attach by wrapping tied end of balloon around line and continue until you reach desired length of arch.

● Flamingo

Build basic frame out of taped aluminum (see illustration). Use nylon net wrapped over frame to shape flamingo—stuff inside of net with crumpled newspaper or small pink balloons until flamingo takes shape. Blow up small pink balloons for body, black balloons for eyes and part of beak, and white for beak. Attach balloons to net using paper clips.

70

Unique Ideas for a Garden Party

When it's time for outdoor parties, you'll wonder if there's an original idea left for those occasions. Fear not—here are enough to get you through an entire summer.

■ Star-Spangled Carnations

▲ *To make, you'll need*:
White carnations, red and blue food coloring, and two clean pint jars filled 3/4 full with water.

▼ *Directions*:
In one of the pint jars with water, put several drops of red food coloring; in the other, several drops of blue food coloring. (The darker the food coloring, the more colorful the flowers will be.)

Beginning at the bottom and being careful not to break the stem, slice stem of each carnation about halfway up the carnation. Put one side of stem in red water, other side of stem in blue water. It takes about 4 to 5 hours before "coloring" takes place. Hint: Let your carnations stay in colored water overnight for best results.

■ Appliqued Tablecloth

Beat the breeze by making your own tablecloth with special pockets shaped like strawberries made from appliqued green and red cotton fabric to hold each person's utensils, napkins, and paper plates.

▲ *To make, you'll need*:
White tablecloth to fit your table, red and green fabric scraps for strawberries, and 1/2"-wide red elastic.

▼ *Directions*:
Enlarge pattern. Cut six each of strawberry, leaf design, and pocket front. Finish top edge of pocket front. Pin strawberry and pocket front to tablecloth. Zigzag edges. Repeat process with leaf design.

To anchor your tablecloth, sew triangular pockets on underside of fabric at each of four corners. Make triangle pocket large enough to hold a good-sized rock (about 2-3" diameter). Put rock in each corner pocket.

■ Fruit Swizzle Sticks

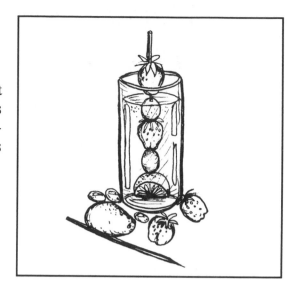

To add an extra bit of fun to summer drinks, make fruit swizzle sticks on bamboo skewers. Alternate fruit on skewers (example: grape, strawberry, grape, strawberry, etc.), ending with a lemon wedge on the bottom. You can store sticks in freezer in a resealable plastic bag up to four months.

■ Whale of a Dessert

This idea can be used for any variety of melon. Draw a whale face on one end of the melon. On a piece of heavy paper or posterboard, draw and cut out flukes. Make slit at back end of melon (opposite face) and insert edge of flukes in melon. When ready to serve, place a lighted sparkler in melon for "spout." Variation: Set melon in large oblong glass baking pan. Using heavy-duty gloves, place small pieces of dry ice around melon. Pour warm water into glass pan and watch the mist "swim" around your whale!

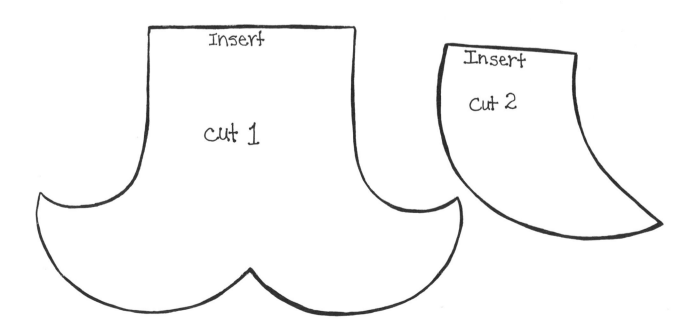

Insert

cut 1

Insert

Cut 2

Flowerpots and More Flowerpots

At this flowerpot party, flowerpots are used for everything else but flowers. Serving bowls with flower spoons, as barbecues, to make a cake, and at the end of a Maypole are some uses you'll see.

One strong word of caution before you try these: Only use unglazed clay pots, and always line them with aluminum foil or plastic so that food doesn't come in direct contact with the pot. Never use glazed pots, which can produce lead poisoning, or ceramic pots, which may contain highly toxic cadmium.

■ Flowerpots—Either Clay or Plastic

To make these bowls even more fun, turn your serving spoons into flowers. Paint the handles of wooden spoons with green acrylic paint. From posterboard or heavy construction paper, cut out flower shapes and leaves, glue them to the spoon handles, and insert in the flowerpots. (You can also purchase thin wooden flower cutouts from craft stores, paint them, and glue to the spoon handles.)

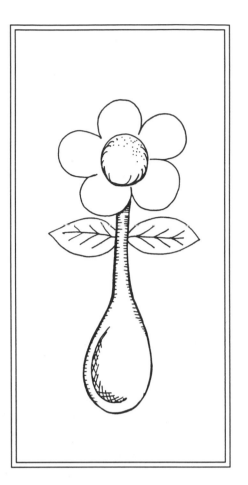

■ Very Large Pots

Pots at least 12" in diameter can be used as portable barbecues. Simply fill the pot with dirt to within 4" of the top. Line the dirt and the top of the pot with aluminum foil and fill with briquets. Use a cake cooling rack across the top of the pot as a grill.

Not only can you barbecue with the clay pots, you can also bake in your oven if you use an unglazed pot that has been lined with aluminum foil before food is put in it. To bake a cake, first line the pot with foil, fill the pot 2/3 full with the cake batter, and bake as usual. Insert a straw vertically in the center of the batter. When you can pull the straw out clean, you know your cake is done. If the cake doesn't rise quite to the top of the pot, you can lift the cake out with the foil, build a fake bottom to lift it higher, and then replace the cake. Frost the cake, sprinkle it with crushed chocolate cookies, and add gummi worms. To further decorate your cake, cut a large flower from posterboard (or use a tissue paper or real flower), glue to a dowel or stick painted with green acrylic paint, and insert in the cake.

To keep your cups from blowing away or tipping over, place each one inside a small pot.

■ "Terra Cotta" Placemat

▲ *To make, you'll need*: Purchased fabric placemats, terra cotta-colored cloth, and fabric scraps for flowers and leaves.

▼ *Directions*: Cut out a pot and flower similar to the ones in the sketch below, making sure that the pot is wider than the diameter of your plate. First, narrowly hem or overcast the edges of the pot and the flower. Applique the leaves and flower to the pot with a wide satin stitch or by hand, leaving the top of the flower open to insert the silverware and napkin. Applique the pot to the placemat, again leaving the top open to insert your plate.

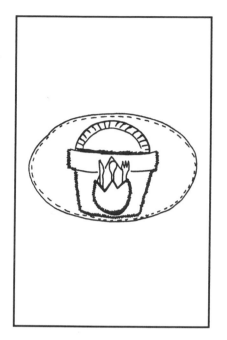

■ For a Maypole

Here's a surprise use for the center pole of an artificial Christmas tree. Attach wide ribbon or crepe paper streamers in a variety of colors to the top of the center pole. You can use a knife or screwdriver to poke the streamers into the edges of the fitting at the top of the pole. Using alternating colors of ribbon, weave the streamers back and forth around the pole until they cover about 8" to 10" of the top. Insert silk flowers and ivy in the holes where you would ordinarily put the tree branches. Extend the streamers, one or two at a time, to within a few inches of the edge of the table and tape down. Serving bowls can be placed over the end of the streamers at the edge of the table for a buffet.

An Oscar Video Party

Lights, action—your video party is ready to roll. Every year at Academy Awards time, I'm inspired with edible recreations of scenes of special significance from the movies nominated for Best Picture of the Year. Here's what I did for a recent Oscar party.

■ The "Oscar"

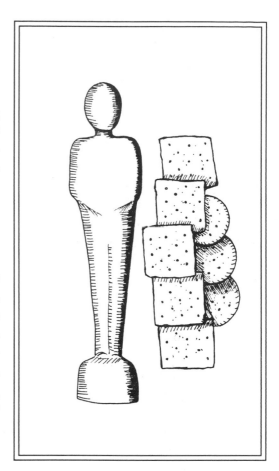

Select a tray large enough to serve about 3 pounds of liver pate and an assortment of crackers of your choosing. Work with a small metal spatula to shape the pate into a sculpture replica of the famous "Oscar" given to the Academy Award winners. The figure should be positioned in the center of the tray. Begin by shaping the silhouette of a man. Then add the details, such as the folded arms, face, etc. Lines can be drawn in the pate with a toothpick or a nut pick. Surround the figure with a variety of crackers of different textures and shapes.

■ Tuxedo Placemat (You can use these at any party).

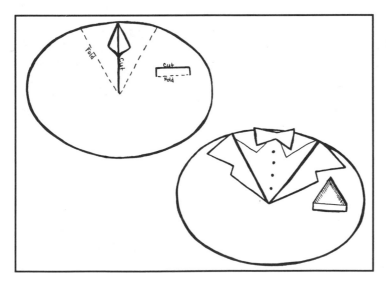

▲ *To make, you'll need*: One large sheet black construction paper, one large sheet white construction paper, and one small piece red construction paper.

▼ *Directions*: Trace an oval placemat on black construction paper and cut out. Halfway along the top long side of the oval, cut a slit 1/3 of the way down the paper. Fold back each side of the slit diagonally to form lapels. On one side of the lapels where the top of the pocket would be on a jacket, cut a 3" slit. Cut down about 1/2" on each side of the slit. Fold down the resulting rectangle of paper to form the top of the pocket.

Trace the same oval placemat on white construction paper and cut out. Glue white mat under black one. (Folded lapels should appear on the outside.) Glue only around outside of the mats.

Draw and cut out a bow tie shape from the red construction paper. Glue it above the lapels where a bow tie would normally show. Fold a white napkin to look like a handkerchief and slip it into the "pocket" slit.

■ Edibles Made Famous

● *Gorillas in the Mist* — Unique Theme Confection

Gorilla
1 cake mix baked in two round 9" pans
Shredded coconut
3 dried prunes
Brown licorice
Chocolate frosting
Food coloring
2 gumdrops

Mist
1 fresh coconut, cut in half (you can scoop out and use the coconut, leaving two half shells)
2 small chunks dry ice
Hot water

To make the gorilla, use one 9" layer as the body. Cut a small circle in middle of other layer, cutting in 2" from edge of cake to form it. Cut resulting 2" ring in four equal parts. Use small circle as gorilla head. Place one of the ring pieces at side of body pointing down for one gorilla arm. Place another part of ring pointing up toward head as the other arm. Arrange the remaining two pieces to form gorilla's bowed legs.

Frost gorilla completely with chocolate frosting. Place coconut in a jar with several drops of brown food coloring. Place the lid securely on jar and shake. (Add more food coloring if the color is too light.) Sprinkle coconut on arms and legs, on edges of body, and on top and side edges of head. Leave tummy and face without coconut "fur."

Use the prunes as nose and ears. Add gumdrop eyes. Cut short pieces of brown licorice and arrange to form toes and fingers.

Just before serving, add the mist. Place the two coconut shell halves on each side of the gorilla. Using tongs or very heavy gloves, place chunks of dry ice in each shell. Pour a little hot water over the dry ice. The dry ice will form an impressive mist.

● *Field of Dreams*

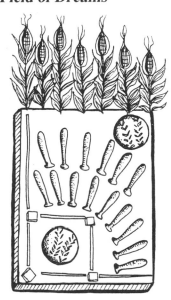

Cover a 2' x 2' piece of plywood with contact paper in either brown or green. Use adhesive tape to "mark out" a baseball diamond. Cut small squares of cheese and pile one on top of another to make the bases. Make baseballs by forming a cheese ball mixture into round shapes. Use strips of beef jerky for the lacing on the baseballs and place them on the field. Add a pile of baseball bats by taking pieces of frozen bread dough and baking them into bat-shaped bread sticks. A cornfield for one side of the completed scene can be made by cutting paper twist to lengths of about 6". Wrap the paper twists around 5" pieces of foil that have, in turn, been wrapped around fuzzy yellow pipe cleaners. The pipe cleaners resemble ears of corn if you attach small pieces of yarn for tassels.

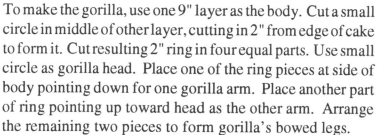

76

● *Driving Miss Daisy*

Purchase ready-made marzipan (made from ground almonds) from the gourmet section of a food store. Use paste food coloring in the appropriate colors for a green turtle, yellow ducks with orange bills, and a black Cadillac. Color and roll out portions of the marzipan and then shape the figures. Marzipan is easy to work with. To make the car, shape the bottom part of it first. The wheels and windows should be of white marzipan and the tires, hood, and trunk of black. After the lower part of the car is completed, shape the top (windshield, windows, and roof) and place it on the lower part.

Select a large tray or cover cardboard with foil or Contact paper to use as the base of your scene. Next melt one bag (12 ounces) of miniature marshmallows and 1/2 stick of margarine in a heavy saucepan over low heat. Stir in six cups of puffed wheat. While the mixture is still warm and pliable, shape it into a highway that curves across the tray or cardboard base. Use strings of black licorice to make a line down the middle of the "road." Use aluminum foil to make a pond or lake on one side of the highway. Line the foil with lettuce leaves and fill with bleu cheese dip. Place cracker ducks on the "water." On the other side of the scene place a line of trees made from leeks, broccoli, or any other vegetable that you want to put on your tray. If you wish, you can add some bushes made from cauliflower. Fill in the other spaces with carrot sticks, green pepper slices, or other vegetables. The scene can be as colorful and imaginative as you wish.

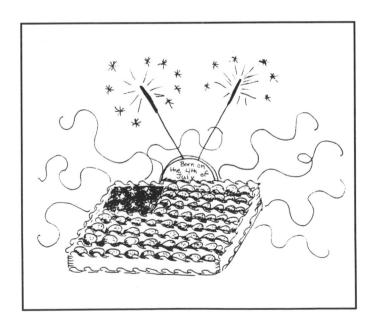

● *Born on the Fourth of July*

Create an American flag by placing a frozen 9" x 13" rectangular cake on a foil-covered piece of heavy cardboard and frosting the cake with white frosting. Use canned cherry pie filling to make red stripes on the cake. Use canned blueberry pie filling to make the blue background. Make white stars by using a star cake decorating tip and some of the white frosting. Fill in the border and white stripes by piping more of the white frosting on the cake.

Straddle the cake across a 9" x 13" cake pan filled with dry ice. (Remember to use gloves to handle dry ice. You can break the dry ice into small pieces by using a hammer.) Pour hot water on the ice to make clouds of vapor. Place miniature American flags about 12" tall along the top of the cake. Add sparklers (out of the way of the flags) stuck along the edge of the top of the cake. Light the sparklers and listen to the "o-o-ohs" and "a-a-ahs."

● *Goodfellas* **and** *The Godfather III*

Serve a shrimp cocktail drink (recipe on page 80) in a "bandito" goblet. To make the goblet, you will need: Scraps of black felt, narrow black ribbon, and 10 1/2-oz. goblets. Directions: Make a Lone Ranger mask from the black felt that is one-half the circumference of the goblet. Glue ribbon to the sides of the mask and tie it onto the goblet. You may need to use clear tape to hold it in place. Tie another piece of ribbon around the stem to look like a bow tie. Fill goblets with the drink and top off with a celery stick.

● *Ghost*

▲ *For the* **Ghost** *scene, you'll need*: 1 large box covered with Contact paper or spray painted, with a small hole cut in the center top and a larger hole in one side; ghosts (directions follow); 1 blond Ken doll; parmesan sesame bundt loaf (recipe on page 80); plates of cold cuts; and lettuce, tomatoes, and other sandwich makings.

▲ *For each ghost, you'll need*: 1 soup can, 1 2" or 3" styrofoam ball, 2 pieces of aluminum foil crumpled to 3" long and 1" diameter, 2 wiggly eyes, scrap of gray felt cut in a circle for the mouth, black spray paint, cheesecloth, and white glue mixed 1-to-1 with water.

▼ *Directions*: Attach the ball to the top of the can. Tape the foil on either side as arms. Dip the gauze in the glue mixture and squeeze out excess. Drape the cheesecloth over the ghost form and allow to dry thoroughly. Carefully remove from form and spray paint. Glue on eyes and mouth. Scene set-up: Place the bundt loaf on the center of the box around the hole. Place the plates of sandwich fixings around the rolls. Put the doll in the center of the rolls just to one edge of the hole. Place the ghosts around the box. At the appropriate time, you can reach into the back hole on the box, grab the doll, and pull him through.

● **Honor** *Awakenings* **with an Ouija Board Pizza**

You will also need slices of mozzarella cheese and alphabet cookie cutters. Cut letters from the cheese and place around the edges of a cooked pizza. Place back in the oven just long enough to soften the cheese.

78

● *Dances with Wolves*

Dessert pays tribute to *Dances with Wolves* by creating a prairie scene complete with a buffalo stampede.

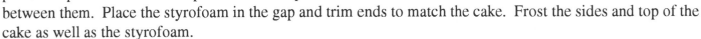

▲ *To make, you'll need*: 1 purchased, unfrosted sheet cake (17" x 25" or adapt the directions to any size cake), 1 extra-large cake pan, sturdy cardboard the same size as the cake, 1 piece of styrofoam 2" x 2" x 32", and light-brown colored frosting (combine 1 can vanilla with 1 can chocolate frosting).

▼ *Directions*: Cut the cake and the cardboard in half diagonally. Place the cake on the cardboard, then place the pieces on the cake pan with a 3" space between them. Place the styrofoam in the gap and trim ends to match the cake. Frost the sides and top of the cake as well as the styrofoam.

▲ *To decorate the cake, you'll need*: 6 small dark sugar ice cream cones, green frosting, purchased tubes of decorating frosting in various colors, rock candy and peanut brittle, pretzel sticks, aluminum foil, red and orange permanent markers, Karo syrup, and blue food coloring.

▼ *Directions*: Frost three cones with green frosting. Turn upside down on one corner of the cake to look like trees. Cut a piece of aluminum foil about 3" x 5" to look like a pond. Place it by the trees. Mix a few drops of food coloring with a small amount of Karo syrup until it is a light blue color, then pour it onto the aluminum foil to look like water. Arrange the other three cones on the opposite corner and decorate with the purchased frosting to look like tepees. To make the fire by the tepees, color a small piece of aluminum foil with red and orange markers. Crumple the foil and place it on the cake. Using the pretzel sticks, form a fire bed over the foil. Scatter rock candy and peanut brittle over the cake to complete the landscape.

▲ *To make the buffalo, you'll need*: Mother's® brand dinosaur cookies (pick out 10 of the ones that look most like buffalo), dark reddish-brown frosting (add red food coloring to chocolate frosting), brown-colored coconut (put coconut in a plastic bag. Mix food coloring according to package directions to make a brown color. Gradually add the coloring to the coconut and shake. To make it an even darker color, you could add 1 tbsp. cocoa), elbow macaroni, 12 popsicle sticks, and glue or royal icing.

▼ *Directions*: With glue or royal icing, attach a popsicle stick to each cookie. When dry, frost both sides of the cookie, then roll in the coconut to cover. Carefully cut the macaroni in half and attach to the head for horns. Push the popsicle sticks into the styrofoam and place dry ice and a small amount of water in the cake pan. Replace the buffalo and, using the end sticks, slide the styrofoam back and forth to create a "stampede."

● **Shrimp Cocktail Drink**

▲ *To make, you'll need*: 1 qt. tomato juice; 1 bottle (32 oz.) shrimp cocktail sauce; 2 cans (4 1/2-oz. each) small shrimp, drained; 2 cups finely diced celery, 1/2 green pepper, finely diced; 1 green onion, finely diced; 1/4 cup sugar; 2 tbsps. lemon juice; 1 tbsp. Worchestershire sauce; 1 tbsp. vinegar; 1 1/2 tsps. horseradish; 1/4 tsp. garlic salt; and salt to taste.

▼ *Directions*: Mix all ingredients and refrigerate overnight. This may be kept several days. Yield: 2 1/2 quarts.

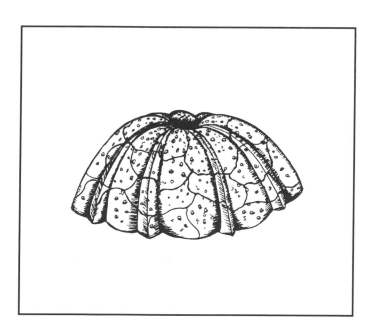

● **Parmesan Sesame Bundt Loaf**

▲ *To make, you'll need*: 24 frozen bread dough rolls, 1/4 cup melted butter or margarine, 1 cup grated Parmesan cheese, and 1 tbsp. sesame seeds.

▼ *Directions*: Thaw the dough for one hour. Roll each piece of dough in the butter and then the cheese. Place in layers in the bundt pan, which has been sprayed with nonstick cooking spray and sprinkled with the sesame seeds. Cover the rolls with plastic wrap and let rise until double in size. Cook at 350 degrees 25 minutes or until golden brown. Remove from pan while still warm.

Super Bowl Party Ideas for Any Time

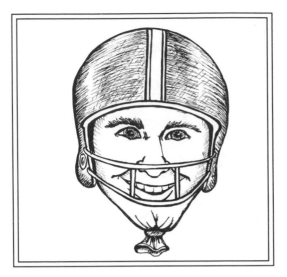

Even if you never want to hear another word about the Super Bowl (regardless of who won or lost), here are some super party ideas that will work for any big football game. Considering how the length of the professional football season is expanding, and adding in college and high school and junior high school games, we soon may be celebrating year round. All you need are a few simple decorations, lots of food, and plenty of friends and family.

▲ *For the decorations, you'll need*:
Green tablecloth, white Contact® paper, two large gumdrops, two straws, two pipe cleaners, two football helmets (you might find inexpensive ones in the toy store or even at a secondhand or thrift shop), spray paint, two pink or brown balloons, glue, and felt scraps.

▼ *Directions*:

Cut strips of Contact paper as long as your table is wide, using the guidelines on the back of the paper. (The number and width of the strips will be determined by the size of your cloth.) Peel off the backing and place in stripes on your cloth to look like a football field. If you have a large table, you may also want to cut numbers from the Contact paper to indicate yard lines. Stick a straw in each of the gumdrops. Twist one end of a pipe cleaner halfway up one straw, then twist the other end around a second straw, forming a goal post. Spray paint the helmets. Blow up the balloons and gently push them into the helmets to form heads. Sketch facial features (eyes, brows, nose, and lips) on paper. Place patterns on felt and cut out. Carefully glue features on the balloons. (A wonderful new glue gun has come on the market to make this easier. It has two temperature settings and uses a special glue that melts at such a low temperature that it can even be used on balloons without popping them. For more information on the dual-temperature glue gun, contact FPC Corporation, 701 Dartmouth Drive, Buffalo Grove, IL 60089; 708-541-3838.)

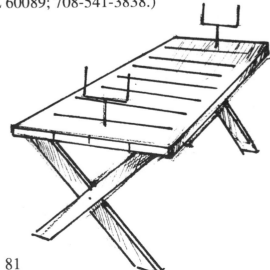

■ Food Ideas

You might try serving "Buffalo" wings, football hoagies, and "Giant" chocolate chip cookies.

● Buffalo Wings—The Wings That Made Buffalo Famous

24 broiler-fryer chicken wings
1 tsp. salt
1/4 tsp. freshly ground black pepper
4 cups vegetable oil
4 tbsps. butter
4 tbsps. bottled red hot sauce
1 tsp. white vinegar
Bleu cheese dressing
Celery sticks

Place each chicken wing on cutting board and cut off tip at first joint; discard tip or save for stock. Cut the remaining wing into two parts at the joint. Sprinkle chicken with salt and pepper. In deep fryer or heavy saucepan, place oil and heat to high temperature. Add half the wings and cook, stirring occasionally, for about 10 minutes, or until golden brown and crisp. Remove chicken from oil and drain on paper towels. Cook remaining wings, repeating process. While chicken is cooking, place butter in small saucepan and melt over medium temperature; add red hot sauce and vinegar. Pour sauce over wings. Serve with celery sticks and bowl of bleu cheese dressing for dipping.

● Bleu Cheese Dressing

1 cup mayonnaise
2 tbsps. onion, finely chopped
1 tsp. garlic, finely minced
1/4 cup parsley, finely chopped
1/2 cup sour cream
1 tbsp. lemon juice
1 tbsp. white vinegar
1/4 cup crumbled bleu cheese

Place mayonnaise in medium bowl. Add onion, garlic, parsley, sour cream, lemon juice, vinegar, and bleu cheese. Mix well and chill in refrigerator for about one hour.

● "Giant" Cookies

To make the "Giant" cookies, simply use your favorite chocolate chip cookie recipe but use the extra-large chips or chocolate chunks and make the cookies double their normal size.

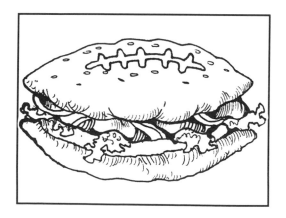

● Football Hoagies

Take frozen whole-wheat roll dough (thawed until pliable) and lightly knead two rolls together. After forming a ball, slightly flatten and stretch the ends to form a football shape. Using a small amount of dough from a third roll, form a long thin piece (just like the snakes you made from clay when you were a child). Press one piece lengthwise on the roll and three smaller pieces across it to look like the stitching on a football. Let rise until about double in size. Bake at 325 degrees for 20 minutes, or until golden brown. To serve, set out trays of sandwich makings (mcat, cheese, lettuce, tomatoes, onions, dressing, etc.) and let everyone help themselves. (If you don't have the time, order "Giant" hoagies from a sandwich shop.)

Surviving Football Season

Have you run out of ideas for the prefootball game partying at the stadium? Here are a few ideas to the rescue.

■ Serving Tips

● Prepare as much food as you can before you leave home. Keep it simple. Save cleanup until after the game.

● To support flimsy paper plates, use frisbees as plate holders.

● Lay down a piece of green astroturf in the parking lot. Stripe with white tape to look like your own football field.

● Use an ironing board as a portable buffet table. Cover with green felt. You can also use a saddle piece of the felt to hold utensils, napkins, and plates.

■ Food Ideas

● **A Baked Potato Bar**: Bake the potatoes at home and store in an insulated bag. Place the sour cream, cheese, chopped onions, etc., in small flowerpots lined with sturdy plastic wrap, cuffed over the top and taped in place.

● **Garbage Can Lid Grill**: Make a grill with a metal garbage can lid. Turn lid over and fill with dirt. Rest on three bricks. Cover dirt with extra-heavy-duty aluminum foil and place briquets in a pile in center of lid. Light briquets. Place three bricks around edge of lid and place grill on top of bricks. (Leave a 4-6" space between briquets and meat.) Cookie cooling racks can be used for grill, but do not use refrigerator racks.

● **Teriyaki Meat Sticks**: Heat 1 cup soy sauce and 1 cup sugar until sugar dissolves. Remove from heat. Add 1/2 tablespoon grated ginger root, 1 tablespoon sesame seed oil, 1/3 cup chopped green onions, and 1 clove crushed garlic. Marinate 2 pounds sirloin tip steak, sliced 1/8" thick, in sauce overnight. Cut steak into strips 1" x 2" long. String meat onto bamboo skewers. Barbecue. Yields 6-8 servings.

● **Fruit Pudding Refresher**: In medium bowl combine 20-ounce can pineapple chunks in juice, 2 sliced bananas, 11-ounce can mandarin oranges (drained), 16-ounce can fruit cocktail with juice, and one cup shredded coconut. Stirring slowly, sprinkle 3 3/4-ounce package instant lemon pudding mix into fruit mixture. Let stand 5 minutes. Pudding will set in fruit juice. Makes 6 1/2 cups. Serving suggestion: Line a football helmet with an extra-large resealable plastic bag or heavy-duty aluminum foil. Put salad in helmet; serve. Tip: Stretch plastic wrap in wooden embroidery hoops. Use as covers over salads and other foods. Food is protected from insects and clear wrap lets guests see what's inside.

● **Potato Hand Warmers**: Wrap potatoes in aluminum foil and bake. Carefully unwrap potatoes and make three slits in each potato. Cut a slice of cheese in thirds. Put slices of cheese down into slits in potatoes. Rewrap potatoes in foil. Line a small ice chest with newspaper (for insulation). Put baked, wrapped potatoes in insulated chest. You can warm your hands with the wrapped potatoes and then unwrap them and eat them for dinner.

● **Football Field Brownies**: Bake your favorite brownie recipe in a dripper pan. Let cool. Frost with green frosting. Using a cake decorator's bag and a writing tip, draw 50-yard line in center of brownies with white frosting. Continue to draw yard lines on brownies to resemble a football field. Decorate around edge of brownies with white frosting using a star tip. For goal posts, glue three popsicle sticks together and wrap with yarn in your team's colors. Push goal posts into brownies at ends of "field." For football, use writing tip and white frosting to make lines on a date to look like football. Place on 50-yard line.

■ Tailgate Runner

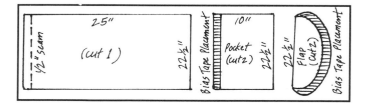

▲ *To make, you'll need*: 2 yards 45"-wide quilted fabric, 3 packages (6 yards each) bias tape, thread to match bias tape, and buttons or Velcro.

▼ *Directions*: Cut fabric in half lengthwise (pieces should measure 22 1/2" wide by 6' long). Using one of the 6' lengths of fabric, cut pattern pieces.

With right sides together, sew remaining 6' length of fabric and the 25" piece together, taking a 1/2" seam. Zigzag seam edges and press seam open. Runner should now measure 8' long (6' tailgate length with 12" overhang on each side for pocket placement). Finish one 22 1/2" edge of each pocket by encasing with bias tape. Baste pockets to each end of runner 1/4" from edge of fabric with finished edge facing toward center of runner. (Be sure to leave encased edge open for pocket.)

Encase pocket flaps with bias tape. With right sides together, sew pocket flap to runner approximately 1 1/2" from pocket. Fold flap down over pocket. Topstitch flap approximately 1/8" from folded edge. Repeat process to apply pocket on opposite end of runner. Finish edges of runner by encasing with bias tape. To keep pockets closed, make buttonholes in pocket flaps or attach Velcro to inside of flap and where appropriate on pocket. Optional: Topstitch pocket making dividers for paper plates, napkins, and utensils.

KIDS

Summer Puppet Fun

When summer is just around the corner, that means it's time to plan ways to keep the kids busy and having fun. Why not hold puppet shows in your garage. All you need for a stage is an old picnic table or plank with chairs, sheets for a curtain and to mask the front to hide the puppeteers, and creative backdrops made from paper or cloth with paste-on designs. Hang a show sign on the side of the garage, put out chairs for the neighborhood audience, and you're in business. Now for the puppets.

■ Three Little Pigs Sock Puppets

You can adapt these to any fairy tale character.

▲ *To make, you'll need*: Three pink socks (adult size works best); one gray sock; three large buttons; six small buttons or small craft-store eyes; two medium craft eyes; red felt, pink felt, and other felt scraps; gray fake fur scraps; yarn; white rickrack or felt; and small black pom-pom.

▼ *Directions*: To assemble, fold toes back to about middle of bottom at arch, then tack to shorten sock. A child's hand fits into what is left of the toe with the thumb in heel of the sock for the bottom of puppet's mouth.

Three Pigs: Glue an ellipse-shaped piece of felt in mouth formed by heel and tacked-back toe of the sock. Cut, then stitch or glue on pink felt area. Use large buttons for noses and small buttons or craft-store eyes for eyes. Add yarn hair and craft-store hats for detail.

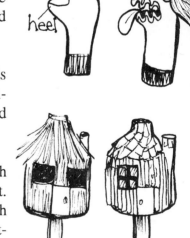

Wolf: Sew white rickrack or felt "teeth" around outside edges of puppet's mouth. Cut and stitch or hot glue fake fur "ears" to the puppet. Use black pom-pom for wolf's nose. To make eyes look mean, place larger craft eyes on top of red felt eye shapes and attach.

Three Pigs' houses: Sock puppets can go up into these houses. For each house, you'll need an empty well-washed plastic bleach bottle with bottom cut out. Bottle top will form roof with handle as "chimney." Cut windows in front of each bottle large enough so that puppets can be seen in the house. Glue or tape a paint-stirring stick on the bottom back of each bottle so that the child puppeteer can hold house with one hand, using other hand to operate sock puppet up inside of the bottle-house. Decorate roofs: Layer squares of masking tape all over roof areas of bottle-houses as shingles. Color by rubbing on shoe polish. House of straw: Place 3" strips of masking tape over entire house area. Glue pieces of raffia (available at craft or basket shops) over tape. House of sticks: Cover roof with masking tape as shown in illustration; glue sticks over outside. House of bricks: Paint entire house with gesso (available at craft or art supply stores); cut small, rectangular piece of sponge. Dip in red-brown paint and sponge on rectangular "bricks" in lines on the bottle-house.

■ Wearable Puppet Stage

▲ *To make, you'll need*: Posterboard and string or yarn.

▼ *Directions*: Cut posterboard so that the narrower side measures a little bit more than width of puppeteer's body. Score posterboard twice in lines parallel to edge of narrow side of rectangular posterboard. Scored lines should divide the board into three equal sections.

Hold posterboard so that bottom of top section comes to about the puppeteer's waist. Fold up along scored line so that second section of posterboard forms a shelf at waist height. Fold down along second scored line so that third section of posterboard forms the bottom of the puppet stage, hiding the puppeteer's hands.

Cut a large square from middle (shelf part) section of posterboard. Puppeteer holds puppets up through this hole to perform shows.

Poke two holes in posterboard, one in each corner of top edge of top section. Poke two holes in middle shelf-like stage section of the cardboard, one in each of the corners farthest from puppeteer's body. Knot one end of each of two 3" to 4" (depending on puppeteer's height) lengths of yarn or string. Thread each length through hole in upper section, tying lengths together around puppeteer's neck so that middle stage section of cardboard lands at about waist height. You may choose to add additional strings or yarn at bottom corners of top section to tie around puppeteer's waist.

Paint a backdrop on top section for puppet show or paint several backdrops on construction paper the size of top section. Attach with paper clips, then change when appropriate.

The portable stage should hang on puppeteer like the portable holder-carriers of drink or popcorn sellers. Use this small stage with small finger or hand puppets, stick puppets, or spoon puppets.

■ Wizard of Oz Spoon Puppets

Paint wooden spoons with acrylic paints and decorate using fabric scraps, craft-store eyes, etc., as desired.

Dorothy: Acrylic-painted face, yarn hair, felt dress.

Scarecrow: Cloth head stuffed sparsely with raffia, face painted on the cloth, felt shirt, denim scrap trousers (spoon handle threads through one leg), with raffia sticking out of the arms and legs.

Tin Man: Spoon painted silver, face painted on, small funnel painted silver glued on for hat, body made from gray felt or heavy foil.

Lion: Spoon painted tawny gold, small pom-pom details on face, yarn mane, pom-pom body.

Edible Jungles to Play In: Tasty Tepees, Tantalizing Tunnels

A neat jungle adventure for kids is right in their own backyard. Green bean tents, sweet pea tepees, tomato tunnels—all imaginative adventures to nibble on. Go on outside and play in the veggies, kids.

Miniature pumpkins, pole beans, and any of the varieties of climbing plants and vines can be planted at the sides and base of frame structures. If the chosen plant varieties are those that grow fruit and vegetables, children have the added bonus of being able to pick and eat the foods growing on the play places. The tepees and tunnels can be any size and shape as long as an open entrance and open exit are provided. Use your imagination. Variations can include the following:

■ Tepee

Seven or eight bamboo poles can be used as the basic frame. Cut all the poles the same length. The longer they are, the more they can be spread out at the base and the larger the circle forming the tepee will be. Tie the poles together at the top about six inches down the pole ends so that you have a bundle of poles. Use very heavy twine or lightweight rope for tying. Spread the bottom of the poles to form a circle. The basic shape is that of a free-standing funnel that is turned upside down. The bottom of the poles form almost a 45-degree angle from the top. There will be open spaces between the poles. Weave heavy twine back and forth through the spaces to provide support for the climbing plants you choose to plant around the base of the tepee. As the plants grow, the bamboo tepee frame will become a covered, secluded, fun place for the kids to play.

■ Igloo

Cut two 2 x 4s into lengths of three to five feet, depending on the length you want the igloo to be. Use a piece of chicken wire that is the length of the 2 x 4s and wide enough to round up to the height you want the igloo to have. Notice that the height of the igloo can also be varied by moving the 2 x 4s farther apart or closer together. Fasten the wire to the wood with staple nails. Plant climbing plants along the base of the 2 x 4s and let the foliage cover the igloo. This design is especially fun for children because the open ends let them use it as a tunnel.

■ A-Frame

Use 2 x 2 soft pine or fir strips. Cut three pieces into equal lengths of three to five feet, depending upon the length you want the finished product to be. Cut six short pieces of equal length to form the triangles for the front and back of the house. The triangles, when finished, need to be large enough for your child to crawl through. Nail the short pieces together to make the two triangles. Nail one end of each long piece to each angle on a triangle. Repeat with the other end. The A-frame should be steady and firm. Cover it with nylon netting. Let the plants grow up and over the frame to cover it and let the kids have a fun and imaginative play space.

Hey, Dad—Did You Get an Edible Tie and a Balloon Family?

Try one of these unique gifts for dad's birthday, special occasions, or a thanks-dad gift. And except for the edible tie, these ideas are good for any favorite person.

■ A Family of Balloons

When it comes time to give dad a party, think about a family of balloons. You can use them for centerpieces, place cards, or as gift decorations. This idea is also suitable for a children's party, a baby shower using a bunch of little ones, or for any occasion that balloons will make more fun.

▲ *To make, you'll need*: Balloons in a variety of sizes, cardboard, scissors, and black and red marking pens. (Marking pens can be used for drawing the features as well as hair, or cut them from construction paper or Contact® paper. Add construction paper ears and hands.)

▼ *Directions*: 1. Blow up balloon to desired size and knot to hold in the air. 2. Cut cardboard feet as pictured. Place balloon on top of feet; pull the knotted end down through front slot and back up again through back slot. By having the knot on top of the cardboard instead of underneath it, the balloon will be more stable. 3. Add features as desired. You might want to tape on two black circles for eyes and a smaller red circle for the nose. 4. Cut construction paper hands and feet and tape or glue to balloon. Decorate further with hair, bows, jewelry, hats, etc.

■ Craft Stick Letter Holder

All that mail that dads receive can be displayed in a creative letter holder.

▲ *To make, you'll need*: Craft sticks (tongue depressors), scissors, heavy craft glue, acrylic paints, and puff paints.

▼ *Directions*: 1. Make a rough sketch of what you want to make (for example, a train). 2. Lay craft sticks on the sketch and cut each to fit along and within the borders of sketch. Cut two sets for the front and back of the letter holder. The sticks can be cut easily with a regular pair of scissors. 3. Glue the sticks together with heavy craft glue and allow ample drying time. 4. Paint with acrylic paints, but use puff paints to make colorful details. 5. Glue front and back together by putting two or three sticks together, flat side down, and gluing them. Then glue both sides of the finished object to these sticks.

Note: Blowing up very small balloons can be an almost impossible task. It's easy if you stretch the rubber by placing the mouth of the balloon over the kitchen faucet. Slowly fill the balloon with water, grab it between thumb and forefinger at the neck of the balloon, and remove it from faucet. Move the water around for several minutes, then empty. You should now have no difficulty in blowing up the balloon. If you do, simply repeat the procedure.

■ Daddy's Snake Tie

Here's a unique homemade tie with a creative and tasty twist.

▲ *To make, you'll need*: One old necktie, scissors, green and red felt, cotton balls, small wiggly eyes or black Contact, glue, a snap or piece of Velcro, and M&Ms®.

▼ *Directions*: 1. Find one of dad's old neckties and cut off pointed end to form a squared end. 2. Draw a pattern the shape of a snake head and cut four pattern pieces out of green felt. Stitch two pieces of felt together along the edges with a running stitch and glue to squared edge of tie on the bottom side. 3. Stitch remaining two pieces along curved edge only. Stuff with cotton balls and close. Glue wiggly eyes on top and glue to squared edge of tie on top side. 4. Tie a bow from grosgrain ribbon and glue on top side at the point where head meets tie. 5. Cut a long, forked tongue out of red felt and glue on the top side of the bottom portion of snake head. 6. Stitch along width of tie about 12" from snake head and fill with M&Ms or dad's favorite candy. 7. Glue two small pieces of Velcro inside snake head on top and bottom pieces to keep mouth closed and candy inside.

■ Pocket Presents

For several special gifts wrapped into one.

▲ *To make, you'll need*: A large sheet of posterboard, clear vinyl, X-Acto knife, glue gun, glue, plastic tape, puff paint, colored paper, scissors, crayons, and pens.

▼ *Directions*: 1. Using a large colored sheet of posterboard, section the bottom three-fourths into nine pockets (3 rows x 3 pockets on each row = 9 pockets total) by using a ruler and drawing the outline of each pocket with a pencil. 2. Cut a piece of clear vinyl (available at fabric stores) to fit over bottom three-fourths of posterboard. Draw borders of pockets on vinyl with markers. About 1/2" from top of each pocket, cut a slit along width of the pocket with an X-Acto knife, leaving 1" uncut on each side. 3. Remove vinyl. Run a bead of hot glue along penciled lines of pockets and lay vinyl back down and press along beaded glue lines. 4. Using plastic tape the color of the original posterboard, tape around each pocket, covering glue marks. 5. At top of posterboard, write with puff paints, "For a Special Dad!" 6. In each pocket place a gift for dad. You might consider the following: * A shoe made from black and white posterboard with brown yarn for the lace reading "Good for one free shoe shine." * An ice cream cone cut from colored paper (a cone made from yellow paper with brown crisscross lines drawn with a brown pen, pink ice cream, and a red cherry on top) reading, "Good for one free trip to the ice cream parlor." * A car cut from blue paper with black wheels reading "Good for one free car wash." * A fish cut from green paper reading "One day of fishing." * A brown teddy bear with a pink heart on its tummy reading "One free bear hug." * Yellow paper cut in the shape of a movie ticket reading "One movie date." * A cookie cut from pink paper with confetti glued on top reading "One dozen free cookies." * A flower cut from colored paper reading "One day of yard work." * An outline of a child's hand cut from colored paper reading "One free back rub."

■ Homemade Camera

Here are two wonderful learning projects that you and your children can make quite inexpensively that will provide hours of active involvement. The first project is a homemade camera.

▲ *To make, you'll need*: A #10 can (such as a large coffee can) with lid, flat black spray paint, black tag board, scissors, clear tape, thin nail and hammer, black tape, and sheet film (available from a photo supply store).

▼ *Directions*: With the nail and hammer, make one very small hole 2" up from the bottom of the can. (Hint: If you fill the can with water and freeze it first, when you make the hole the can will maintain its shape, or drill the hole with a very small drill bit.) Spray paint the inside and outside of the can and lid. Allow to dry thoroughly. Use a piece of black tape to cover the hole. To make the film holder, cut a square of the tag board approximately 1" less than the diameter of the can. Cut three 1/4"-wide strips of tag board. Lay these strips along three sides of the square, trimming to fit. Tape the outer edges together, leaving the inside edge loose for film to slide in (see Fig. 1).

◆ *How to use*: In a completely dark room, slide the film into the holder, then slide the holder into the can, directly opposite the hole (see Fig. 2), and replace the lid. To take a picture, go outside in the sunlight, hold the camera very still, remove the tape, wait for four seconds to expose the film, then replace the tape. Remove the film in a completely dark room and place it in a black envelope to take to the developer.

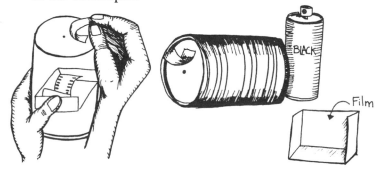

Fig. 1   *Fig. 2*

■ Waterworks

▲ *To make, you'll need*: Colored party cups and bowls (red, yellow, and blue); clear 9-oz. plastic cups; 1/8" to 1/4" diameter clear plastic tubing (any variety of clear cups and bendable straws work just as well); a board (masonite, plywood, or heavy cardboard) to mount it on; glue gun; clear silicone gel; red, yellow, and blue food coloring; and water. Waterworks consists of several towers of varying heights and connecting tubes, which allow colored water to drain from one cup to another.

▼ *Directions*: Build six towers, gluing bowls or cups rim to rim or bottom to bottom. Arrange on the board and glue into place. To connect the tubing (it will go out at the bottom of one cup and into the top of another), hold the tip of the hot glue gun against the side as close to the bottom as possible and melt a small hole in the clear cups. Insert tubing and seal around the edges with the glue or silicone gel (gel will take overnight to dry completely). Where tubing runs into the top of a cup, hold securely in place with more glue. Place bowls in positions 7 and 8 to catch the water. Do not glue them in place; you will want to remove them to empty the water. Test the water works for leaks by pouring water into the tallest tower. Once everything is sealed tight, the fun begins. Put ten drops of yellow food coloring in each of towers 4 and 5. Put one drop of blue in tower 2 and one drop of red in tower 6 Fill the cup in tower 1 with water and watch as it flows through the tubing and changes colors. Now use your imagination and experiment with different heights and colors.

Clever Caps

Use pandas and elephants to solve the age-old problem of kids losing their stocking caps in the cloakroom when all caps look alike—turn them into animal hats. The panda caps are good for four- to ten-year-olds; even adults will like the elephants.

■ Elephant Stocking Cap

▲ *To make, you'll need*: 1 stocking cap, felt squares or scraps, scissors, needle, thread, fiberfill batting, and two buttons.

▼ *Directions*: Begin by cutting two elephant's trunks and four ears out of felt. Adjust the size of the pattern to fit the cap you are using. Baste the trunk pieces together, leaving a 1 1/2" to 2" space open. Very lightly stuff the trunk with the fiberfill through the opening. Sew again around the entire trunk. You may wish to use a blanket stitch for a more decorative look. Sew the ears together (two pieces of felt for each) following the same steps as for the trunk. Securely attach the trunk to the brim of the cap using a blind stitch. Sew button eyes about 2" above the brim. To attach the ears, make a tiny pleat on either side of the cap. Insert the ear into the pleat and sew through all thicknesses. Variations: By adapting the basic pattern, you can make a panda bear, a bunny, or a kitten. Look through coloring books or picture books for more ideas.

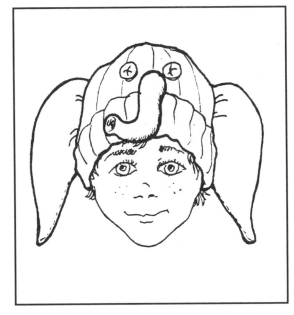

■ Panda Bear Hat

▼ *Directions*: From black felt, cut four ears and two outer eyes. From white felt, cut two muzzles and two inner eyes. Machine or hand stitch the outside edges of the ears and the muzzle together using a 1/8" seam. Stuff each piece lightly with fiberfill and position on the stocking hat. Slip stitch the muzzle on with white embroidery floss. Chain stitch a mouth with black embroidery floss and stitch on a black button for the nose. Slip stitch the white inner eye to the black outer eye, position it on the hat, and attach with black embroidery floss. Enclose the flat edge of the ear in a small fold of the hat and stitch through all three layers (hat, felt, hat). This makes the ear stand up when it is worn.

Kids' Decorating Ideas

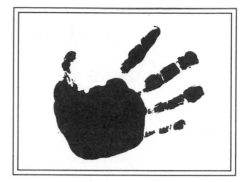

High-level decorating ideas for kids' rooms are fun and easy if you combine individual characteristics of the child with a few craft store items and a lot of imagination. For example, instead of wallpaper, mix some water-based acrylic paint. Use a paint roller to cover the bare feet of your child with a coat of paint. Let the child lie on his or her back and make footprints on the wall. For variation, dip the palms of the child's hands in paint and let him or her make handprints in the same or in contrasting colors. If you wish, you can put names and dates by the prints and show how old the child is as the prints grow.

■ **Graffiti and writing on the wall** can be especially fun if you invest in a pad of "static image" which can be purchased for about 75 cents per sheet (about $20-25 for a 30-page pad) at a stationery store. It sticks to the wall. Children can write on it, make lists, draw pictures, erase it, and generally have fun "writing on the wall" without actually marking on it.

■ **Mirrors** can become fun decorations for a child's room if they are turned into large paper dolls. Choose mirrors that are about 10" in diameter. Place yarn around the mirror to resemble hair. Cut a child's silhouette out of foam core and glue it to the mirror to form a body. When purchasing the child's clothes, buy some matching fabric and cut out matching clothes for the mirror doll. Fasten clothes to the silhouette with small strips of Velcro. Children are delighted to see themselves in the mirror. A variation is to make a clown instead of a doll. Simply substitute a clown suit for the doll clothes and add a clown hat to the yarn surrounding the mirror face.

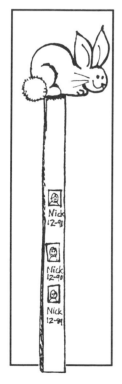

■ **A grow stick** is a good addition to any child's room. One can be made of yardsticks or measuring sticks covered with felt or hopsacking. A personalized variation can be easily made by adding a wallet-size photo of the child showing what he or she looks like as each measurement is periodically marked off.

■ **A private puppet theatre** made from the closet door can be the ultimate in decorating for a child. Obtain a piece of fabric long enough and wide enough to cover the open door of the closet. Use two hooks to secure the fabric to the top of the door. Mark off an 18" square located about 1/3 of the way up from the bottom of the fabric. Cut along the sides and bottom of the square. Zigzag around the raw edges. Roll the cut-out fabric up and secure it with ribbons or Velcro from an open window in the fabric door. Line the window with a square of black fabric, sewing it to the top and sides of the square opening. Leave the bottom undone so that it forms an open slit. Children kneeling in the closet, behind the fabric door, can be

hidden from view as they place puppets "on stage" through the bottom slit in the fabric window. The fabric puppet stage can be quickly taken down and folded for easy storage.

New Twists on Old-Fashioned Games

If it's late in the summer and your backyard games have lost a wicket, here's a solution—some new twists in homemade backyard games that will make you yet again the cleverest neighbor on the block. A special thank you to friend Dave Nielsen for sharing these great ideas.

■ Fiesta Horseshoes

▲ *To make, you'll need*: 3-4' board, 9" wide and 1 1/2-2" thick, and 3 1/2" metal washers for each set. Spray paint each set a different color (these will be the horseshoes.)

▼ *To assemble*: Cut three 5" holes in the board, equal distances apart. Paint numbers 1, 2, and 3, indicating point value, in each hole. Option: Paint whole board white except top. Cover top with outdoor carpet or turf.

◆ *To play*: Each player chooses three washers (horseshoes) of the same color. The board is placed from 1 to 20 feet away (depending on the age and skill of players) with the "3" end farthest away from the player. Player then tosses horseshoes into the holes in the board. The player with the highest number of points after tossing all three horseshoes is the winner.

■ Ring Toss

▲ *To make, you'll need*: Garden hose (cut into 10" lengths); dowel cut into 1 1/2" pieces (dowel should be of a thickness to allow easy insertion of hose ends); black electrical tape; circular board (about 18" in diameter), painted and decorated as desired; bicycle hooks or nails pounded into round board at an upward angle; and standard or platform to which round board can be attached.

▼ *To assemble*: To make a "ring," insert one dowel piece into each end of hose, work hose ends together until they meet, and wrap securely with electrical tape. On a circular piece of plywood (about 18" diameter), paint and decorate a clown face (or other desired design). On the nose area and on the other areas of the face, insert bicycle hooks that extend away from the face when in place. Attach face to a standard, and you're ready to play. Option: If you do not have a standard, you can set the circular board on a table and lean it against a wall for support.

◆ *To play*: Each player tries to toss his or her rings onto the bicycle hooks. Ten points are given for a successful nose hit, five points for the other parts of the clown face.

■ Beanbag Toss

▲ *To make, you'll need*: Heavy fabric (enough for desired number of beanbags), gravel, and 1 powerline spool (or tree stump or small round table).

▼ *To assemble*: Cut 4 1/2" squares from heavy fabric (two squares for each beanbag). With right sides together, take 1/2" seam on three sides of square. Turn right side out. Fill bag loosely with gravel. Whip stitch or zigzag beanbag closed (tucking raw edges to inside of bag while sewing). Decorate the tops of the powerline spool with numbers indicating point values. (It's harder to throw bags onto the top of spool, so number values on the top should be higher.)

◆ *To play*: From a distance of four to five yards, each player tosses his or her bags onto the spool. The one with the highest number of accumulated points wins.

■ Soccer Croquet

▲ *To make, you'll need*: 8-10 one-yard pieces of iron rod (about 1/2-3/4" thick), 2 soccer balls, and 1 "goal" ball (such as a tennis ball).

▼ *To assemble*: Band iron rods around a telephone pole or column to give each an arch form. With pliers, twist the top of one of the 3' pieces of iron rod to form a resting place for the goal ball.

◆ *To play*: Push wickets (arches) at intervals in lawn, leaving a space large enough for a soccer ball to pass through (same number of wickets for each player). Place goal wicket at the end of designated course and set small "goal" ball on top. At a given signal, two players must kick their soccer ball through an equal number of wickets to the goal wicket. The first one to reach the goal wicket, knocking the ball off, is the winner.

An Edible Answer to "What Do I Do Now, Mom?"

After three days of being locked in the house because of snow, flu, or the winter blahs, even kids join fish in becoming unsavory little characters. The solution: Let them bake bread in the shape of hippos, dinosaurs, or alligators.

Frozen bread dough comes in several varieties, including white, whole wheat, and cracked wheat. It requires a little special handling, as it comes "awake" or thaws and rises. It needs to be covered with plastic wrap during this process and will take about 3-5 hours at room temperature. It will also thaw in the refrigerator overnight. Before you handle the dough, you need to lightly grease the countertop and your hands so it doesn't stick. For sculpturing, you use the dough when it is thawed but still cold.

■ Hippopotamus—Fun to make and eat

▲ *To make, you'll need*:
One loaf ready-made frozen bread dough
Two raisins
Six wooden matches
Aluminum foil
One egg, well beaten
Six pieces of candy corn

▼ *Directions*:
With kitchen scissors or a knife, cut about 3" of dough off the loaf and divide into four pieces. Reserve large piece of dough for body. Dip the small pieces of dough into the egg and attach to the body for legs. Make small holes and push the raisins in for the eyes. Strike the matches, extinguish, and wrap the ends of them (two at a time) with the foil. Cut the mouth open and use the matches to prop it open during baking. Brush the entire hippo with the egg wash; this makes it shiny when it is baked.

Bake 20-30 minutes in 400 degree oven until golden brown. After the hippo cools, remove the matches from his mouth and put candy corn in the holes for teeth.

■ Dinosaur

Cut 3" off one thawed loaf of Rhodes® bread dough for feet and plates. Set aside. Using remaining dough, pinch one end to form a small head. With scissors, cut open a 1"-deep mouth. Open mouth with a small ball of foil. Cut one raisin in half for eyes. Stretch rest of loaf to form a tail. Cut into back of dinosaur from tail to 1" from head a slit 1/4" deep. Place dinosaur body over a 4" roll of crushed foil on greased cookie sheet.

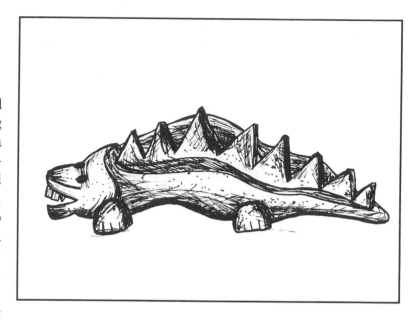

Cut 1" x 3" piece from reserved dough for the four legs. Cut into four pieces. Cut five toes in each leg. Place on either side of foil. Flatten slightly the remaining pieces of dough. Cut into eight triangles of graduating size from 1 1/2" tall to 1/2". Place in slit. Begin by putting tallest in middle of back. Secure plates with toothpicks. Cover with plastic wrap and let raise 1/2 hour. Bake at 350 degrees for 20 minutes. Remove foil before serving.

■ Alligator

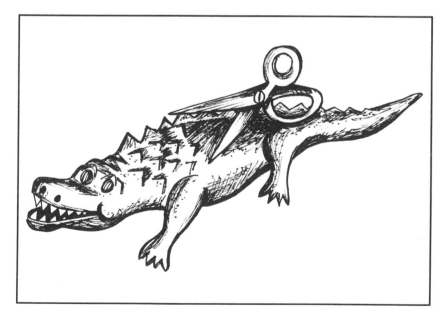

Cut a 2" section from one loaf of thawed bread dough for the legs and eyes. With the remaining dough, start forming a tail by rolling and stretching the loaf to 18" long. Cut a 3"-deep mouth at the wide end. Clip teeth with scissors. Pinch the nose to form nostrils. Curving the body, place alligator on greased cookie sheet. One and one-half inches from the nostril, pinch eye sockets. From the 2" reserve section of dough, pinch off two pea-sized balls of dough for the eyes. Place in eye sockets. Cut the remaining reserve dough into four equal pieces for the legs.

Stretch each leg to 5". Cut four 1"- long toes. Stretch and splay toes on cookie sheet. Cut triangular scales on body with scissors. Brush with whole beaten egg and sprinkle with poppy seeds.

Cover with plastic wrap; let rise until nearly double. Bake at 350 degrees for 20 minutes. Remove foil from mouth before serving.

Ant Farms, Hold the Mustard

For a project that will hold you and your child's interest, make an ant farm with him or her.

▲ *To make, you'll need*: One large (one gallon or larger) clear plastic or glass jar with a tight-fitting lid; one tubular can, such as the kind potato chips come in; soil; black construction paper; and ants. Optional: Miniature farm, houses, trees, etc., purchased at crafts stores.

▼ *Directions*: Place the smaller, tubular can inside the large jar. (This small can forces the ants to build their tunnels, etc., near the edge of the jar, rather than in the middle out of view.) Spoon soil into jar all around the smaller can to within two to three inches of the top of the jar (not into the small can). Punch many small holes in lid of larger jar. (If lid is plastic, use a warmed ice pick to punch holes.) Tape black construction paper all around outside of jar so that the ants, as they tunnel along the inside edge of the jar, will think that they are underground.

If you live where you have access to ants, find an anthill. You can find anthills under rocks in your yard, in orchards or gardens, and in vacant lots. Capture many ants. Find the little white globular eggs and larvae, and try to find a queen, an ant two to three times larger than the other ants. The queen may have wings. Place the ants, queen, and some of the eggs in the soil in the jar.

If you have no access to ants, hobby supply shops should have access to suppliers, or send a letter of inquiry to: Ant Farm Supplies, Uncle Milton Industries, P. O. Box 246, Culver City, CA 90230. (Regular ants cost about $2.50/set, giant ants about $3.)

For decoration, after the ants have begun to build their tunnels, you may want to glue miniature houses, barns, and trees to toothpicks or popsicle sticks and stick them down into the dirt so that they stay secure in the top of the farm. After one to two weeks, when the ants have established tunnels and chambers, remove construction paper so that you can watch your ants at work.

You'll want to feed your ants small bits of fruits, vegetables, and bread dipped in sugar water or honey solution. You may want to place a small piece of sponge soaked in water in the jar for liquid, though most of the ants' liquid will come from foods they eat.

Keep your ants in a warm, not hot, place. If they seem agitated and try to climb out of the jar, place the farm in a cool place, or place the jar in a pan of water with the level quite high on the outside of the jar. (The ants won't climb into the water.)

Kids Can't Wait to Buckle Up
with These

It's guaranteed that your kids will plead "Please, let's go for a ride so we can all buckle up our seatbelts" if you add "seat paws" in the shape of fanciful well-known characters.

■ Mickey Mouse

Start with a white cotton glove from a costume store. Stuff and pad it with polyester fiberfill. Tie the glove shut with a narrow piece of ribbon. Get a Mickey Mouse pin or medallion from a novelty shop and fasten at wrist of glove. Attach the finished "hand" to the seatbelt with a Velcro strip.

■ Goldilocks and the Three Bears

Use a garden glove. Make each finger of the glove into a finger puppet by using pom-poms for puppet heads. For Goldilocks, use a 1" pale yellow pom-pom. Cut a half-circle from a piece of white, pale peach, or pink felt and glue it on the pom-pom to make a face framed by the fluffy yellow hair. Use a scrap of fabric or piece of wide ribbon and gather it under the pom-pom to make a dress. If you wish, put a tiny bow in the hair. Use a one-inch brown pom-pom for Mama Bear's head, a larger one for Papa Bear's head, and a smaller one for Baby Bear's head. Glue a tiny black or dark brown pom-pom in place for the bears' muzzles. Use a small bead glued on the muzzle for the nose. Add tiny beads for eyes. Use tiny fabric scraps or pieces of ribbon to make a bow tie for Baby Bear, a tie for Papa Bear, and a dress for Mama Bear.

■ Ninja Turtles

Use one of your own hands to make a pattern by holding the pinky and ring fingers together and the index and pointer fingers together so that they form two fat fingers with an open V-shaped space between them. Trace around the two fat fingers and your thumb. Make the thumb a little fatter than it actually is. The result will be a Ninja Turtle hand. Cut out the pattern and trace it onto felt pieces so that you have two identical hands. Use mossy green-colored felt for the color of a turtle. Place the two cut-out hands together and stitch around the fingers, the thumb, and down the sides, leaving the bottom open to stuff. Stuff until firm with polyester fiberfill. Fasten the wrist with a narrow piece of ribbon drawn around and tied into a bow. Attach to seatbelt with a Velcro strip.

■ Bear Paw

Cut a bear paw from fake fur. Cut an identical piece from felt to use as a facing for the fur. Cut two large felt bear toes and six smaller ones from the remaining felt. Stitch around the edges and stuff. Position the felt toes on the felt paw piece. Stitch them in place. Stitch the felt paw to the fake fur paw so the felt "faces" the fur. Stitch around the outer edge, leaving a small opening to turn and stuff. The toes will give the bear paw movement and dimension. Fasten to the seatbelt with a Velcro strip.

100

A Bed in the Castle for Your Child

Children's bedrooms are their castles. Here's an idea to make the very beds they sleep in a castle—complete with arches, towers, and medieval flags—for less than $10. Use recyclable material to make the headboard (use what you have on hand and check with furniture and appliance stores for the rest).

▲ *To make, you'll need*: A large piece of corrugated cardboard (from an appliance box) cut 2' to 2 1/2' high and as long as the bed is wide; two pieces of 4-foot-long heavy cardboard tubing (obtained from a carpet store); two papier-mache cones about 12" tall (from a craft or floral supply store); pieces of styrofoam such as those packed around TV sets or appliances; four pieces of 1" x 8" lumber (two pieces 4" longer than the sides and two pieces 4" longer than the top); two small dowels; scrap material or felt for the flags; duct tape; hot glue gun (the cool-melt type will work best; however, if you do not have one, simply allow the glue to cool a few seconds before attaching the styrofoam); a sharp knife (electric or X-Acto knife); brown acrylic paint and brushes; and Fleck-Stone spray paint in Gotham Grey and Manhattan Mist.

▼ *Directions*:

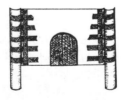

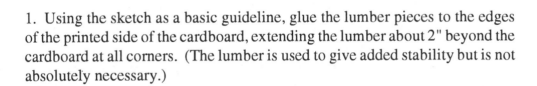
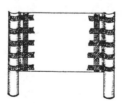
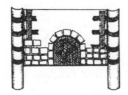

1. Using the sketch as a basic guideline, glue the lumber pieces to the edges of the printed side of the cardboard, extending the lumber about 2" beyond the cardboard at all corners. (The lumber is used to give added stability but is not absolutely necessary.)

2. Turn it over and attach the tubing to the sides with the duct tape, securing it well to the lumber extensions.

3. In the center of the cardboard, draw an arched doorway approximately 1' x 1'. Paint the doorway brown, using alternately heavy and light strokes to give the look of wood.

4. Using the knife, cut 1"-thick blocks from styrofoam. The blocks can be of varying sizes and shapes and need not be perfectly smooth, as the rough appearance makes them look more like stone. First, glue a row of "stones" around the arched doorway. Then, starting at the bottom edges, build the castle with more blocks, leaving a small space between each. As you reach the top, you may want to use a row of thicker styrofoam (or one row on top of another) to form the battlements.

5. When your castle is complete, carefully cover the door area and spray paint the entire castle with the Gotham Grey® paint. (Note: It will be easier to paint the cones separately and put them on the tube towers after everything is dry.) When the paint is dry, carefully use the darker Manhattan Mist® paint to spray between the blocks and in a random pattern on the towers and cones to make them look like stone.

6. Place the cones on the towers. Cut pennant-shaped flags from felt or scrap material, glue to one end of the small dowel, and insert the dowel into the top of the cone to complete your castle.

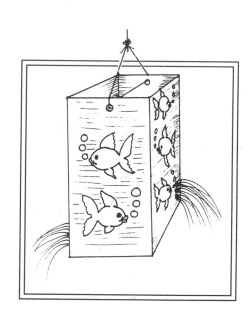

Bath Merry-Go-Round for Kids

Some engineering whiz can probably come up with the logical explanation for this fascinating milk-carton-turned-merry-go-round for the tub.

■ Bathtub Merry-Go-Round

▲ *To make, you'll need*: An empty 1/2-gallon milk or juice carton, two 15" pieces of strong string, scissors, Contact® paper, stickers, crayons, permanent markers, and large nail.

▼ *Directions*: Cut the top off the milk carton at the base of the slope. Cover the sides of the carton with a plain color of Contact paper. With the nail, punch two holes about 3/4" from the top of the carton and on opposite sides. Thread one piece of the string through the holes and knot the ends together. Tie one end of the second string to the knot in the first string. At the bottom of the carton, punch three holes 1/2" apart on each side (see illustration). Finish your project by decorating the sides with more Contact paper cut into shapes, or use stickers, crayons, markers, etc. To make your merry-go-round twirl, fill the carton with water and hold it up by the string.

Shoestring Vacations

If you have a family of three or four or more and want to vacation away from home, at a theme park, for example, it can be very expensive. But here are some shoestring examples that, with a little research and planning, will allow you to have an exciting five-day vacation for under $500. In fact, I got the cost down to $220.50, not including food for the final two days' camping.

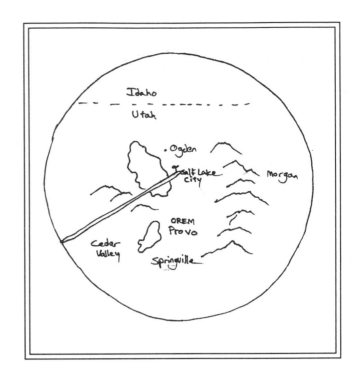

The key is to mark the area where you live on a map and draw the circumference of 100 miles around the mark. You then plan all your activities within the specified area, allowing you to make a round trip to any point of interest in one day, without the extra cost of hotels. After you have designated the area, you then go to your local Chamber of Commerce to obtain a packet of information containing details on all the sites in your area.

You might also select your site by sticking a pin in a map blindfolded. For example, Lafayette (pronounced laFAYette), Tennessee (near Nashville), may come up. Contact Lafayette's tour guides, local hotels, and the Chamber of Commerce for regional information. Local families are also good sources, and this is what you might do if you were to spend vacation time in Lafayette.

● **A Country-Style Day**: The first day of your shoestring vacation you might go country-style. Take a self-guided tour of Macon County, Tennessee, and spend a few hours at a local dairy farm. After lunch, visit a Tennessee walking horse farm, a free public attraction tourists travel hundreds of miles to visit. The total cost of the first day: $67.50.

● **A Day in the City**: On the second day, take a city excursion to Nashville, a 90-minute car trip each way. Your itinerary might begin at the home of Andrew Jackson. Then, proceeding into downtown Nashville, visit various public attractions such as the city's re-creation of the Greek Parthenon, an antique toy museum, and one of Nashville's famous science museums. Total cost: $103.

● **An Exotic Day in Greece**: Get up early on the third day, drive around the block, and return home to a make-believe exotic vacation town in Greece. This low-cost getaway involves theme food, music, activities, and costmes. You might even locate an authentic Greek restaurant and order a take-out Greek meal. Total cost: $50.

On a shoestring vacation, most of your traveling is done in the car, so here are several suggestions to keep your children occupied while traveling to your designated destinations.

● **Decorated Egg Cartons**: Before leaving on vacation, have your children decorate empty egg cartons with paint or markers, stickers, and crayons. Each carton then becomes their own personal treasure box to be filled with all their souvenirs.

● **Story Books on Audio Tape**: While the children are busy preparing their treasure boxes, parents can prepare an audio tape for use in the car. Record a favorite storybook and change the lead characters' names to the names of your children. Later, a cassette tape recorder can be used for an audio scavenger hunt for the children to record the sounds of their vacation.

● **Traveling Bingo**: Make up a traveling bingo game by using small pictures of outdoor scenery from magazines and travel guide books. Paste the pictures on paper in a pattern similar to a bingo card. Even small children can mark off the pictures as they see them while traveling in the car.

● **Disposable Cameras**: Children love to take pictures. You'll be surprised at the pictures three- and four-year-olds can take.

● **Final Two Days of Camping**: To top off your vacation, spend two days camping. While the kids are off on a sound scavenger hunt, the older ones can try a little pit cooking. Here's how. First, dig a large hole in the ground. Place flat rocks around bottom and sides and build a fire on top of them. Let it burn to ashes for about an hour and a half. This drives the heat into the rocks which cooks the food. While the fire is burning, prepare your food by wrapping it tightly in aluminum foil. Your menu might include corn on the cob, potatoes, and barbecued chicken. Wrap the corn, husk and all, individually in foil; oil the potatoes and wrap each of them; and put barbecue sauce on the chicken and double wrap in foil. To cook, take coals from the pit with a shovel and place chicken in the bottom of the pit. Place some coals on top of the chicken and then a little soil. Next place the potatoes in the pit and top with some coals. Put the corn on top and cover with a few layers of newspaper. Lastly, cover the newspaper with six inches of soil and let it all cook for about 3 1/2 hours.

■ And Sleeping Arrangements Were Never So Easy

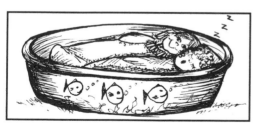

● **Double Bed for Children**: Make a double bed for your kids by placing their blankets or sleeping bags inside a small wading pool.

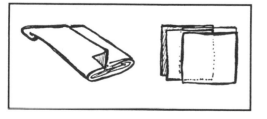

● **Homemade Sleeping Bags**: For those who don't own a sleeping bag, here's how to make your own. First, lay a large ground cloth out. Then layer several blankets by placing them halfway across each other. Start folding them in by bringing in the top blanket from one side, the second blanket from the other side, and so on. When you have completed this, fold under the bottom.

Turn Children's Drawings into Folk Art

The charming pictures that your children do just for you sometimes pile up and get lost in drawers. This is a lovely way to turn them into family folk art via wood cutouts.

▲ *To make, you'll need*: Your child's drawing, graphite paper or carbon paper, appropriate-sized plywood, white paint, wood sealer, acrylic paints, and polyurethane spray. Optional as needed: Turpentine, foam core, and paste.

▼ *Directions*: To provide a pattern, photocopy your child's artwork. You may want to enlarge the drawing as you photocopy it.

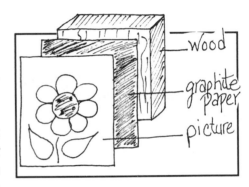

To transfer the drawing to wood, choose one of the following methods: Place graphite paper or carbon paper directly on the wood, carbon or graphite side down. Lay the copy of your child's work on top of the graphite or carbon paper and trace over the drawing's outline. Carbon paper smears more easily than graphite paper, but either works well.

A cheaper but more time-consuming method involves using only a soft-lead pencil. Scribble thoroughly all over the back of the copy with a soft-lead pencil (#2). Place the drawing right side up on the wood. Pressing hard, trace over the outline of the drawing. When you lift up the copy, you should see clear, light lines outlining the drawing on the wood.

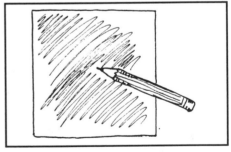

Next, cut out the resulting figure. If you do not have proper wood saws for the job, arrange to have your lumber supply store cut the figure. If the store does not offer this service, someone there can probably refer you to someone who will cut the figure for you for a minimal charge. (Foam core may be used instead of wood.)

You'll probably want to seal the wood next. Although this step isn't absolutely necessary, this makes the paint go on smoother and easier.

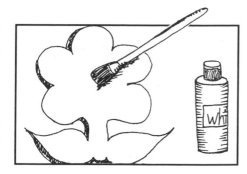

After sealing and painting the wood white, transfer all important detail lines of the drawing onto the wood using the same method you used to transfer the outline of the drawing.

Next, using the original drawing as a guide, paint the wooden copy with acrylic paints, duplicating colors and details as closely as possible. If leftover carbon or graphite lines show up and distract from the drawing, use a little bit of turpentine on a cotton swab to "erase" them.

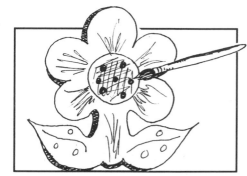

When the wooden drawing is complete, spray or paint on polyurethane to seal and protect the drawing.

You may want to add a dowel or plywood base or brace with foam or felt underneath so that the drawing can stand alone on shelf or table.

You can add real objects like balloons, ribbons, or other whimsies. If you'd rather save the original, paste it on a board cut-out and preserve with polyurethane. Whatever the method, put the child's name and date on the back.

A Dirty, Messy, Wonderful Project: Garbage Time Capsule

Talk about getting your hands into a project. Here's a dirty, messy, smelly garbage time capsule for Earth Day that kids can have fun with and use to see how nature recycles itself. They'll also see for themselves that certain manmade trash will never decompose. At the end of a month, they'll have the best beginning for a compost heap.

▲ *To do this experiment, you'll need*: One terra cotta (clay) pot about 10" high and 12" in diameter, ordinary garden dirt (potting soil will not work), 1/2 to 1 cup of lawn fertilizer (to help speed up the process), glass pie plate or plastic bag, and assorted garbage (such as banana peels, carrot peels, breadcrusts, paper towel, styrofoam cup, and plastic wrap or aluminum foil).

▼ *Directions*: Begin by mixing the fertilizer with enough dirt to fill the pot. Cover the drainage holes in the pot with small rocks, then add dirt to 1/3 full. Cut, crush, tear, or break the garbage into quarter-sized pieces and place in the pot. Lightly spray with water, then finish filling the pot with the soil. Spray with enough water to thoroughly dampen, but not soak, the soil. Cover the pot with the pie plate or plastic bag and put in a warm, dark place. Check every day and add water as necessary to keep it moist. After four weeks, empty the contents onto a large piece of newspaper and stir with a stick to see which pieces of garbage were decomposed by the bacteria and organisms in the soil. It will be obvious that nature can recycle some of our garbage, but not all. It is up to all of us to find alternative ways to recycle those things that are nonbiodegradable. Teach your children to separate the garbage and recycle. If your community does not have a program for recycling, call your local leaders and encourage them to begin one. You can also begin your own compost pit; buy a commercial container or build one of your own. All it takes is chicken wire formed in a circle the size of a large garbage can. Add grass clippings, vegetable peelings, and other organic matter. Doing this can help save Earth and your money too; you'll be making your own garden fertilizer.

C'Mon a My Playhouse

If you always wanted a playhouse when you were a child, there's still time if you help your child build one. Easy and fun, these instructions show how to do it using masonite pegboard.

▲ *To make, you'll need*: Four 4' x 8' sheets of pegboard; paper on which to design your playhouse; marking pen; jigsaw (a hand saw can be used, but the edges will not be as smooth); spray paint (optional); heavy nylon cord (burn the ends with a match so they will not fray); twine, heavy string, yarn, or leather; and bobby pin (to be used as a needle). For decoration, you could also use one-inch strips of fabric.

▼ *Directions*:

1. Draw and cut out your patterns (the sketch below can easily be adapted to your own designs). Place them on the pegboard, making sure that the sides and bottom edges line up evenly with a row of holes. Trace with a marking pen and remove the paper. With the jigsaw, cut the outside edges of the house as well as any windows or doors.

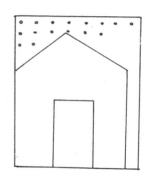

2. Optional: Lightly spray paint the house and allow to dry thoroughly.

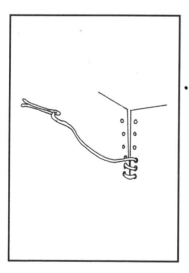

3. To join the boards together, thread a long piece of cord through the bobby pin. Place two adjoining sides together, lining up the holes on top of each other. Starting at the bottom, "sew" the cord through two holes and tie a square knot (right over left and then left over right). Bring the cord down through one set of holes, then up around the outside edge and down through the next set, continuing to the top. Now reverse the steps and sew back down the sides, making a crisscross design. If the cord isn't long enough, just tie on another piece and continue sewing. (This is the time to really get your child involved.) Repeat this step with all sides of the house. If you have decided to put a roof on your house, attach it in a similar manner. Sew down through a hole on the roof, then through a hole on the house, back up to the roof again, and on to the next set of holes until the roof is firmly in place. For the door, simply sew down one long side, allowing the door to move freely.

4. Now that your house is put together, you can have the fun of decorating it. Using the fabric strips, whipstitch (down through a hole, up and around the edge, and then down through the next hole) the edges of the roof, windows, and door. Use the strips to attach a wreath on a door, a basket of flowers under a window, or to make a door handle. Use a basic embroidery outline stitch to make flowers bloom by the front door or to give your house a name. Baskets can be put inside the house to store toys or coloring books. Put your imagination to work and create a whole village. (An added bonus: If the roof is removed, these playhouses can be easily collapsed for storage.)

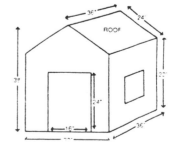

Pop Up a Winner for a Few Cents

Many popular pop-up books can cost $20, but you can create your own for just the cost of the paper. For children, you can personalize fairy tales, print their own story with their drawings, or use the pop-ups as any-occasion cards.

■ Pop-up Strip

Take two pieces of paper (8 1/2" x 11"). Fold each in half—set one aside. In the middle of the folded edge of first paper, mark two dots, 1/4" apart. Starting at dots, draw two 1" parallel lines toward paper's edge. Cut lines starting from folded edge. Fold cut strip back; fold it forward again. Open card and fold like a tent. Push strip through to other side of card. Close card and press firmly. Open to see pop-up strip. Draw a person or animal on a sheet of paper. (Figure can be a little taller and wider than your strip.) Color in figure and cut out. Apply glue on one side of strip. Place figure on glue. Glue card to paper put inside. (This now becomes outside of card.) When card is opened, the little cut-out figure will pop up. Decorate front and inside.

■ Talking Mouth

Take two pieces of paper (8 1/2" x 11"). Fold each in half—set one aside. On one, put a dot in approximately the center of folded edge. Draw 2" line from dot toward outer edge and cut, starting at folded edge. Fold back flaps to form two triangles. Open up flaps again. Open whole page. Hold paper like a tent. Put your finger on top triangle and push down. Pinch two folded edges of top triangle so that triangle is pushed through to other side. Repeat on bottom triangle. Top and bottom triangles will now be pushed out to form a mouth inside card. When you open and close card, the mouth will "talk." Glue inside and outside cards together. Important: Do not apply glue in area of pop-up mouth. Variations: Draw a jagged line instead of a straight line for talking mouth. Your figure will now have teeth.

■ Springs (accordion strip)

Fold a heavy piece of paper (8 1/2" x 5 1/2") in half. Put it aside. (This will be the card.) Make a large spring using two strips of paper measuring 1" x 11". Glue one end of spring about 1/8" away from middle fold line of your card. Put glue on top part of spring and close card, holding firm for about a minute while glue dries. When you open card, the spring will be pulled open and can become a crown, accordion, etc. Draw a person or animal around spring. Springs can also be used anywhere inside card to give the appearance of objects jumping out at you. Glue only one side of spring to inside. Then glue an object to top part of spring.

■ Opening Door

Fold two pieces of heavy paper in half. Put one aside. On the right side of card, draw two vertical lines 2" long and 4" apart. Label left slot A, right slot B. Cut lines with X-Acto knife. Cut a strip of heavy paper 7" x 3/4". Start at right side of strip and measure 1 1/2"; fold at this line. Cut out a thin rectangle of heavy paper about 1 1/2" x 1/4". Glue strip against left side of folded line on inside of strip. Insert short end of strip into Slot A so that thin rectangle is facing outside. Put opposite end of strip through slot B. Turn paper over and fold other way. Cut door out of heavy paper measuring 6" x 6". Fold this square in half. Apply glue to inside of folded square. Fold paper over short tab. Press edges of door firmly. Push and pull strip to make door open or close. On long side of strip, write "PULL." Apply glue around edges of card away from strip. Important: Don't apply glue near strip. Place card on paper set aside. Press firmly. Make a drawing under flapping door and on rest of page to complete your card/picture.

110

Nasty-Day Activities for Kids

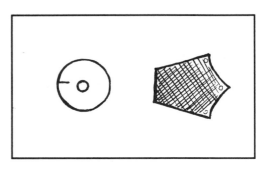

If bad weather brings out the blahs in your kids' activities, here are a couple of nifty how-to's. The finished items are so much fun, in fact, that the age of enjoyment of these will go well into retirement.

■ Walking Duck Tot Toy

▲ *To make, you'll need*: Duck pattern from comic book, etc.; one 12" x 18" x 1" pine board; one old auto tire inner tube or vinyl; 30" length 7/16" dowel; 4" length 1" dowel; wood; glue; and acrylic paints.

▼ *Directions*:

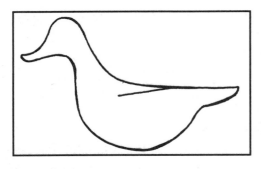

Using pattern as guide, draw duck's body on the pine board. Use compass to draw wheels 3" in diameter on the same board. With jigsaw or sabre saw, cut parts out (the lumber yard will cut this for you, if you prefer). Make sure to cut the slit in the duck's body as shown. The opening should end 3/4" below the center of the duck's back. Also cut a 3/4" slit into each wheel as shown. Sand body and wheels. Paint them in colors and designs attractive to you.

Cut a 3" piece from one end of the 7/16" dowel to form wheel axle. Drill a 7/16" hole through center of each wheel and on the wooden duck as shown. Thread dowel through duck. Glue wheels to each end of dowel.

Bore a 7/16" hole into top of duck's back at a 45-degree angle. Insert the long 7/16" dowel into the hole, securing it with wood glue. Drill a 7/16" hole into center of the 1" dowel and fit it to end of long dowel. Use glue to secure it.

Cut wings and feet from the inner tube or vinyl using the pattern as guide. Paint as shown. Attach wings to body by sliding them into the slit cut along center of duck's back. Insert feet into slits cut into wheels. Use glue to secure.

■ Marionette Animal Friends

▲ *To make, you'll need*: 1/2 yard long-pile artificial fur fabric (buy in craft store), 1/2 yard cotton/polyester fabric, polyester batting, two 30mm wiggle eyes, three 2" pom-poms, one 1" pom-pom, plastic craft eyelashes, felt scraps, 14" length 3/4" x 1/8" oak furring strip, 11" length 3/4" x 1/8" oak furring strip, and 6-8 pound test fishing line.

◆ *Note*: As you cut the artificial fur, be careful to push far away from backing so you cut only backing. Trace pattern pieces on back of fur with dark pencil (arrows on pattern pieces indicate direction of nap).

▼ *Directions*:

Body: Place circles with right sides together, then seam, leaving three 2" openings, 4" apart, on one side of the circle. Turn to right sides through one opening. Stuff loosely with batting.

Head: Place right sides together and seam, leaving 2" opening for turning (see pattern marking). Turn fabric to right side through opening. Stuff loosely. Using a hot glue gun or other craft glue, glue wiggle eyes on two of the 2" pom-poms. Cut half-circle eyelids from felt scraps. Glue eyelashes to straight side of eyelids. Attach pom-poms on head as shown on pattern. Glue eyelids so that they cover top portion of the eye pom-poms. Use glue gun to attach the 1" pom-pom as shown on pattern to form nose.

Feet: Place one circle of fur with one circle of cotton/polyester, right sides together, and seam, leaving 2" opening in the seam. Turn to right side through opening. Stuff loosely. Repeat with remaining two circles.

Legs and Back: Cut three straight strips of fur fabric 4 1/2" wide and 12" long. Fold each strip of fabric lengthwise so that long edges are together and right sides are together. Seam. Turn to right side.

To assemble marionette: 1. Slip end of neck piece into opening in head. Turn under edges of head opening. Zigzag stitch on machine, or slip stitch by hand to attach neck and close head opening. 2. Use same procedure to attach other end of neck to middle opening in body, one end of each leg to remaining openings in body, other ends on legs to feet. Glue remaining pom-pom to back bottom of body for tail. 3. Sand both furring strips until smooth. Stain or paint if desired. One-half inch from each end of each strip, drill two small holes 1/4" apart. Holes need only be large enough for fishing line to spread through. Glue shorter strip 4" from end of longer strip to form a cross. 4. Cut a 20"-21" piece of fishing line. Thread through needle. Attach one end to the top of the head (marked by dot on pattern). Take a small stitch through backing of holes in the end of longest stick closest to crosspiece. Pull through until length of line between stick and top of the head measures exactly 16". 5. Cut a piece of line at least 30". Use same procedure to attach line to center of back of body and other end of long strip. Fishing line between the center of body and stick should measure exactly 26". 6. Cut two pieces of line at least 38" long. Using procedure described above, connect center of one foot to an end of the short strip and center of other foot to other end of strip. Fishing line should measure exactly 34" between each foot and the wood strip. Operate marionette by moving the cross of wood up and down, tipping in, and so on.

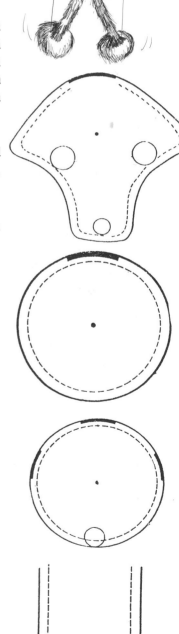

112

Turn Sneakers into Watermelons

Back-to-school time means new shoes as well as new everything. Here's a way to turn ordinary sneakers into watermelons and other A+ designs for little money.

Decorated shoes can be teamed with similarly decorated shirts, slacks, shorts, etc., to create ensembles kids will love to wear. Here are several techniques for creating designer shoes that will add color, interest, and excitement to kids' school wardrobes.

■ Painted or Dyed Shoes

▲ *To make, you'll need*: Puff paint, fabric dye, any permanent fabric paint, and acrylic paint.

Watermelon Shoes: Purchase red canvas shoes and paint the rubber sides with green acrylic paint (green permanent marker can also be used). With black puff paint, draw "teardrops" in the shape of watermelon seeds in groups of three on the shoe canvas. If desired, complement with a tie-dyed T-shirt to match.

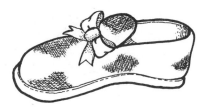

Sponge-Painted Shoes: Using a sponge dipped in acrylic paint, make designs on shoes as desired.

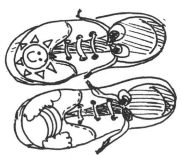

Permanent Marker Shoes: If you prefer, permanent markers can be used to paint designs on shoes.

Fabric-Dyed Shoes: You can also apply fabric dyes onto shoes using a brush and then "wetting" the designs with a fabric enhancer. (Spraying fabric enhancer on wet dye will cause it to run, giving you a "watered" effect.) Carry the shoe design onto a T-shirt to create a matching set.

■ Shrink Art Shoes

For shrink art shoes, you'll need 8" x 10" shrink art sheets (clear sheets yield a finished product which is clear, and opaque sheets yield a finished product which is cloudy), scissors, paper punch, and permanent markers, colored pencils, crayons, or other media.

Draw a design onto a sheet and color with one of the above. Cut out designs with scissors, rounding off sharp corners. Punch holes into the finished artwork where you want the ties to lace through.

Set pieces on brown paper and place into a 250-degree oven for one minute (for larger pieces, leave in slightly longer). Remove pieces from the oven using a smooth spatula (remember to then remove the brown paper from the oven immediately), let them cool for a moment, and they're ready to thread onto shoelaces. Note: Your artwork design will shrink up to four times the original size, so be sure to allow for shrinkage.

■ Decorated Shoes with Sequins, Beads, Lace, Beaded Lace, and Ribbon

For attractive variations, sew designs onto shoes using sequins or beads. If desired, repeat design on shirts and other clothing. Ribbons, lace, and beaded lace can be substituted for shoelaces. If using ribbon, a heavy-ribbed ribbon is recommended.

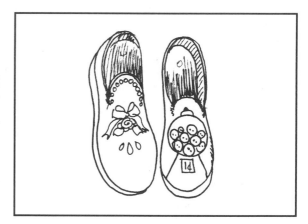

Rhinestones or other costume jewels can be "glued" onto shoe canvas by placing a dollop of puff paint on the shoe. Place gem onto the paint, and when it dries, the gem is set in place.

■ Wood Cutout Art

Small wooden cutouts can be purchased at most craft stores for anywhere from 10 cents to a dollar. Drill or punch a small hole in each cutout where you want the shoelaces to go through. Decorate cutouts with acrylic paint or any other permanent nontoxic paint. Varnish and thread onto shoelaces.

■ Applique Shoes

Almost any type of fabric can be made into an applique, but felt works especially well. Cut out desired applique design and place together. Attach Velcro to the applique underside. Place Velcro on shoes (Velcro-fastened shoes or slip-ons, which have no laces to get in the way, work best) and match Velcro strips together so that the applique adheres to the shoe. Applique designs can be interchanged as desired to create different outfits.

Take One Loved but Forgotten Teddy Bear

There are so many loved stuffed animals sitting in closets that if they could talk, you'd hear, "Use me, use me." I have heard them and have brought them back as hand puppets. Starting with one devoted teddy bear, for instance, you will also need muslin (amount will depend on the size of the bear), scissors, and sewing machine or needle and thread.

▼ *Directions*: Begin by cutting a hole in the bottom of the bear's body (behind the area where the legs join). Make sure it is large enough for a hand to be inserted. Using the glove pattern adjusted to fit the size of your bear, cut two pieces from the muslin. Stitch 1/4" around all sides except the flat side. Turn the open edge under 1/4" toward the seamed side and press. Carefully remove a small amount of stuffing from the bear. Put your hand in the glove, then insert your hand into the bear. Gently work your hand and match the opening of the muslin to the opening on the bear. Whip stitch the bear and muslin together to finish your puppet.

◆ *Variations*: Following these same steps, you can make a puppet from any stuffed animal. An especially fun puppet can be made from a cloth doll and a blanket. Again, use the basic steps except make an opening in the back of the doll (along a seam line if there is one). After the glove is inserted, place the doll on a blanket in which you have cut a slit the same size as the one in the doll. Whip stitch the muslin to the doll and blanket together. Pajama bags (or secret hiding places) can be made using the same technique. Simply make a rectangular pocket instead of a glove, inserting it into an opening in the back or the stomach of the stuffed animal. You may also want to remove a little more of the stuffing than you would for the puppet.

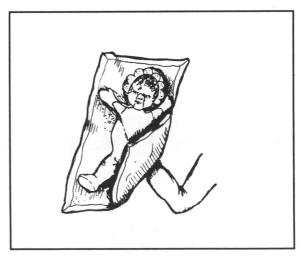

Teddy Bears, Pandas, and Elephants

Here are some sweet animals: teddy bears, pandas, and elephants that make no noise or mess but produce lots of giggles and pleasure.

Use any premade dough bought in stores. You can also use a mixture of white and whole-wheat flour. Apart from the dough, you will need decorating ingredients, a large greased baking pan, and kitchen scissors or a knife.

● Making the Bears:

1. Break a ball of dough in two. Roll half of it into a big ball for the bear's body. Put it on the baking pan and flatten it a little. 2. Break the remaining dough in two. Roll half of it into a small ball. Roll the other half into a sausage shape about 6" long. 3. Brush one side of the small ball with egg. Stick it to the bear's body, tucking it slightly underneath, to make the head. 4. Break off a piece of the sausage-shaped roll. Brush one side of it with egg and stick it to the bear's face. Pinch it into the shape of a snout. 5. Cut two small pieces for the ears and four bigger ones for the legs. Pinch them into position under the bear's body and head. 6. Using the kitchen scissors or a knife, snip or slash the ends of the bear's legs to make them look like paws with claws. Make all the bears this way.

● Letting the Bears Rise:

7. Cover them loosely with a dish towel and leave them in a warm place to rise for about an hour, until they have doubled in size. Then brush them lightly with beaten egg to glaze them and use raisins to make their eyes. Now you can add other decorations if you like.

● Baking the Bears:

8. Bake the bears in the oven at 350 degrees for about 25 minutes, depending on their size, until they are golden brown. Then put them on a wire rack to cool.

116

A Wonderful, Magical Zoo for You

This imaginative zoo is full of animals made of foam for your children to create and enjoy. When I saw small Mexican children playing with some like these recently while on a trip, I knew just about everyone would love the idea. Lizards that walk, centipedes that crawl, chickens that cackle as they lay eggs, dinosaurs claimed by no prehistoric era—you can't wait to begin, I'll bet. (Note: Enlarge pattern pieces to desired size—suggested size of lizard body: 12".)

■ Foam Rubber Toys

▲ **To make the toy lizard,** use 1/4" to 1/2" thick foam, which can be purchased at a craft or fabric store (or check with your local upholstery shop). Draw the pattern on the sheet of foam with a marking pen and cut it out with an electric knife. If one is not available, use sharp scissors and cut with long, even strokes.

Thread a piece of medium-gauge wire (about one foot long) lengthwise through the middle of the foam for each leg. Clip off excess wire and fold the ends under to eliminate sharp edges. To attach the legs to the body, place a leg piece horizontally across the top of the body about 4" from one end. Gathering the body slightly, twist the leg piece around and under the body, crossing and extending out the opposite sides. Repeat procedure about 4" from the other end with the second leg piece. Fold down about 1" on all four legs to form the feet. Using a nontoxic spray paint, decorate it any way you like. Cut a small slit in the tip of one end for the mouth. For the eyes, glue on sequins, buttons, or movable eyes.

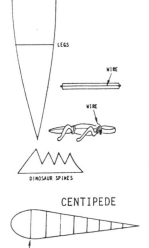

LIZARD AND DINOSAUR

ELASTIC BAND LEGS

LEGS

WIRE

WIRE

DINOSAUR SPIKES

CENTIPEDE

PIPE CLEANERS

To make the lizard move, put an elastic band around the neck area. Using a long piece of heavy-gauge wire (a straightened coat hanger is great), form a small hook at one end. From the top side near the elastic band, push the wire through the foam. Hook the elastic band and pull the wire back into the foam. Bend over the other end of the wire and tape to make a safe handle.

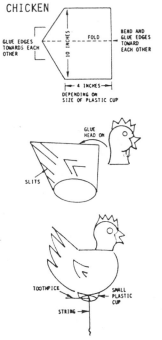

CHICKEN

GLUE EDGES TOWARDS EACH OTHER

FOLD

BEND AND GLUE EDGES TOWARD EACH OTHER

10 INCHES

4 INCHES

DEPENDING ON SIZE OF PLASTIC CUP

GLUE HEAD ON

SLITS

TOOTHPICK

SMALL PLASTIC CUP

STRING

▲ **To make a centipede,** cut out the body according to the pattern and spray paint it. To make the legs, place the center of a pipe cleaner horizontally across the top of the body. Gather the body slightly and twist the pipe cleaner around and under the body crossing and extending out the opposite side. Attach legs at 1" intervals down the entire body of the centipede. Form a head and attach eyes.

▲ **To make the dinosaur,** trace and cut out the body. Cut out the spine and glue to the top of body. Follow lizard directions to attach legs.

▲ **To make the chicken,** trace the pattern and cut the pieces from foam. Poke a tiny hole in the bottom of a small plastic cup. Break a toothpick in half and tie about 18" of string to the middle of it. Thread the toothpick (with string attached) through the hole in the cup and let the string hang down. Glue the body piece around the plastic cup. Glue on the head and attach the eyes. To make the chicken cackle and lay an egg, wet a small piece of foam rubber and hold it around the string, next to the cup, with your thumb and index finger. Pull the foam down the string in short jerking motions. As the chicken cackles, drop the egg into a nest.

Creative Ways to Give Money

■ Money Shower

Take an umbrella and tie ribbons 10 to 12 inches long on spokes. Tape $1, $5, or $10 bills on the end of each ribbon. With umbrella upside down, close so money will be inside umbrella. When recipient pushes button to pop it open, she will be showered with money.

■ Box of Carnations

In small folds, accordion-pleat $1, $5, or $10 bills and wrap end of a 16-20" wire around center of each bill. Wrap with florist tape, adding one or two leaves from craft store as you wrap. Place tissue in bottom of long rose box; add baby's breath and floral greens. Wrap and give to a special friend.

■ Dump Truck

Load toy truck with 10-15 rolls of pennies. Wrap with plastic wrap and put a bow on it. You can also open the packages of pennies and place pennies in the dump truck. Give the recipient the paper rolls. When child is ready to roll them, he or she can count them into piles of 50 and roll into paper wrappers.

■ Money Worm

At the craft store purchase 3" pom-pom, two wiggly eyes, small pom-pom (for nose), yellow pipe cleaner, green felt, and yellow rickrack. Start with a piece of green felt 2" long by 4" wide. Fold felt together and insert yellow rickrack along the 2" edge and sew. Place rolls of pennies, dimes, or quarters in the center of felt and tie off with yellow ribbon between rolls. On the top end glue a 3" craft pom-pom and other facial features. Fold yellow pipe cleaner in the center and twist like antennae.

■ Gift Coupons

Gift coupons are exciting ways of giving a service to a special friend or family member. Out of construction paper, make an object that resembles the service you want to give. For example:

Object:	Service:
Scissors	Good for haircut
Taxi cab	Good for taxi fare
Bus	Good for bus fare
Snowman	Good for shoveling snow
Gingerbread man	Good for baking home-made cookies

We Could All Be Albert Einsteins

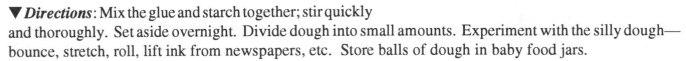

You're an Einstein who can make learning fun for your children if you try these with them.

■ Make Your Own Silly Dough

▲ *To make, you'll need*: 2 cups white glue, 1 cup liquid starch, a mixing bowl, and a big spoon.

▼ *Directions*: Mix the glue and starch together; stir quickly and thoroughly. Set aside overnight. Divide dough into small amounts. Experiment with the silly dough—bounce, stretch, roll, lift ink from newspapers, etc. Store balls of dough in baby food jars.

■ How Plants Breathe

▲ *To make, you'll need*: A healthy potted plant, plastic bag, bag twist tie, petroleum jelly, and water.

▼ *Directions*: First, water the plant well. Be sure to let excess water drain out through the bottom. Put a plastic bag over the plant. Tie the bag around the stem of the plant. Set the plant near a sunny window where it will get good light. Check the plant the next day. You should see drops of water on the inside of the bag.

More experiments with plants: Smear a thick coat of petroleum jelly on the tops of two or three leaves. Smear a thick coat of petroleum jelly on the bottoms of two or three other leaves. (The petroleum jelly will block the stomates so that the leaves can't breathe.) Water the plant well and set near a sunny window. Next day, see what happened to the jelly-coated leaves.

Tips for Parents: When Your Child Is Sick in Bed

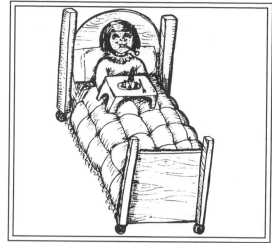

Here are some imaginative ways to take the strain off Mom or Dad when a child is sick in bed.

● **To monitor a bedridden child** without an intercom system: If your child is old enough, use a pair of inexpensive two-way radios to keep in touch as you work around the house. Your child keeps one at the bedside to call you when you're needed. You keep the other one with you to check on the child periodically.

● **Thermos Cooler**: Keep cool water handy by filling a thermos or other insulated beverage container with cold or ice water and placing it near the bed. The water stays cool and convenient for you to serve your child. If you're dealing with an older child, set the container near enough that the child can serve him/herself.

● **Sanitary Can**: If your child's symptoms include stomach upset, you'll want a handy throw-away container. Thoroughly clean a large, empty can (a three-pound shortening can, coffee can, etc.). Place a large, heavy, self-sealing plastic bag inside the can. Pull the top edges of the open bag up and over the edge of the can. Keep this at the child's bedside. Cleanup is simple. Just zip the bag closed and dispose of it, then line the can with another bag.

● **Cardboard Box Lap Table**: You can make a lap table handy for eating, as well as doing homework, coloring, or playing in bed. Cut a sufficiently large cardboard box so that it's just the right height for your child to eat or write in bed. Cut half circles from the long sides of the box so that the box fits comfortably over the child's legs. Cover the box/lap table with cheerful Contact paper.

● **Muffin Tin Server**: Try serving your child's meal in a muffin tin. It makes foods easier to manage for your bedridden child and easier for you to carry from the kitchen. Nest a small beverage glass in one muffin tin compartment and small portions of tempting foods in the other compartments.

● **Pear Clown**: Set two canned pear halves together to form a whole. Place a sugar cone over the smaller end of the pear to hold the pear halves together and form the clown's hat. Use whole cloves for the clown's eyes; cut a sliver of maraschino cherry to form the clown's mouth. Add shredded cheese "hair."

● **Fruitsicles**: Make popsicles from a large (28 ounce) can of fruit. Add corn syrup to sweeten the fruit, if needed. Puree the fruit in a blender. Pour the fruit mixture into paper cups. (Small 4-oz. cups work best for smaller children. Use 6 or 8-oz. cups for older children.) Invert a popsicle stick in the center of each cup of fruit. Freeze until firm. Peel off the cup to serve.

● **Licorice Straws**: Hollow-centered red or black licorice makes a sweet, flexible straw to tempt children to drink the liquids they need.

Crafts

An Energy-Saving Caterpillar

This caterpillar was created to stop drafts. It'll stop your windy doors and windows too if you follow these easy instructions.

■ Caterpillar Draft Stopper

▲ *To make (for a 36" door), you'll need*: One 9" x 38" piece of green felt, 1 yard giant yellow rickrack, 2 1/2 yards yellow ribbon, one 2"-diameter green pom-pom, one 1/2"-diameter pink pom-pom, one yellow pipe cleaner, one pair plastic eyes, one pair long curly plastic eyelashes, craft glue or hot glue gun, and pea gravel or coarse sand. (Hint: Do not use beans, as they will sprout if they get wet. If you cannot obtain the gravel or sand, you could use aquarium gravel or even kitty litter.)

▼ *Directions*:

Fold the felt in half lengthwise, cutting the corners in a rounded shape as in the drawing. Narrowly stitch the rounded end, leaving the long side open. Insert the rickrack along the long edge and stitch the side closed, leaving a 2" opening at one end. Solidly fill the caterpillar's body with the gravel, then hand stitch it closed. Starting about 6" from the long end, tightly tie the yellow ribbon around the body, ending in a bow on top. Space the ribbon every six inches.

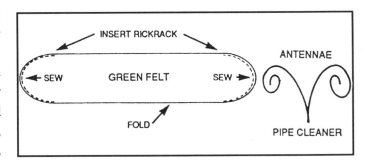

Glue the pink pom-pom on to the green one for the nose. Glue on the eyes and lashes. To make the antennae, fold the pipe cleaner in half. Twist each end of the pipe cleaner into a flat, curly shape. Insert the center of the pipe cleaner into the top of the pom-pom and glue into place. Glue the head to one end of the caterpillar's body. Now lay it on the floor along the edge of your door to prevent drafts from entering your home. Use your imagination to create other draft stoppers or look in the craft section of pattern books for the doll draft stoppers.

Open Your Linen Closet, Find a Doll

For all the old pillowcases, napkins, and men's large handker-chiefs that are sitting in closets and drawers, let me suggest an innovative use—turn them into dolls for about $3.

■ Pillowcase Doll

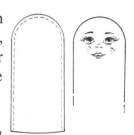

▲ *To make, you'll need*: 1/4 yard muslin, one standard-size pillowcase (preserve an heirloom pillowcase this way), 21" of 1/4"-wide elastic, fiberfill stuffing, acrylic paints, textile medium and brushes, one piece heavy paper (cardstock), purchased doll hair or 1/2 yard 100 percent cotton material for fabric hair (use colored fabric or white and dye to the color of your choice), fabric glue or hot glue gun, lace, and ribbon.

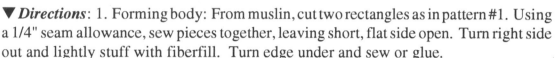

▼ *Directions*: 1. Forming body: From muslin, cut two rectangles as in pattern #1. Using a 1/4" seam allowance, sew pieces together, leaving short, flat side open. Turn right side out and lightly stuff with fiberfill. Turn edge under and sew or glue.

2. Painting the face: On a piece of paper, enlarge one of the face patterns (about 2" from outside eye to outside eye). Fold the pillowcase in half lengthwise and mark the midpoint at the seam line. Slip the face pattern (pattern #2) inside and center it about 2" below the mark. Trace the pattern on the pillowcase with a pencil. Remove the pattern and place the piece of heavy paper inside under the face to protect the back while painting. Using the acrylic paints mixed with textile medium, paint the face. If you wish, you can use your own blush for the cheeks.

3. Constructing the doll: After the paint is completely dry, remove the paper and insert the doll form, centering the rounded part under the face. Tie a 5" piece of elastic at the neck area to form the head. Evenly adjust the gathers around the neck. Put one or two handfuls of stuffing (depending on how puffy you wish it to be) in the corners of the pillowcase to form the arms. Tie each off with a 5" piece of elastic. Using a 3" piece of elastic, make hands by tying off about one inch of the corner of the pillowcase of the puffy arms (see elastic placement guide). Glue or stitch gathered lace around top of head on pillowcase seam so lace faces forward. This will give the doll the appearance of wearing a bonnet. Glue curly craft hair under lace next to seam.

4. Decorating the doll: Glue or sew several layers of lace trim around the bottom of the pillowcase. Tie narrow ribbon around the neck with a bow and streamers hanging down the front. Variations: Now that you know how to do the basic doll, use your imagination; make a ghost, a pilgrim, or a Christmas angel.

Birds Will Think Twice About Flying South

There are so many wonderful birdhouses to cleverly care for and protect the neighborhood birds in the winter, it's doubtful that any will want to fly south.

With any type of birdhouse, remember: 1. Houses must be well ventilated. 2. Houses should have small holes in the bottom for drainage. 3. Think ahead—houses need to be cleaned yearly. Construct your birdhouse to include some type of access for you to clean (such as a hinged roof, etc.). 4. Cut hole for doorway large enough to accommodate types of birds you want to attract (1" to 2" in diameter). 5. Hang birdhouses where birds will be reasonably safe from cats, dogs, or curious children, and out of direct sunlight.

■ Wedge Birdhouse

▲ *To make, simply cut* pieces of wood following diagrams. Using small nails and wood glue, assemble house. (Remember to hinge roof for cleaning.)

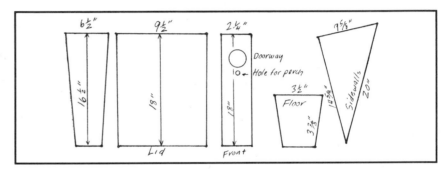

■ Kleenex® Box House

▲ *To make, you'll need*: Wicker Kleenex box (with oblong opening), barn wood (2 pieces), and dried flowers and raffia for decoration (optional).

Cut barn wood large enough to allow approximately 3" extra extension at both top and bottom of Kleenex container. Miter one end of back piece. Attach roof to back piece at mitered edge using small nails and wood glue. Wire Kleenex container to back piece. Decorate as desired with dried flowers and raffia.

■ Watermelon Birdhouse

Because this birdhouse is less protective of birds, it is recommended for warmer climates.

▲ *To make, you'll need*: Two fruit baskets (5-6" in diameter, one with handle); red, green, and white acrylic paint; raffia; and wire. Attach basket without handle to basket with handle by placing basket over handle (as you would put a lid on a pan), securing with wire. Paint inside of baskets red, including handle, and outside of baskets green and white to look like a watermelon. Tie bows around handle on each side using raffia. Use heavy-gauge wire attached to top of "watermelon" to hang birdhouse.

■ Bleach Bottle Birdhouse

▲ *To make, you'll need*: Any type of plastic bottle. Make sure it is cleaned out thoroughly.

Cut a 1 1/2" hole in bottle approximately 6" from bottom of half-gallon bottle. One inch below hole, make another small hole with a paper punch, insert a 3" piece of dowel, and super glue in hole. This is the perch. Use a small nail to poke holes in bottom of bottle for drainage. Paint outside of bottle to look like a house.

■ "Larry Bird" House

▲ *To make, you'll need*: Basketball, funnel, 3-wire plant hanger, and 3" piece wooden dowel.

Cut hole in top of basketball large enough for your hand. In front of basketball, cut a 1 1/2"-2" hole for "doorway." One inch below "doorway," cut a small hole and insert 3"-piece wooden dowel. Super glue in place. This is the perch. Holding funnel with small end up, insert 3-wire hanger through small opening. Attach wires to ball around large hole made in top of ball. Poke holes in bottom of ball for drainage. Slide funnel down to cover top opening of ball.

■ Bird Condo

▲ *To make, you'll need*: 6 pieces of 2"-3" diameter PVC pipe cut in 4" lengths, purple spray paint, silk leaves, and raffia.

Paint inside and outside of pipe with purple spray paint. Let dry thoroughly. Glue PVC pipe together using hot glue gun or wood glue. Tie raffia bow and glue to top of cluster along with a few silk leaves. This unique and easy-to-assemble birdhouse was made to look like a cluster of grapes when looking at open ends of pipes.

■ Scarecrow Birdhouse

▲ *To make, you'll need*: Wooden stand (wooden box with hinged top), scarecrow head (can purchase precut head at craft store or cut your own), pair of cotton garden gloves, old men's shirt, and raffia.

Paint front of scarecrow head to look like face and hat. Cut hole in wood at the base of the painted hat for "doorway." Attach hinged wooden box to back of head for birdhouse. Attach head to center of a piece of wood that measures 24" long, 1 1/2" wide, and 3/4" thick. This will be the "shoulders." Pull shirt over scarecrow head and put sleeves over board. Attach head and shoulder boards to wooden stand. Button shirt. Gather up bottom of shirt around wooden stand and tie with raffia. Stuff cotton gloves slightly. Tie with raffia to end of sleeves forming hands. Tie shirt closed around neck with raffia.

Birdfeeders

■ Coconut

Poke small holes in top of coconut; drain out coconut milk. Cut hole approximately 2" in diameter on side of coconut. Pull heavy-gauge wire through top of coconut and hang from tree. Birds will fly inside and eat the coconut.

■ Pinecone

You'll need 1/2 cup bacon grease, 1/2 cup cornmeal, 1 tablespoon peanut butter, and 1/4 cup birdseed (or sunflower seeds). Mix cooled bacon grease, peanut butter, and cornmeal together. Push mixture up into and all over pinecone. Roll pinecone in birdseed. Hang with string or wire from tree.

■ Bird Trail Mix

You'll need a small plastic margarine container with lid, three empty thread spools, heavy-gauge wire, sunflower seeds, birdseed, raisins, and cracked corn.

Poke small holes in bottom of plastic margarine container for drainage. In center of container, poke hole large enough to accommodate heavy-gauge wire. Bend end of wire so it won't pull through hole. Thread empty spools onto the heavy-gauge wire. Poke hole in center of plastic lid. Thread onto wire. Make a loop with end of wire to hang in tree. Fill margarine container with seeds, raisins, etc. Hang in tree.

Garden Tool Wall Art

When I looked through the excellent book *Flower Style* by Kenneth Turner (Weidenfeld and Nicholson, $35), I saw a beautiful wall sculpture made of old gardening tools. You can make one following this adaptation.

▲ *To make, you'll need*: Old or broken garden tools, watering cans or flower pots, white flat spray paint, enamel spray paint of your color choice, green florist's wire, medium- to heavy-gauge wire, raffia, hot glue gun, artificial flowers, ferns, and moss.

▼ *Directions*:

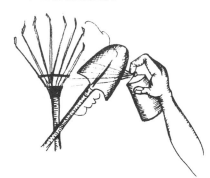

1. Clean tools and then spray with white flat paint. When dry, spray with enamel paint.

2. On a large table or flat surface, begin by crisscrossing the largest tools. Wire together wherever they cross. Tie with raffia for extra support and decoration.

3. Attach the rest of the pieces individually with wire and raffia. When all pieces are securely in place, decorate with artificial flowers using florist's wire and glue gun.

◆ *Helpful hint*: Since this sculpture can be very heavy, you will probably need two or three heavy-duty hooks to hang it. Make sure the hooks are placed in wall studs for extra strength.

My inspiration came from Kenneth Turner's book; now use your imagination to create wall sculptures for other rooms in your home using objects appropriate to each room: kitchen, nursery, den, or even the bathroom. Yard sales and Goodwill stores would be great places to find interesting pieces for your sculptures.

String Baskets to Really Tie Up Decorations

String baskets being all the rage now, here's a way to make baskets costing up to $20 in stores for about $3.50. This delicate basket adds a light touch to any festive decoration. Easy to make, it doubles as an attractive gift as well.

■ String Basket

▲ *To make, you'll need*: Balloon (rounded, tear-shaped), string (use "crochet-cotton" string from fabric or craft stores; thinner and stronger than regular string, it costs about $1.50 a roll), sugar, and bow or other trims.

▼ *Directions*:
To make your basket, make up a solution of one cup of sugar to one cup of hot water. Stir until the sugar is dissolved. While the solution is cooling, blow up the balloon, tying the end securely. Tie one end of the string to the knot in the balloon. Wrap the string around the balloon in crisscrossing patterns. Hold the wrapped balloon over a large bowl in a sink or bathtub. With the other hand, pour the sugar water over the balloon, patting string to make sure all string is saturated with the solution. Hang the covered balloon over a sink or bathtub. (Use the end of the string or another length of string tied to the knot of the balloon to hang it from shower head or curtain rod. The string will drip stickily.)

When the string is completely dry (in about 24 hours), pop the balloon with a straight pin. Cut the string carefully to disattach it from the balloon. Then carefully cut away string to form the top edge and handle of the basket. Trim with a bow or ribbon. Fill with "grass" and lightweight decorations and candies.

Use your imagination when cutting out the openings and planning the designs for specific occasions—deeper sides, wider handles, window openings, etc. Use red and green string for winter, pink or blue for baby showers, browns and yellows for autumn, etc.

129

Make a Wonderful Wooden Basket

■ Wooden Basket

▲ *To make, you'll need*: 3 16' lengths of parting stock (1/2" thick x 3/4" wide), carpenter's wood glue, and a large sheet of freezer wrap.

▼ *Directions*:

1. Cut parting stock into pieces measuring 4 1/4" (at base) by 3 1/4" on top (see Fig. 1). You will need 125 pieces to complete each basket. Using black marker, draw a 15"-diameter circle on the freezer wrap. This will serve as a guide.

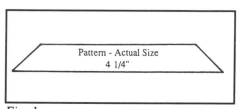

Fig. 1

2. First Row (Base): Set 11 wood pieces around circle on freezer wrap. Lay pieces on their side with 4 1/4" side facing outward.

3. Second Row: Put wood glue on ends of 4 1/4" side of wood piece. Center wood piece over gap between base wood pieces. Press in place. Continue putting glue on ends of wood pieces and centering over gaps of base wood pieces until you have 10 pieces of wood in place around circle (Fig. 2).

Fig. 2

4. Third Row: Follow instructions for second row, only gluing 9 pieces of wood to second row of basket.

5. Fourth Row: Follow instructions for third row, only gluing 8 pieces of wood to third row of basket.

6. Fifth Row: Follow instructions for fourth row, only gluing 7 pieces of wood to fourth row of basket. Let dry completely.

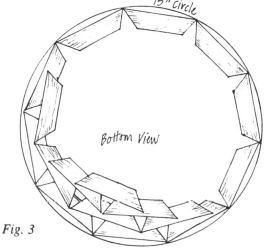

Fig. 3

7. Turn basket over. Glue rows 1-5 following same directions given above for 1st-5th rows on opposite side. After these rows have dried completely, finish with rows 6-10, decreasing wood pieces used in each row by one until your final tenth row has only one wood piece (see Fig. 3). Let dry completely.

8. Again, turn basket over and finish rows 6-10 on opposite side. Let dry completely.

● *Optional*: Paint, stain, or varnish basket to create the look you want.

130

Your Beach Mat Is in the Bag

No more lugging and toting a lot of little bundles when you go to the beach if you follow this clever idea—carry it all in what's called a "tote-n-mat." Everything goes in an attractive shoulder tote that opens into a mat, which has pockets to hold the other stuff. And that includes a nifty paddle game.

■ Beach Mat

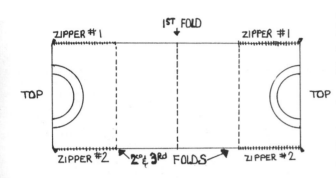

▲ *To make, you'll need*: One piece of foam 72" x 24" x 1/2", 2 pieces of cotton fabric (preshrunk) 74" x 26", 1 yard cotton webbing for handles (or 2 pieces of fabric 18" x 4"), and 2 18"-long separating zippers.

▼ *Directions*:
1. Position the zippers on the right side of the fabric, according to the diagram, with the teeth facing inward and the edges even with the material edges. Stitch in place.

2. Cut the webbing in half and stitch at each end according to the diagram. (If you wish to make fabric handles, fold each fabric piece in half lengthwise and sew together using a 1/2" seam. Turn right side out and press.)

3. With right sides facing, sew the two pieces of fabric together, leaving one short end open.

4. An easy way to encase the foam and turn the material right side out all in one step will take two people. One person slides his or her arms into the fabric, with a hand at each corner, and holds onto the corners of the foam. The second person holds onto the opposite end of the fabric and pulls it down, turning the fabric right side out as it encloses the foam. Smooth and straighten the fabric over the foam, making sure that the zippers are on the edge. Pull out the handle on the open end, turn under the edges, and topstitch closed.

5. To turn your mat into a bag, simply fold the bag in half, then fold each side in half again, bringing the ends up to the first fold. Match the zippers and zip.

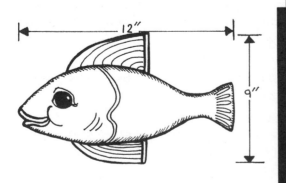

■ Beach Paddle Ball
A fun and easy-to-carry-along game to play at the beach is paddle ball. It is even more fun when you've made it yourself in a unique design. Or you can try these fish paddles to use with a soft foam ball. To make the paddles, you will need: Two pieces of 1/4" plywood and 2 pieces of 1/8" foam, each 10" x 12"; saw; sandpaper; varnish; spray adhesive; sharp scissors or X-Acto knife; acrylic paints and brush; and permanent ink pen. Directions: 1. Begin by enlarging the pattern (or draw your own). Trace it onto the plywood and cut out. Sand the edges smooth, then varnish to prevent splinters. 2. Spray the adhesive on one side of the wood, carefully positioning the foam on top, and press firmly in place. 3. When the glue is dry, cut the foam to match the wood. 4. Paint the foam with the acrylic paints (thinned with a little water to make painting easier) and outline with the permanent ink pen. With a purchased soft foam ball, your game is complete.

Your Glasses Are in Your Bed Pocket

Where are your glasses when you're lying in bed ready to read the latest news? Or a note pad and pencil to write tomorrow's reminders? These and other things can be organized for you in bed pockets. The following instructions are planned for the child who has to stay still in bed while getting over the flu, but they can be adapted to any age.

■ Bed Pockets

▲ *To make, you'll need*: Fabric cut to the following sizes (you may use one color or several coordinating colors): 2 pieces 16" x 16" (A and B); 2 pieces 16" x 6" (C and D); 1 piece 5" x 5" (E [for a small box of crayons]); 1 piece 5" x 4" (F [for a package of tissues]); 1" wide elastic, 5" long (to hold a plastic water bottle); 1 piece of Velcro 16" long; 1 piece of cardboard 16" x 6"; decorative trims if you choose; sewing machine; and hot glue gun.

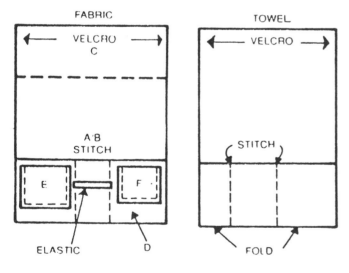

▼ *Directions*: With the right sides facing, sew pieces A and B together on three sides with a 1/4" seam allowance. Turn right side out and press. Press raw edges under 1/4". Narrowly hem three sides (6", 16", 6") of piece C. Insert the raw edge 1/4" into the opening on piece A/B and topstitch closed. Sew one half of the Velcro on the opposite long side of C. Hot glue the other piece of Velcro to one edge of the cardboard. To make the pockets (D, E, and F), turn under 1/4" on all edges and press. Position pockets E and F and elastic on pocket D (see illustration) and topstitch into place. (If you wish to add decorative trim, do it before sewing pockets into place.) Place pocket D on A/B opposite the Velcro. Topstitch edges. To determine the necessary width of individual pockets on D, position story books, coloring books, flashlight, etc., inside pocket and mark. Remove items and topstitch to finish. To use the bed pockets, fasten the Velcro, then insert the cardboard between the springs and mattress, allowing the pockets to hang over the edge.

◆ *Variations*: You can vary the size and shapes of the backing and pockets to fit your needs. * Use fabric (even sheets) that coordinate with the bedroom. * For a teenager, use denim and shape the bed pocket to look like a pair of blue jeans. * A very simple version can be made using a bath towel. (It is best if you use a towel without an obvious right and wrong side.) Sew the Velcro on one end of the towel. Fold the other end up about 6" or 7", depending on how deep you want the pockets. Again, position the items on the towel to determine how wide you want the pockets to be. Mark, remove the items, then sew (or even glue) to finish.

Your Own Candle Power

The premise is this: you're standing in one of those fancy gift shops looking at a myriad of candles—wonderful shapes, hand-painted, floaters, layered—and you wish someone could teach you to make your own so you didn't burn up your money. Here's the magical solution.

● General hints and tips

❒ Never allow wax to exceed 300 degrees. Use a candy thermometer (or special candle-making thermometer) to monitor temperature.

❒ Be prepared in case wax ignites. Keep a lid handy to cover pot to smother flames, or have baking soda or sand ready to douse flame. Never use water to extinguish wax fire.

❒ Put wooden dowels in bottom pot of double boiler to rest "melting" pot on. This will assist in keeping wax temperature low.

❒ Use an old pan for bottom of double boiler and an old coffee pot or other spouted can to melt wax in.

❒ Cover your work area with paper.

❒ Coat inside of molds with salad oil. This allows for easy removal of candles when they are cooled and set.

▲ *To make,* choose wax best suited for your needs (block candle wax—good for molded candles; paraffin wax—good for molded candles; tapered candle wax—good for tapered candles; sheet wax—good for hand-molded candles), wicks—cotton cord or cotton-wrapped wire wicks, double boiler, molds, crayons (paper peeled off) or colored wax chips for coloring wax, pencil or wooden dowel, and salad oil.

■ Parfait Sundae

Tie cotton cord wick to center of pencil or dowel. Cut wick long enough to reach bottom of sundae dish. Lay pencil or dowel across top of sundae dish. (Tape in place to keep wick from moving when pouring in wax.) Melt clear wax in double boiler. To add color, melt half of a red crayon in with wax. Pour wax into sundae dish. For "whipped" topping, add one tablespoon laundry soap flakes and one teaspoon cornstarch to one pound of melted clear wax. Whip with beater until fluffy. Spoon on top of wax in sundae dish. Optional: Before wax has hardened, put straw in to look like a soda. Mold a cherry from red molding wax or use a red bead.

133

■ Chocolate Kiss

Coat inside of plastic funnel with salad oil. Make notches in top of funnel to hold pencil or dowel in place. Tie cotton cord wick to center of pencil or dowel; bring wick through small end of funnel. Cut a potato in half and rest it cut-side down; push small end of funnel into potato to keep wax from seeping out and to hold mold in place while pouring wax in. Melt paraffin or candle wax in double boiler. Add a brown crayon to melted wax to give "chocolate" color. Pour wax into mold. Let sit for at least two hours to harden. Loosen edge of candle from mold with butter knife. Pop out of mold. Trim wick and any residue wax on bottom of "kiss" so candle sits level.

■ Swiss Cheese

A cottage cheese container works well for a mold. Coat inside of container with salad oil. Melt candle or paraffin wax in double boiler. Add color to wax by melting a small piece of yellow or orange crayon. Put small tapered candle in center of mold. Cut to desired height (to top of carton). Put a few ice cubes in container. Pour wax over ice. Fill container to within 1/4" of top. Let wax harden (about 1 1/2 to 2 hours). Loosen edges with knife. Pop out candle. Water will run out, leaving holes in "cheese." Optional: Set candle on cutting board and mold a mouse from soft molding wax.

■ Painted Candles

Melt wax and put in desired molds. When candles are hardened and cooled, paint with water-based varnish. Let dry. Add second coat if desired. Paint design on with acrylic paints.

■ Molding Wax Candles

Put sheets of colored wax in tepid water for 2 to 5 minutes until wax is workable. You can mold in any shape your desire or skill allows. When you have finished molding, use a toothpick or bamboo skewer to make a passageway for wick through middle of candle. Pull wick through passageway using a small crochet hook or needle. To make braided candles, soften wax in water. Cut in strips and roll to round out strips. Braid as desired. Cookie cutters can be used with this molding wax. Cut desired shapes out of softened wax. Cut three of the same shape out of different colors of wax and layer together. Remember to add wick to center of candle using the above technique.

Chime Right In

Make your own wind chimes out of objects found around your house—keys, flatware, cookie cutters, bolts, and even bones left over from dinner serve the purpose.

Wind chimes can be produced from almost any object that can be suspended from another symmetrical object. Try to overlook the object's original intended use. Experiment with the sound. Strike one metal object with another. Find combinations that please you—gentle tinkles in the backyard, soothing symphonies in the patio, and for the home gardener, the happy singing sounds of a wind chime that do a superb job of protecting seeds from birds or other small animals.

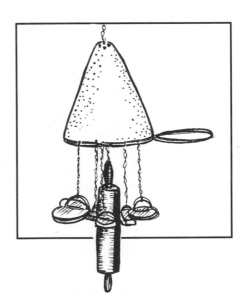

■ Kitchen Chimes

Remove handle from old metal colander. Spray colander and eight metal cookie cutters (about two or three inches in diameter) with bright-colored enamel spray. Let dry. Spray with spray webbing, purchased at craft and hardware stores. Drill hole in one handle of a wooden rolling pin; attach to colander using 3" of small chain which can be obtained at a hardware store for about 30 cents per foot. Drill a hole in the other handle of the rolling pin; tie a metal cookie cutter to it with heavy twine. Use chain cut to 8", 8 1/2", 9", and 10" lengths to attach the other cookie cutters to colander. Suspend them at equal distances around the large end of colander. Use pliers to open and close links of chain pushing through holes of colander. Adjust lengths of chain so cookie cutters clang into each other when set in motion. Put a hook in top of colander and suspend from the ceiling.

■ Conduit Pipe Chimes

Buy conduit pipe (about 33 cents per foot at hardware stores). Drill two small holes in one end of pieces of pipe that have been cut to individual lengths of 17", 19", 15", 16", 20", and 22". Using heavy fishing line or leader, tie each pipe to one end of 6" pieces of lightweight gold chain. Cut a 5" diameter circle from wood or plastic. If you wish, use a piece of chain 30" long suspended from the center of the circle. Cut a plastic bell or tree shape from the wood or plastic and tie it to the end of the center chain. Suspend the conduit pipe wind chime from a 2" diameter metal ring wired through the wood or plastic circle to the center chain. Hint: The longer the pipes, the lower the tone.

■ Dinosaur Cutout

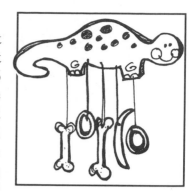

Use a pattern from a child's book, or buy a wooden dinosaur cutout from a craft shop. Dinosaur should be about 6" x 9" and cut from 1/2" soft pine or other soft wood. Paint dinosaur to match the room. Put a 1/2" brass screw eye (size 216 1/2) in the top so the wind chime can be suspended from an 8" loop of macrame or other heavy twine. From the butcher, get two rib bones cut in 6" lengths and five round bones cut about 1" thick and measuring about 2" in diameter. Boil bones to remove all scraps of meat and marrow. Dry bones. Suspend bones from plastic string cut to 6" lengths and tied to the bone by threading the string through small round holes drilled in the center of each bone. Tie the other end of the plastic string to small screw eyes placed along the bottom of the dinosaur cutout.

■ Early American Barn

Use a tracing from a child's paintbook or picture book as a pattern and cut the shape of a barn from 1/2" thick pine or other soft wood. The barn should be painted as desired. Place five screw eyes that are size 216 1/2 at equal intervals along the bottom of the barn. Attach five plastic strings, one to each screw eye, by knotting one end of the string through the eye. The strings should measure 7", 5 1/2", 4", 6 1/2", and 5 1/2", respectively. Using patterns from children's books, trace onto plastic shrink art sheets a cow, a duck, and a lamb. Color the animals. Cut out the animals' tracings and place them in the oven to "shrink." Follow directions on the shrink art package for this procedure. Tie small Christmas bells to the neck of the cow, the lamb, and the duck. Tie the finished cow cutout to the 7" string. Tie a Christmas bell to the 5 1/2" string. Tie the duck to the 4" string. Tie a Christmas bell to the 6 1/2" string. Tie the lamb to the 5 1/2" string. Suspend barn from a brass ring or a heavy twine loop and let the bells ring!

■ Key Chimes

Use household and car keys. Brass-colored ones work well if combined with gold chain and suspended from a 6"-diameter wooden ring. Try tying four keys to 9" of chain, three keys to 8 1/2" pieces of chain, and one key to a 7" piece of chain. Stretch a piece of chain across diameter of the ring and attach to both sides of the wooden ring. Put a brass ring in the center to suspend the chain. Hang a key on an 11" piece of chain and suspend it from the center of the chime.

■ Pie Tin and Old Silver

Use a 9" metal pie tin. Punch holes or use a metal bit on a drill to drill holes at intervals and wire lightweight chain cut to 10" and 16" lengths to the pie tin. Flatten two soup spoons, three teaspoons, three dinner forks, and two salad forks by pounding them with a sledge hammer. Drill a small hole near the end of the handle of each piece of silver. Attach the silver to one end of the chain. Use pliers to open and close links of the chain to facilitate attaching to the pie tin. Hang the pie tin by suspending it from chain attached to two holes drilled or punched in the center of the pie tin. If you wish, pie tin can be decorated with fluorescent plastic sticks purchased from craft stores. Plan your design, cut sticks to desired size, and follow directions on the package for softening in the oven or in hot water. The plastic sticks will adhere to the sides of the pie tin and you can create colorful artistic designs that match any decor.

Let These Smiles Be Your Umbrella

It'll be a lovely day to be out in the rain if you follow these steps for decorating umbrellas. You can use any size or color of umbrella. Create your own designs—use beads, slick pens, pompoms, yarn, almost anything. You can find umbrellas for as little as $6; finished, the designs run about $10. But they're really priceless.

If you want your decorated umbrellas for use in the rain or snow when you have finished trimmimg them, spray with Scotchgard® or water repellent spray. If you want to be able to close the umbrella or parasol, use materials that will lie flat and bend or fold easily without crushing.

■ Auto Umbrella

This colorfully trimmed umbrella will appeal to both boys and girls.

▲ *To make, you'll need*: A bright, solid-colored umbrella; red (or other primary color) fabric; black calico print; yellow calico print; Wonder-Under® or other iron-on adhesive webbing with paper-peel backing (can be found in fabric stores); and puff paint for outlining.

▼ *Directions*: Cut one large or two small car outlines for each panel of the umbrella from the red or other solid-colored fabric. (You can draw the car pattern or use one from a coloring book or illustration.) Cut wheels from black calico and round suns (one for each panel) from yellow calico. Iron cars with wheels and suns onto the iron-on adhesive. Cut around car with wheels and suns. Peel off paper backing from adhesive and iron cars and suns onto umbrella—cars along edge of umbrella and suns at top of each panel.

Use puff paint to outline and put details on cars and sun. Puff paint not only adds depth and detail, it also seals the edges of the appliqued cars and suns so that fabric does not peel off. Puff paint should be allowed to dry for 24 hours.

■ Ladybug Umbrella

This cute-as-a-bug umbrella can serve as an umbrella or decoration.

▲ *To make, you'll need*: Red umbrella, one square of beige iron-on felt, two 2" red pom-poms, two 30mm wiggle eyes (purchase at crafts store), scrap of black felt, plastic craft eyelashes, two heavier black pipe cleaners, two 1 1/2" red pom-poms, red puff paint, 10-15 1/2" black pompoms, 10-15 1" black pom-poms, and hot glue gun.

▼ *Directions*: Cut a half circle using most of the square of iron-on felt. Iron it onto one panel of the umbrella with the straight end of the circle at the bottom of the section to form the bug's "head." Glue two 2" red pom-poms about 2/3 of the way up on the half circle for "eyes." Glue the wiggle eyes onto the pom-poms. Cut eyelids from the black felt. Glue the eyelashes to underside bottom edge of eyelids. Glue eyelid with lashes to form an eyelid half covering the pom-pom "eye."

Cut 3" off the end of each pipe cleaner. Poke each pipe cleaner carefully through the fabric of the umbrella on either side of the felt half-circle "head" to form feelers. (On underside of umbrella, attach ends of pipe cleaners to metal ribs of umbrella.) Glue the 1 1/2" pom-poms to the ends of the pipe cleaners to complete the "feelers." Use puff paint to draw on a smiling mouth on the head of the ladybug. To complete the ladybug, glue 1/2" and 1" black pom-poms randomly over the rest of the umbrella.

■ Rainbow Parasol

This beautiful umbrella will attract any young girl, or add beauty to any delicate pastel room.

▲ *To make, you'll need*: Sky-blue umbrella; three yards each of six different pastel-colored, 3/4-1" pregathered lace; 1/2 yard each of the same colors in 1/8" satin ribbon; and glue gun.

▼ *Directions*: Glue one of the pastel-colored lengths of lace along the outside edge of the umbrella. Repeat the process with each of the other five lengths of lace, working your way up the umbrella, forming a rainbow of lace along each panel edge. Overlap each successive layer of lace over the adjoining lower layer to cover its glued top edge.

Make eight small tassels from lengths of 1/8" ribbon (use several colors in each tassel). Attach a tassel at the exposed metal end of each umbrella rib. If any umbrella decorations pull in places after a time, put a dab of glue under spots.

138

Hey Lady, There's a Harp in Your Laundry!

A harp from a bleach bottle? Popsicle sticks for piano keys? A glockenspiel out of electrical conduit? These "musical instruments" work and are fun and instructive for kids to build.

■ Harp

▲ *To make, you'll need*: 3 sticks or dowels 12" long and 1" thick; 1 dowel about 6" long and 1/4" thick; 1-gallon bleach bottle, well rinsed and dried; 7 heavy-duty, long elastic bands, cut to make 7 long strips; drill with small bit; twine or string; and scissors or sharp knife. Optional: Permanent markers for decoration.

INSERT LONG STICK

Fig. 1

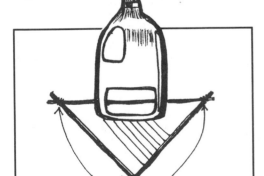

LASH AT CORNERS

Fig. 2

▼ *Directions*: Begin by cutting a rectangular hole (about 2 1/2" high x 4" long) in the side of the bottle about 1" up from the bottom. Make a small hole (just big enough for the stick to go through) 2" up from the bottom and directly under the handle. Make a second, similar hole exactly opposite on the bottle (see Fig. 1). Make seven drill holes 1/2" apart. Place the dowel inside the bottle and thread the elastics through the drilled holes. Slide the bottle onto a large stick through the two holes. Drill seven small holes in a line in the middle of one of the two remaining sticks. Form a triangle with the other two sticks and lash joints together. Thread the other end of each elastic through the holes in the stick and tie a knot (see Fig. 2). Your harp is now complete; tune by tightening or loosening the elastics.

● *Hint*: When the elastic is at the right pitch, wedge a toothpick in the hole to hold the elastic tight. Decorate with the permanent markers.

139

■ Thumb Piano

▲ *To make, you'll need*: 1 block of wood 6" x 6" x 3/4", 1 piece of wood 6" x 1" x 1/2", 3 wood screws, 1 dowel 6" long and 1/4" thick, and 8 popsicle sticks.

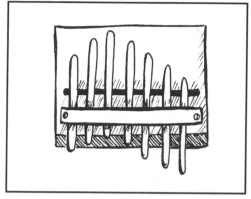

Fig.

▼ *Directions:* Loosely attach the small piece of wood about 1 1/2" from the edge of the larger piece with the wood screws. (Place a screw close to each end and one in the center.) Arrange the popsicle sticks parallel to each other, with one end under the cross stick (see Fig. 3). Now tighten the screws so the cross stick almost touches the popsicle sticks. Wedge the dowel under the popsicle sticks, pushing it as close to the cross stick as possible. Tune the piano by pushing in the popsicle sticks or pulling them out. The longer the vibrating part, the lower the pitch.

● *Hint*: You can increase the resonance of the piano by placing it on another box with a thin top, such as a shoe box.

■ Tubular Glockenspiel

▲ *To make, you'll need*: Hacksaw or a plumber's pipe cutter and 1/2"-diameter electrical conduit.

▼ *Directions*:

Fig. 4

Cut the conduit exactly to the following sizes: 11", 10 1/4", 9 3/4", 9 1/2", 8 7/8", 8 1/2", 8 3/8", and 7 5/8". You now have a set of tubes already tuned to a major scale. There are several ways to use them. The simplest is to set the tubes (in the graduated lengths) on two strips of foam or felt (similar to a xylophone). If you have access to a drill press, there are two other ways to use the pipes. The first is to drill holes at either end of the pipes (this will change the pitch slightly). Using string or twine, thread it through the holes (see Fig. 4), spacing the pipes about one inch apart. The second method is to drill holes at one end only. Tie a loop of string through the hole and hang the pipes from a broomstick.

● *Hint*: Shorten tubing by sanding to raise pitch or add a drop of solder inside tubing to lower the pitch. To ring the chimes, you can use a spoon, a large nail, or another piece of conduit with tape wrapped around one end to mellow the ring.

140

Wooden Fireplace Screens

When it's time to cozy up around the fireplace, what do you do when the embers have died and that black hole is staring at you? Try this decorative camouflage: wooden fireplace screens you can make easily and inexpensively.

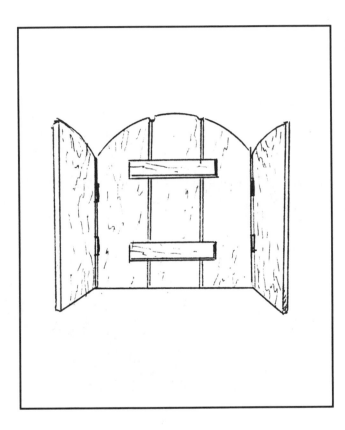

■ Basic Wood Screen

▲ *To make, you'll need*: 5 pieces of 1" x 10" pine or other inexpensive wood (for height measurement: measure the height of your fireplace opening; add 2-3" to this figure), two wooden braces (approximately 1 1/2" x 1 1/4" x 20"), four hinges, screws, wood sealer, and stain or acrylic paint.

▼ *Directions*: Using a strong wood glue, glue three of the 1" x 10" planks together. Let dry completely. Attach braces to back of three-plank panel by using wood glue and small finishing nails. (Braces should be placed horizontally, approximately 5" from top and bottom of panel.) Attach side pieces (1" x 10" plank on each side) using hinges—two each side approximately 5" from top and bottom of planks. Note: Attach hinges to back side of planks so they are not visible on front of screen. Brush wood sealer on entire wood screen. Let dry. Paint as desired.

■ Painting Techniques

Wash: After sealing wood and letting dry completely, dip a sponge-type paintbrush in water, shake out excess, then dip in acrylic paint. The more water, the lighter your "wash" will be. Experiment on a piece of scrap wood for the desired effect, using up and down strokes.

Speckle: Dip a small artist's brush in water, shake out excess, then dip into desired color of acrylic paint. Hold brush over wood and lightly tap your finger against the brush.

◆ *Variation*: To make screen look like a row of houses, before assembling planks, cut tops to resemble different rooftops, pitched, barn-shaped, etc. After sealing wood, trace design on front of wooden screen and paint as desired.

■ Quilt Fireplace Screen

Follow instructions for basic wooden screen, except front panel will be built as a "frame" for your quilted square. Use 1" x 6" pieces of wood. Measure fireplace opening for height and width of frame. Be sure frame allows enough overhang in center to tack quilted square into place, but first seal and stain wood.

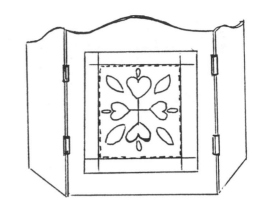

■ Wooden Shutters

If you prefer something easier to assemble, purchase ready-made wooden shutters and assemble as you would the basic screen. Depending on size of fireplace, you may only need two shutters for front panel. Glue shutters together for front. Attach side panels (one shutter each side) with hinges. Finish as desired.

■ Picket Fence

With a few accessories, this can be altered for different holidays or seasons. Measure width of fireplace opening. Cut length of 1" x 8" plank to equal this (approximately 3'). This will be your base. To make "pickets" for fence, use 1/2" thick by 1 1/2" wide by 8' tall pine. Cut 9-10 10" pieces of wood. Cut tops to look like "pickets." Attach to base plank with wood glue and small finishing nails or thin tacks. Place pickets between 2 1/2"-3" apart on base. Add seasonal decorations.

■ Mirrored Screen

Enjoy a fireplace without having one. A mirrored screen with many lighted candles can give this cozy effect. Follow instructions for basic wooden screen, but instead of painting or staining, attach mirrors to front of screen. To avoid having custom mirrors made, purchase mirrors first, and cut wood to accommodate. For "fire," place different sizes of candles on an oval mirror (such as a make-up mirror) and set in front of your mirrored screen. Light and enjoy your cozy "fire." *Caution*: Do not leave lighted candles unattended!

Flowers Held in a Linen Napkin or Handkerchief

If you're tired of your flower containers, here's how to turn a linen napkin or handkerchief into a vase to hold dried flowers. A fresh nosegay can be put into a plastic bag held with a rubber band.

▲ *To make, you'll need*: 12" x 12" linen napkin or handkerchief, 11" x 11" heavy-weight interfacing (nonwoven), 11" of white ribbon, ruler, scissors, quilter's or disappearing fabric marker, and decorative ribbon or flowers.

▼ *Directions*:

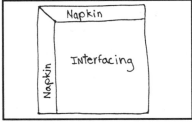

Fig. 1

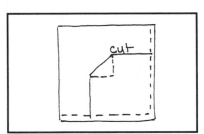

Fig. 2

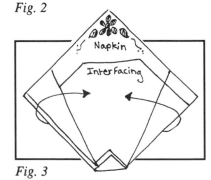

Fig. 3

1. Lay interfacing on wrong side of napkin. Put bottom edges and right sides together.

2. Fold over bottom and right side edges of napkin and interfacing 1/4". Machine stitch folded edges into a hem (Fig. 1).

3. Fold down upper left corner of interfacing 3" toward the center. Finger crease and then cut off interfacing only along the crease (Fig. 2).

4. Fold up bottom right corner 3", toward the center crease. (Note: To crease the fabric, rub the side edge of a pencil, ruler, or your finger along the fabric. This will press in a crease.)

5. Using disappearing ink fabric marker, make a small mark at a halfway point along top edge. Make another small mark at a halfway point along top edge. Make another small mark at halfway point along left side edge (Fig. 3).

6. Make two small marks 1/3 and 2/3 of the way along the bottom folded edge (Fig. 3).

7. Using your ruler and a disappearing ink pen, draw a line as a guide that connects left side halfway mark to 1/3 mark at bottom folded edge. Then connect the 2/3 mark on the bottom folded edge in the same manner (Fig. 3).

8. Fold along the lines you have just drawn. Fold toward center, following arrows shown in Fig. 3. Crease folds so that result is a cone-shaped holder.

9. Use a hot glue gun and glue the outside edges in place to hold cone shape permanently. Continue to glue along bottom 1/3 (Fig. 4). Fold and let cool.

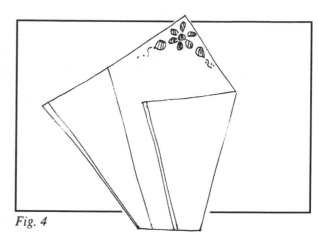

Fig. 4

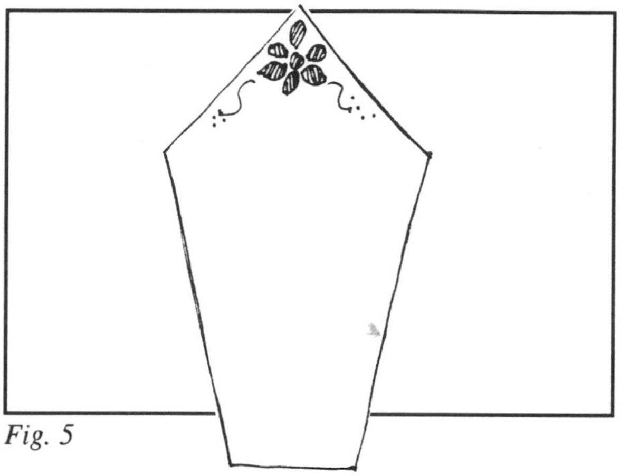

10. When glue is cool, turn cone over and fold decorative corner of handkerchief or napkin down toward center. Use hot glue gun to fasten narrow ribbon to outside edges of remaining peak of cone (Fig. 5).

Fig. 5

11. To check for accuracy in following the directions, insert your hand inside the cone shape and make sure the bottom flap is folded toward the back. There is no opening in bottom of the holder. Note: If using a larger napkin, adjust the size by cutting down napkin on right side and bottom. If using a smaller one, remember the 1/3 bottom to 1/3 side rule.

Fig. 6

A True Footstool

I had a great idea for a footstool—and that's exactly what I meant—using an old pair of shoes for the base of these delightful stools to rest your feet on. (If I ever come up with an idea for head scarves, you'll know we're crossing into monster movies.)

■ Granny Footstool

▲ *To make, you'll need*: Two boards 1" x 2" x 15"; 1/2" to 1" plywood cut into an 18" x 9" oval; four 3" wood screws; bonded batting cut into the following sizes: two 23" squares, two 6" circles, five 18" x 9" ovals; fabric: one 22" x 13" oval, one 5" x 2 2/3 yard strip (hem each edge, then gather one side); 50" of lace (optional); one pair of nylons; one pair old shoes; two small plastic bags filled with child's clay; sand or dirt (enough to fill the toe of the shoe); staple or glue gun; cotton swab; and felt-tip pen.

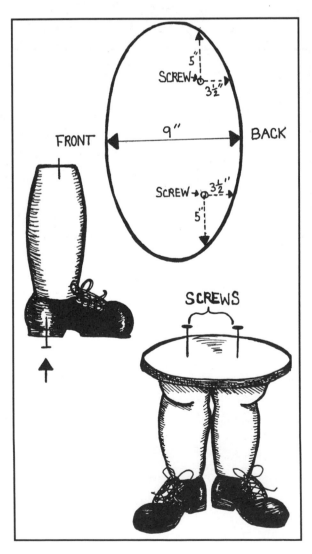

▼ *Directions*:

Drill screw holes in the center of both ends of the long boards. (If the shoes you are using have more than a one-inch heel, cut one end of each board on a slight angle to compensate and make a steadier stool.) Mark and drill holes in the heel of each shoe, snip a cotton swab in half, and insert stick into drilled hole in long board. Using a felt-tip pen, color the end of the swab and quickly press board down into heel. Drill through to outside of shoe. Roll each long board in one piece of square batting, leaving about seven inches of batting on one edge. Bend the extra batting at right angles to the board, forming the foot. Snip a small hole in the batting at the heel area to expose the screw hole. Pull stocking over foot and up the leg. Slip the 6" circle of batting inside the stocking to form the knee. Put the bagged weights into the toe of each shoe, then put foot into the shoe, attaching securely with the screws. Join each leg to the oval board with screws. Center the five layers of batting on the wrong side of the oval piece of material. Place the stool upside down on the batting. Carefully pull material up around the board and staple securely on the underside. (A glue gun will also work.) Using the staple gun or glue gun, attach the ruffle to the edge of the board. Glue the lace (if using) around the edge of the stool.

◆ *Variations*: This would be a fun way to preserve a special dress or pair of shoes or even a child's first sports uniform, using the team logo from the shirt for the top of the stool.

Making Your Own Traveling High Chair

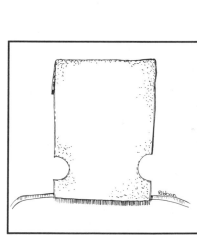

You're off to visit the family and there's no high chair for your little one? Not to worry—make one out of a bath towel.

▲ *To make, you'll need*: One large bath towel, one package 2" seam binding, two yards 1" grosgrain ribbon or cording, scissors, thread, and pins.

▼ *Directions*:

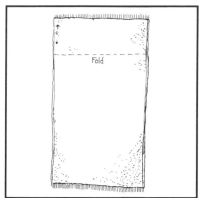

Fig. 1

1. Use a standard dining or kitchen chair to help construct this seat. Lay the bath towel over the chair with 6" hanging down the back. Pin the towel on each side (Fig. 1). Test to see if the towel can easily slip off the chair. Sew sides together.

2. After sewing, place towel on chair and let the rest of it hang down the front of the chair and over the seat. Set child on seat. Bring towel up around legs. Cut both sides of towel in half circles to resemble legs of baby plastic pants (Fig. 2). If the towel is too long, trim it to fit the child at the waist. Finish raw edge around legs with seam binding.

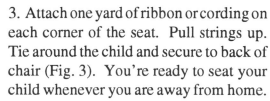

Fig. 2

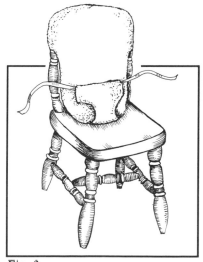

Fig. 3

3. Attach one yard of ribbon or cording on each corner of the seat. Pull strings up. Tie around the child and secure to back of chair (Fig. 3). You're ready to seat your child whenever you are away from home.

Art and Mops Serve Dual Purposes

Most picture frames hold a work of art, but they can also hold a safe for documents, jewelry, or for kids to hide their personal possessions.

▲ **To make,** have a frame shop work with you to cut a frame to the exact dimensions that you want, or buy a precut unassembled frame. The length and width should correspond to the picture chosen and the wall space in which you will hang the picture. The depth of the wooden frame should be 2" and the width of the frame should be 1 1/2".

▲ **You will also need**: Plexiglas instead of glass (to prevent breakage), two pieces of furring strip the length of the height of the frame, one piece of 1/4" dowel cut the length of the width of the frame, three (or more for a larger frame) pieces of 1/4" dowel cut 1 1/2" long, one piece of masonite for the back of the frame, one piece of velvet the size of the masonite and the Plexiglas to be used for backing on the finished picture frame, a picture of your choice, a mat the width and color you desire, and a tube of two-sided epoxy glue.

▼ **Directions**:

1. Assemble the bottom and sides of the frame or have the frame shop fasten them together for you. Leave top of frame apart from other three pieces.

2. Drill small holes in the masonite, spaced so that when the short pieces of dowel are glued into the holes, they will serve as pegs to hang necklaces or other jewelry on. Once the pegs are glued in place, glue velvet on back of masonite to form an attractive and protective backing for the frame.

3. Glue the two furring strips to the sides of the frame so that they form a trough on the back of the sides for the glass to slide in and out.

4. Glue the masonite to the sides and bottom of the frame. Be sure the velvet is on what will be the back of the finished product, since the purpose of the velvet is to protect the surface on which the picture will be hung.

5. To finish the top, glue the Plexiglas to the top of the frame. Place the mat and then the picture on the underneath side of the glass. Hold them in place by gluing the dowel stick along the top and back of the frame piece that will be at the top of the picture. The picture mat, top frame piece, and Plexiglas will be combined to form a very sturdy unit.

6. The top unit will slide into place between the furring strips and the sides of the bottom unit. Once the bottom and top units are combined, the result will be a wall safe for small valuables that looks like any other picture hanging on your wall.

■ Mop Dolls

Mops turn into unusual, inexpensive, huggable dolls when you follow these simple directions.

▲ *To make, you'll need*: Two 4 1/2" x 5 1/2" ovals cut from muslin or tricot in white, pale peach, pink, or beige, as desired; one size 12 or size 16 mop head made of string; two 3/8" black buttons; a small amount of fiberfill or quilt batting; one 6" straw hat purchased from a craft shop; 1/2 yard of 1/8" elastic; one cotton ball or makeup brush; powder blush; assorted ribbon, lace trim, beads, flowers, etc., as desired; hot glue gun; and scissors.

▼ *Directions*:

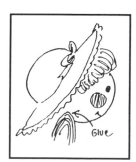

1. Separate seven strands of the mop from the right side and pull them over the binding to the center. Repeat on the left side. With the strands smoothed and glued in place, pull the mop up over back binding to hide the binding. Glue in place. This makes some strands shorter than others. Pull one left and one right strand apart. Bring them to the center. Tie on a bow.

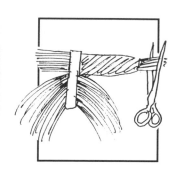

2. Mark a point not quite one-half of the way down the length of the mop. Use the finger to separate the strings into two bunches to form arms. Lay the mop on a table with the two arm bunches out to the side. The longer strings forming the skirt should be laying down below the arms. Begin twisting the right strings away from you to form a right arm. Temporarily tie with a string or ribbon. Repeat with the left side. Pick up the doll by the two arms and twist both away from you. As you continue to twist, the arms will position themselves in a curve toward each other. Pull them together, hold them with one hand; fasten them together using the 1/8" elastic. Fasten them securely at about the point where the wrist should be. There will be some straggly excess lengths of mop strands. Cut these off evenly with the scissors close to the elastic. They will be used to make hair.

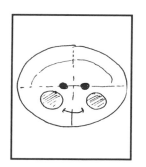

3. The head of the doll is made by sewing the two oval pieces of fabric together with the fiberfill placed inside. Sewing can be done by hand or by machine. Pencil in a hairline and use the scraps of mop strands left from making the arms to form loops which make hair when glued into place on the hairline. Add blush with a cotton ball or a makeup brush. Use makeup pencils to draw a smiling mouth (or embroider it if you wish). Glue the two buttons in place for eyes.

4. Glue the head to the body. Decorate the hat and glue it to the head. On the back of the doll, glue the hat to the mop body to give solidity and to hold the head up. Make a small bouquet of artificial flowers and ribbons. Glue it to the hands. Decorate the doll with ribbons and lace as you wish.

Stencil and Applique Quilting

Quilts have always been valued heirlooms in families. In the last generation, quilt design has taken on more graphic creativity. Here's a solution to the problem of those who can't sew—a stenciled quilt. And for those of you who have a few basic sewing skills, there's the basic applique technique, using a heart as a block in quilt top or as a pillow top.

■ Stenciled Country Quilt

For this quilt top, you can buy a commercial, pre-prepared stencil, or make your own from freezer wrap or Contact® paper.

▲ *To make, you'll need*: Stencil, Contact paper or freezer wrap (one side waxed), unbleached muslin to make the size quilt top you desire (prewashed), acrylic paints, and stencil brush.

▼ *Directions*: If you're making your own stencil, draw the design on freezer wrap or Contact paper in pencil. Use a craft knife or small, sharp scissors to carefully cut the outline of the design and lift out all portions you'll want to color. Use what remains as the stencil.

To use the freezer wrap stencil, place stencil, waxed side down, on muslin. Press with hot iron. The stencil can only be used once. For the Contact paper stencil, peel off paper backing. Carefully smooth stencil onto muslin. If you remove it carefully after painting is done, you may be able to use this stencil more than once.

To paint, dip stencil brush into paint and blot. Carefully dab paint onto portion of the muslin with the stencil where you wish paint to appear. Do not brush paint onto the fabric. When all areas shown through stencil are painted, carefully lift off stencil. When paint is thoroughly dry, spray fabric with mixture of one part vinegar to one part water, place an ironing cloth over design, then press with an iron. This procedure "sets" the design, making it washable. Quilt or tie as you would any quilt top.

■ Heart Applique

▲ *To make, you'll need*: Background fabric, such as unbleached muslin, and more colorful fabric for the heart, such as lightweight cotton/polyester mix.

▼ *Directions*: Draw a heart the size desired on a piece of lightweight cardboard, and cut out to use as pattern. Trace heart with pencil on colored fabric to begin applique and on background fabric where applique will go. Stay-stitch along penciled heart outline on colored fabric. Draw the seam allowance about 1/4" from the penciled heart outline. Cut out heart along the seam allowance line. Carefully cut notches in the seam allowance along the two outward curves and at the point of the heart. Turn under heart's seam along the original, penciled, stay-stitched line. Baste and press the seam.

Pin (or secure with some sort of fabric adhesive) heart in place where outline appears on the background fabric. Using a slip stitch, hand sew around edge of heart to attach. Carefully remove basting and any stay-stitching that might show. Remove any remaining pencil lines.

When you are ready to quilt, you'll want the quilting stitches to outline the heart. If you are tying instead of quilting, tie at each corner of the heart block as usual. Pull a complementing color of yarn up through the middle of the heart, then tie a small bow to add a decorative touch to your heart.

150

No More Plain Old
Window Sun Screens

Here's a thought: why should we have to use boring, plain, roll-down blinds when we need a sun screen on a window? Let's have jungle scenes, lush gardens, and overlapping patterns. They're easy to do, if you follow these simple directions.

▲ *To make, you'll need*: Fiberglass window screening (available at most hardware stores in a variety of sizes), ripstop nylon fabric (windbreaker material that comes in a wide range of colors from the fabric shop), Fray-Check™ (also available at fabric or craft stores), 1" wooden dowels, screw-in hooks and eyes, measuring tape, paper, pencil, scissors, pins, masking tape, clear nylon thread, and sewing machine or sewing needles.

▼ *Directions*:

1. Measure the area that you want screened. Will you need one or several screens? Now the fun of designing your own screen begins. It can be as simple as three overlapping squares of color or as elaborate as a multi-paneled jungle scene. (Hint: If you are going to make a multi-paneled screen, you may wish to draw your design on graph paper first.) Be sure to allow for 4" hems on the screening material at the top and bottom.

2. Pin the pattern on the nylon material and cut it out. Use the Fray-Check on all material edges so that your screen will always look like new.

3. Pin and tape the pattern to the screening. (Don't forget to leave space for the hem.) When your pattern is positioned exactly as you want it, baste it in place. Applique, using a wide zigzag stitch set on a medium length on your machine or a running stitch if doing it by hand. Straight stitch the hems at either end.

4. Insert the dowels in the hems. Screw in the eyes and hang your sun screen from hooks screwed into the roof or porch beams.

◆ *Note*: *With just a little more work, you could make these "screen scenes" freestanding around a hot tub or sand pile. Simply twist-lash the top and bottom dowels (extend them 2" or 3" beyond the screening) to upright poles pounded into the ground. For additional stability in the wind, run four twine lines from the frame's bottom dowel diagonally out to short stakes.*

Dip 'N Drape®
Southwestern Style

With the use of Dip 'N Drape, which is a material with starch, you can make a nifty prickly pear cactus or Indian doll.

■ Prickly Pear Cactus

▲ *To make, you'll need*: Dip 'N Drape fabric (available at craft stores), 15 styrofoam eggs in various sizes from 2" to 4", gesso, acrylic paint, brushes, terra cotta pot or basket, styrofoam to fill container, moss to cover styrofoam, 1 poppy-type silk flower, glue gun, and toothpicks.

▼ *Directions*: To give a cactus-like texture to the eggs, carefully line them up in your driveway and drive your car tire over them. (Please be sure children and pets are out of the way.) Now trace each shape on the dry Dip 'N Drape, adding about 3/4" all around. Cut two for each one. Clip in 1/2" all around edge of fabric. Soak fabric in water until pliable. Set flat and allow to soften for another minute or two. Press and mold fabric onto flattened styrofoam one side at a time. Let them air dry, then paint with a coat of gesso. Glue different sizes together to form branches of the cactus, then paint a soft green. Glue each branch into your container and finally glue on the flower. Add toothpicks for spines.

■ Indian Doll

▲ *To make, you'll need*: Plastic foam cup, 2 1/2" styrofoam ball, Dip 'N Drape fabric, gesso, paint, brushes, and hot glue gun.

▼ *Directions*: Turn cup upside down. Wet and soften a 6" square of Dip 'N Drape. Cover the sides of the cup, tucking any excess under and inside cup. Glue the ball to the bottom part of the cup. Soften a 9 1/2" square of fabric and cover the ball, being sure to mold it close where ball joins cup to form the neck. Carefully mold excess fabric over cup. To form blanket, cut a 12 1/2" square of Dip 'N Drape. Dampen it and turn under a small hem on all edges. Fold fabric in half (hems to the inside) and press together. Drape around the body, bringing it part way up on the back of the head and overlapping in the front. Spread the excess fabric out at the bottom. Let it air dry, then paint with a coat of gesso. When dry, paint the doll's face a light tan and the hair black. Paint the blanket any colors of your choice, painting an Indian-like motif around the edge. After the blanket is dry, finish painting the braids that lay on top of the blanket.

Boodles of Backpacks to Make

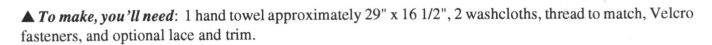

This easy basic pattern for backpacks uses towels and other fabrics.

■ Backpack

▲ *To make, you'll need*: 1 hand towel approximately 29" x 16 1/2", 2 washcloths, thread to match, Velcro fasteners, and optional lace and trim.

▼ *Directions*:

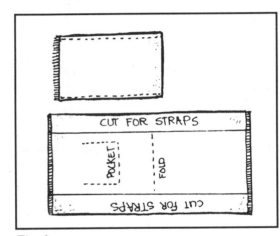

Fig. 1

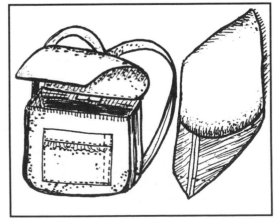

Fig. 2

● **Straps**: Cut 2 1/2" off each side of hand towel lengthwise. Fold strap in half lengthwise. Turn under unfinished edge 1/8" and zigzag edges.

● **Front Pocket**: Cut washcloth to make 7 1/2" x 8" piece (measure and cut, using finished edge of cloth on two sides). Fold edge of washcloth down 2". Optional: Sew 1 1/2"-wide eyelet lace to edge of pocket flap. Fold bottom of towel up approximately 11 1/2". Mark with chalk along fold line. Measure up 2" from first chalk line and center washcloth. Topstitch to towel (edges of washcloth should already be finished; if not, turn under 1/8" and then topstitch). Be sure to leave top edge open for pocket.

● **Attach straps**: On back of hand towel, measure up 2" from bottom of towel and mark center. Attach one end of each strap side by side by topstitching to towel (see Fig. 1). Leave other end of strap loose at this time. Turn pack inside out and sew seam 1/2" up each side (about 11 1/2"). To give backpack more depth, make dog-ear seams (2 1/2") in bottom corners of pack. Turn right side out.

● **Flap**: Using second washcloth, cut cloth to measure 7 1/2" x 12". Gather cloth to fit across back of pack. With right sides together, attach cloth 3 1/2" from top of pack by zigzagging to back of pack. Sew Velcro fasteners to center of flap and center front of pack (3" down from top of pack).

● **Straps**: Hold pack up to child and measure straps to fit accordingly. (Make sure straps are loose enough to permit easy removal.) Attach straps about 3" from outside edge of pack (one on each side) and 1/2" down from where flap folds down. Topstitch at an angle (see Fig. 2).

153

■ Drawstring Bag

▲ *To make, you'll need*: 1 hand towel, 1 washcloth, thread to match, 7" of 1"-wide bias tape, 1 24" shoelace, and 1 45" shoelace.

▼ *Directions*:

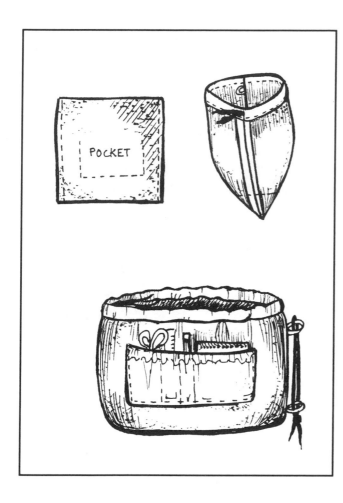

● **Attach pocket**: Cut washcloth to measure 7" x 12". Measure 2 1/2" from top of towel and center cloth. Topstitch cloth to towel on three sides, leaving opening at top of pocket. Topstitch slats on washcloth for pencil, ruler, etc.

● **Bag**: Fold hand towel in half. With right sides together, take 1/2" seam on one side of towel. Make bias tape loops by folding bias tape in half lengthwise and zigzag edges together. Cut in half (you should have two 3 1/2" pieces). Fold each piece in half to form loops. Place one loop 2 1/2" from top of towel and other loop 10 1/2" from top of towel with loops between right sides. Take 1/2" seam in side of towel, catching edges of loops in seam. Make 3" dog-ear seams on both sides of bottom of bag. Turn right side out.

● **Drawstring**: To form casing, fold top edge of bag 3/4" down on outside of bag. Stitch close to edge all around bag, leaving opening at seam line where loops are attached. Thread 45" shoelace through casing and tie a knot in shoestring to prevent slipping through casing. Thread 24" shoelace through loops and knot ends together.

◆ *Variations*: * Instead of flap closure at top, set in a zipper. * To make a drawstring underneath flap, fold top of pack 3/4" down to outside of pack and stitch close to edge to make casing. Leave a 1" opening to thread cording through for drawstring.

154

Make Your Own Veggies

Here's a way to make your own veggies from paper twist that you can buy in craft stores. Your holiday table is going to look festive.

■ Paper Twist Vegetables

● Cauliflower

Cut 5" styrofoam ball in half. Wrap cotton balls with small pieces of white paper twist. Wrap wire around stem. Glue paper-wrapped cotton balls to flat side of styrofoam ball. Cut five pieces of green paper twist, varying in length from 5-7". Wire together about 1" from one end. With a pencil, poke a hole in bottom of rounded side of styrofoam ball and insert ends of paper twist that are wired together. Pull paper twist up around outside of styrofoam ball. With a hot glue gun, glue strips of paper twist to styrofoam ball. Roll ends of paper twist around a pencil to curl edges.

● Lettuce

Cut 11 strips of 3 1/2"-wide light green paper twist, varying in length from 11" to 13". Wire together about 1" from one end. With a pencil, poke about 1/2"-diameter hole in bottom of 5" styrofoam ball. Push wired-together end of twist into hole and hot glue in place. Pull paper twist up over ball, covering whole styrofoam ball with four of inside lengths of paper twist. Curl end of outside lengths of paper twist and hot glue to styrofoam ball at varying places (to resemble a head of lettuce).

● Tomato

With a pencil, poke hole in top of a 3" styrofoam ball. Cut two 5" pieces of red paper twist. Cut 2" of green paper twist (do not pull paper twist apart). This will serve as the stem. Gather the two pieces of red paper, twist around the 2" green twist serving as stem, and wire all together. Turn right side out. Insert stem in hole made in top of styrofoam ball. Pull twist down over ball. Poke ends of paper twist in bottom of ball and hot glue in place. Cut small piece of green paper twist in six-point star shape for "leaves." Push down over green stem; glue in place.

● Turnip

Roll a 2" styrofoam ball to make an oval shape. Cut piece of green paper twist 4" long and two pieces of lavender paper twist 3 1/2" long. With green twist in middle, gather all strips of paper twist and wire together, approximately 1/2" from one end. Turn right side out. Poke hole in top of oval-shaped styrofoam with pencil. Push wired-together ends of paper twist into hole and hot glue in place. Pull lavender twist down over oval styrofoam to cover. Poke paper twist into bottom of styrofoam and hot glue in place. Cut small strips of white paper twist and wire together. Glue these small strips into hole on bottom of "turnip" to resemble roots. Cut green twist at top of turnip to resemble "turnip greens."

155

● Radish

Follow instructions given for turnip, except use 1" styrofoam ball. Cut red paper twist in 2 1/2" lengths and half the width.

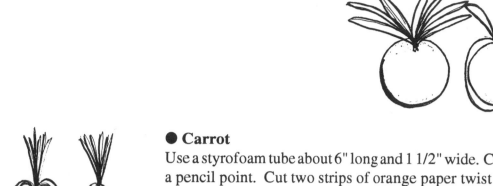

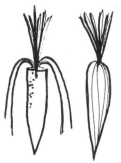

● Carrot

Use a styrofoam tube about 6" long and 1 1/2" wide. Cut bottom end to resemble a pencil point. Cut two strips of orange paper twist 9" long and two strips of green paper twist 4 1/2" long. Wire all paper twists together with orange strips on outside. Using a pencil, poke a hole in top of tube and insert ends of paper twist that are wired together. Pull orange paper twist down over tube, making sure the styrofoam is completely covered. Twist ends of orange paper together for root. (A dab of hot glue on the inside will hold it together better.) Cut the green paper twist into strips.

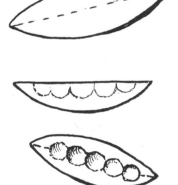

● Peas

Use five 1/4" light green pom-poms for each pea pod. Cut green paper twist into 5" pieces. Cut in shape of leaf. Glue 1/4" pom-poms to center of leaf shape. Fold in half, hot glue edges together. Glue pods to wire. Wrap wire with green floral tape. For added touch, curl green-wrapped wire around a pencil. While wrapping green floral tape around wire, attach ends of curled green wire to give a "vine" effect.

Wedding Album with Heart for the Bride

Here are some indispensable items you can make yourself to help keep your wedding from costing a fortune.

■ Custom-Made Wedding Album: An elegant, fabric-covered album for about $12.

▲ *To make, you'll need*: Three-ring looseleaf binder, 3/8 yard plain-colored fabric (your wedding color), 3/8 yard lace fabric, one yard pellon fleece (like thick felt), 2 3/4-yard-wide pregathered lace, lightweight cardboard, polyethylene photo protector sheet, 1/2 yard narrow pregathered lace, and hot glue gun.

▼ *Directions*:

Cut two layers of fleece the same size as the binder opened up flat. Cut fabric and lace fabric the same size as fleece with 1" added all of the way around as overlap. Lay fleece with plain-colored material over cover of binder. Fold overlap and glue to inside of the binder cover. Do not stretch fabric tightly across cover, or binder will not close when you have finished covering it. Add lace material over fabric and glue overlap to inside cover. Use knife to wedge overlap under metal edge that holds binder's rings. Next, glue gathered edge of wide lace around edge of inside of binder cover so that lace shows around edge of closed binder. Pad outside cover of the binder, covered with material and lace fabric and edged with wide lace.

For inside of album, cut two strips of plain-colored fabric 6-8" wide and the height of binder, with about 1/2" excess to turn under. Fold one strip of fabric in half lengthwise. Use a knife to wedge fold of fabric smoothly under length of metal holding binder rings. Turn remaining edges of fabric under and glue in place. Repeat with the other strip of material on other side of metal. This fabric strip allows the album cover to shut easily against binder rings.

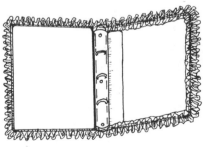

Cut two pieces of cardboard the height of binder and the width of inside front cover minus the 2 1/2"-3" already covered by fabric. Cut pieces of fabric the same size with 1/2" additional fabric all the way around to turn under. Cover each piece of cardboard with fabric, folding fabric edges to cardboard's back side, and glue in place. Glue fabric-covered cardboard inside album's front and back covers, hiding glued fabric and lace edges.

For a decorative pocket to hold a photo of the couple on the album cover, trace and cut an appropriately sized oval-shaped frame from the cardboard. Then cut pieces of the plain-colored fabric and lace fabric the same size with 1/4"-1/2" excess on each edge to turn under. Cover cardboard with the plain-colored fabric, fold the excess to back of cardboard, and glue. Repeat with lace fabric. Cut an oval from photo-protecting clear plastic and glue to the inside of oval to cover frame opening. Glue gathered edge of narrow lace around the back outside edge of oval to form a lacy edge to frame. Position oval on album cover, then glue, leaving top open so that photo can be slipped into pocket. Add a bow or flowers or more trim to complete album.

For the inside of the album, purchase acid-free paper and special photo-protecting clear plastic pages at a photo supply or stationery store. Use permanent markers with high carbon content to label and letter pages. Your custom album will last longer than commercial albums.

■ Photo Display Tree

A "tree" for hanging photos of the bride and groom from birth to wedding adds a special personal touch to the wedding or shower.

▲ *To make, you'll need*: Three or four tree branches, one large clay flowerpot, rocks or gravel to fill the pot, white spray paint, glitter, small twinkling white Christmas-type lights on a white cord, large bow of the wedding colors, and photos of the bride and groom from birth on in inexpensive frames or lace-trimmed fabric frames.

▼ *Directions*: Spray branches and pot with white paint. Spray adhesive or hair spray on branches, then sprinkle with glitter. Fill pot with rocks, gravel, or sand so that the branches stand upright in the pot like a tree. Arrange lights in tree. Hang photos on branches. Decorate with small bows of wedding colors. Trim pot with a large bow.

■ Wooden Heart Memento

Instead of a guest book, wedding guests can sign this attractive wood plaque. Decide the size and shape you want. Have your plaque cut from lumber or plywood. (Edges should be routed to make sides decorative.) For a medium-sized reception, a heart-shaped plaque made from plywood measuring 19" x 21" is a good size.

Seal plaque with a clear wood sealer. Mix parchment-colored acrylic paint with water, and then paint the plaque with this light wash. Use acrylic paints to stencil, paint, or tole paint decorations around the plaque edges. Paint the names of the bride and groom and the date of the wedding at the top. Trace straight lines with pencil or graphite paper to guide guests as they sign their names. Provide an extra-fine-point permanent marker for guests to sign. After wedding, erase guide lines with turpentine or gum eraser. To make plaque permanent, spray or brush on clear varnish. Nail hanger hardware on back for hanging.

Write-and-Erase T-Shirt Messages

Just when you think you've heard it all on T-shirt decorating, here come some new products relating to the word "message." Available in craft stores, these will allow you to use your T-shirt as a blackboard, to paint on stretchy fabrics without cracking, and to watch colors change through some kind of temperature magic.

■ Happy Chalk® (about $2.99)

This product lets you turn your T-shirt into a chalkboard. Just iron on one of the six colorful designs, allow it to cool thoroughly, then remove the paper. Your T-shirt now has a chalkboard that you can write on, erase, and write on again and again. (Do you have an important message for the babysitter? Just write it on the transfer's chalkboard and it won't be lost or forgotten. Do you like to paint on T-shirts but hate the mess? This product eliminates all that.)

■ Brush Top® (about $3.49)

This product is a paintbrush right on the fabric paint bottle. It comes in 12 vivid colors that allow you to create big, bold designs that fill in quickly and easily. It works great with iron-on transfers, too.

■ Stretch® (about $5.99 for 4 ounces)

This elastic paint, which comes in 24 different colors, lets you turn ordinary active wear into something special. Since it won't crack or peel when stretched, you can use this paint to put your own unique design on swimsuits, stretch pants, aerobic wear, fleece wear, knits, and stretch belts.

■ Color Switch® ($5.99/3 pack)

This product lets you double the fun. Simply paint any design you like, then watch as rich cool shades turn to vibrant warm shades as the temperature changes. And the paint will switch back and forth endlessly. These nontoxic, permanent, colorfast paints come in 12 two-in-one colors.

◆ *Hints*:

● When working with transfers or fabric paints, prewash the clothing. This will help avoid puckering and the paint will adhere better as well.

● Slip a piece of cardboard or waxed paper between layers of fabric before painting to prevent the color from bleeding through to the other side.

● Carefully follow the directions that come with the transfers or paint. It's always better to take a few minutes to read the manufacturer's suggestions so that you won't be sorry later.

Instant Foam =
Instant Creativity

■ Insta-Foam™ Floral Arrangements

Have you ever wanted to make a floral arrangement in an unusual container, but couldn't figure out how to get the floral cushiony foam in it? Here is a new product that will solve that problem and many others. Insta-Foam (available at most craft stores) lets you pour a liquid chemical into any container. It will then foam and grow, filling the space and hardening just like styrofoam (1/2 oz. of the chemical will grow to completely fill a 4" flowerpot). There are safety precautions that should be followed when using Insta-Foam. Always cover the work area with newspaper or plastic to avoid damage from accidental spills. Have everything ready before you mix the chemicals; the reaction is immediate and it sets up within three to four minutes. When mixing the chemicals, use only disposable containers and mixers, such as paper cups and popsicle sticks. To show Insta-Foam's versatility, you might try making this decorative wall hanging using silk flowers and a brass horn.

▲ **To make, you'll need**: A jelly roll pan covered with heavy-duty aluminum foil, an 18" square of heavy-duty aluminum foil, scissors, masking tape, acrylic paint (green), paintbrush, moss, wire or glue, a decorative brass horn (circle type), silk or dried flowers, and ribbon.

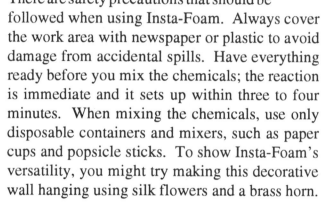

Fig. 1

▼ **Directions**: Begin by folding the piece of foil to make a 2" x 18" ribbon. Form it into a circle, holding the ends together with a paper clip. (You may need to adapt the size of the circle to an appropriate size for the form you use.) Place the horn on the foil-covered pan. Then center the foil circle over the horn at the point you want to attach the flowers. Using the scissors, cut a small circle from the edge of the foil ribbon where it touches the horn, thus allowing the ribbon to sit flush with the pan, but bridging the horn. Tape the circle to the pan on the outside, making a firm barrier. Following the instructions that come with the Insta-Foam, mix the chemicals and pour into the foil ribbon circle. Spread the foam around as it begins to grow (using a popsicle stick or a paddle made from aluminum foil) to make an even layer. You might also wish to place a piece of foil across the top of the ribbon to force it to spread to all the edges. After the foam has thoroughly cooled, carefully peel off the foil. Paint it with the acrylic paint and let dry. Cover with moss and attach the flowers and ribbon with wire or glue. Now that you've tried Insta-Foam once, let your imagination go—use it in baskets, bottles, or on hats—anyplace you would use styrofoam (see Fig. 1).

Out in Your Backyard, a Pretty Picture Frame

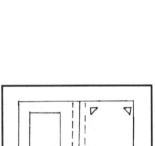

There are always uses for materials right under our noses—like twigs and sticks in our own backyards. Turn them into pretty picture frames.

■ Rustic Twig or Pinecone Picture Frame

▲ *To make the twig or pinecone frame, you'll need*: One precut picture framing mat, 1/4" plywood board cut to the same size as the mat, brown spray paint, photograph, mounting corners, duct tape, hot glue gun, and hand pruning shears. In addition, for the twig frame, you will need: Small, straight twigs; large cinnamon sticks from a craft store; ribbon; and a small piece of Velcro.

▲ *To make the pinecone wreath, you'll need*: Small pinecones.

▼ *Directions*:

1. Spray paint the plywood and mat. Let dry thoroughly.

2. Cut the twigs to the width of the mat frame. Using the hot glue gun, attach them to the frame in a pattern similar to Fig. 1.

Fig. 1

3. To miter corners, draw a diagonal line from the inside corner to the outside.

4. Cut the twigs progressively smaller and glue in place. When the entire frame is covered with the twigs, glue the large cinnamon sticks along the outer and inner edges.

5. To hinge the front to the back for ease in replacing the photograph, lay two like edges together and join with the duct tape (see Fig. 2).

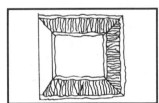

Fig. 2

6. Attach the photo mounting corners to the plywood.

7. Make a bow from the ribbon (the size of the bow will depend on the size of the frame). Glue half of the Velcro to the bow and the other half on the top of the frame (see Fig. 3). By doing this, you can easily change the bow as the seasons change.

Fig. 3

To make the pinecone frame, use the same techniques as above, gluing the cones as closely together as possible. To fill in bare spots, separate pinecone pieces and glue in place.

◆ *Variations*: Use your imagination and create other fun accessories from twigs or pinecones such as a notepad holder, tissue or treasure boxes, napkin holders, or wall hangings. Experiment with other natural fibers such as tree bark, monkey grass, or dry moss. Use silk flowers, paper twist ribbons, or even a small bird's nest as additional decoration.

Make a Dress in a Jiffy

If you follow these instructions, you can make a dress, once it's cut out, in a very short time—so start your timers!

▲ *To make, you'll need*: An interlock knit with 50 percent stretch.

▼ *Sewing hints*: Sew with a 5/8" seam allowance, using a straight stitch with about nine stitches per inch. Stretch the fabric as you sew. When topstitching, sew 1/2" from seam with a medium zigzag. Do not stretch fabric.

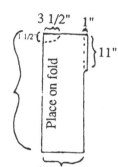

▲ *Pattern*: The basic dress is a modified rectangle. 1. To determine the width of the rectangle, measure the hips and add 5", then divide by 4. (Example: 35" + 5" = 40"/ 4 = 10". Ten inches would be the width of the rectangle.)

2. Measure from the base of the back of the neck to the knee to determine the length of the rectangle. Remember, it's better to err on the long side; you can always cut it shorter afterward.

3. To make the armhole, extend the width of one end of the rectangle 1" for an 11" length for a medium adult size (9" for a child's size 10). To make the dress, cut two of the rectangles with the long straightedge placed on the fold each time. To make the front neck opening, measure 3 1/2" (3" for child's size 10) from the folded edge toward the sleeve and mark. Measure 1 1/2" down the fold and mark. Draw an elongated quarter circle between the two marks (see pattern example) and cut out. To make the back neck opening, repeat on the second rectangle, except measure only 1" down on the fold.

▼ *Directions*: Sew the shoulder seams together. Press open. Starting at the outside shoulder edge of the front piece, topstitch toward the neck. Turn the neck edge under 5/8" and continue topstitching around the neck and onto the other shoulder. Repeat procedure on the back piece. Sew the side seams together, beginning at the bottom edge. Clip armhole curve and press seam open. Turn armhole edge under 5/8" and topstitch. Hem dress by turning under 5/8" and topstitching, being careful not to stretch the material. If you want to add a sleeve, cut two rectangles the same length as the armhole opening (20 3/4" for adult size and 16 3/4" for child's size 10) and as wide as you want the sleeve to be long. Sew in the sleeve after the shoulder seam has been completed. Press seam open and topstitch before sewing side seams.

▲ *Knotted Belt*: Cut two rectangles 12" wide and as long as the waist measurement. Sew the narrow ends together to form a circle. Press seam open and topstitch. Hem both sides of the circle. Slip a circle on each arm. Sliding arms together, with the right hand, catch the edge of the circle closest to the left elbow and with the left hand, the edge closest to the right elbow. Pull arms apart forming the knot. Fold the two circles together to form the belt.

Food and Outdoors

Miscellaneous

Set Up a Texas-Style Barbecue in Your Backyard

The hot trend is the Texas barbecue—from the backyard at the White House to your backyard. Make the cooking comfortably down-home with these ideas.

■ Turn a Wheelbarrow into a Barbecue Grill

You can make a versatile barbecue that will handle a whole meal by using a wheelbarrow, a few bricks, some foil, and dirt. You can wheel it wherever you want; it's just the right height for you to sit on a lawn chair while doing the work, and there's enough space for a rotisserie and a grill, as well as for direct cooking on the coals. Fill wheelbarrow with gravel, sand, or dirt about six or more inches deep (enough to insulate from heat). For efficient briquet cooking, cover area where briquets will be placed with extra-heavy aluminum foil. The foil keeps briquets from nestling into sand or dirt and insures that air will circulate to keep briquets burning. Stack the briquets in center of wheelbarrow and light. When hot, spread over foil. Once briquets are burning, line sides of wheelbarrow with bricks, then place a large heavy grill across for barbecuing flat pieces of meat. (For easy cleaning, spray rack with nonstick cooking spray before using.) You can regulate cooking temperature by adding or taking away bricks to raise or lower grill. The most efficient grill height is about 4-6" above the coals.

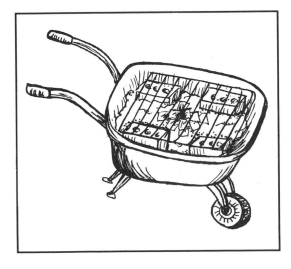

■ Alternative Arrangements

1. Rotisserie, grill, and open coals—use bricks on the back for a rotisserie, bricks just in front to support a wire rack, and leave an open space for cooking over open coals.
2. Rotisserie and open grill—stack bricks at back for rotisserie and bricks along the side with a rack on them for a grill.
3. Grill—place bricks in four corners and put rack on top.
4. Open coals—cook directly on or over coals using foil or stick (wooden dowels) cooking methods. Good for corn in the husks, top sticks removed. Place on coals for about five minutes per side.

■ A Couple of Tips

1. Don't use refrigerator racks as grills. Some contain a harmful substance that is released by the heat.

2. Cover the wheelbarrow after briquets are out so the dirt doesn't get wet from rain or dew. Moisture will tend to rust the bottom of the wheelbarrow.

3. Slide a pair of mitt-type pot holders onto the handles of the wheelbarrow so they will be handy while you are grilling.

4. If you use bricks with holes, you can use them for storing roasting sticks.

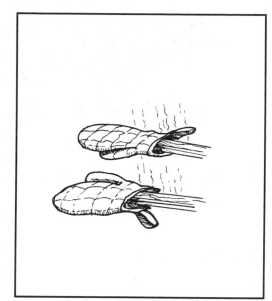

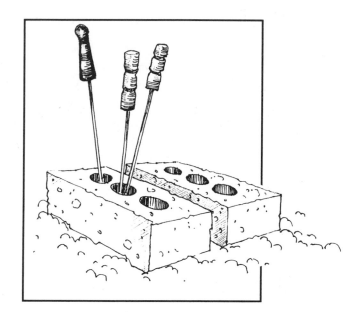

Watermelon Delight

■ De-Seed a Watermelon

1. Cut the ends of the watermelon off and set the melon in front of you on a table.

2. With a paring knife, cut the melon from the top to the bottom into the seed base, which is about 3" deep in the melon. Cut the opposite side of the melon from the top to bottom into the seed base.

3. Repeat procedure three to five times.

4. With the palm of your hand, hit the melon up and down each wedge until it becomes loose. Then remove the wedge.

5. With a knife, scrape out the watermelon seeds, and you'll have a watermelon without the seeds.

■ Watermelon Slush—A Cool Summer Treat

2 12-oz. cans frozen orange juice concentrate
1 12-oz. can frozen lemonade concentrate
1 12-oz. can pineapple juice concentrate
5 ripe bananas, mashed
6 cups water
4 cups sugar
2 pkgs. powdered strawberry Kool-Aid® (unsweetened)
1 gallon watermelon juice*

In a large bowl mix orange, lemonade, and pineapple concentrates and bananas which have been mashed. In a saucepan bring water and sugar to a boil until sugar is dissolved. Add sugar water to concentrates, then mix together. Fill blender with mixture, blend, then pour mixture in freezer containers. Continue the process until all the mixture has been blended. Place mixture in freezer. Before serving time, take out of freezer and allow to soften. Then add strawberry Kool-Aid mix and watermelon juice for a wonderful slush.

*To make watermelon juice, take two large watermelons and push through a strainer.

■ Melon Pie—Not Your Traditional Pie

3 cups watermelon, cubed, 1/2" thick
Grated rind of one lime or lemon
Juice of 1/2 lime or lemon
1/3 cup sugar
1/2 tsp. vanilla
3 tbsps. flour
3 tbsps. butter or margarine
Pastry for a double-crust pie

Mix melon with the lime or lemon rind and juice, sugar, vanilla, and flour. Put in pastry-lined pan and dot with butter or margarine. Cover with lattice top. Bake at 400 degrees for 15 minutes, then at 350 degrees for 20 minutes longer. Melons that are not good enough to be eaten raw may be used.

■ Watermelon Soup— A Refreshing Soup for Summer

1 envelope unflavored gelatin
1/4 cup cold water
6 cups diced fresh watermelon
1/4 cup sugar
1/3 cup fresh lime juice
1/4 tsp. salt
Fresh mint sprigs

Soften gelatin in cold water. Microwave on high 45 seconds. Press watermelon through a sieve. Add sugar, lime juice, and salt. Stir in gelatin. Chill until mixture has thickened slightly, 3 to 4 hours. Serve in chilled mugs or bowls. Garnish with sprigs of fresh mint. Makes 1 quart or 5 servings.

Fun Breakfast Ideas

Cooking can be fun. Here are a few ways to add interest to your breakfast.

● **Smoking Fruit Cup.** You'll need a brandy snifter and a bowl larger than the snifter. Fill snifter with hot water and a drop of food coloring. Fill bowl with fresh fruit. At serving time, place dry ice in brandy snifter and set bowl with fruit on top.

● **Muffin-Tin Breakfast:** Preheat oven to 375 degrees. In a nonstick muffin pan, fill six spaces with muffin batter. In the other six, put a slice of ham and break an egg over the ham. Bake for 15-20 minutes.

● **Puff Pancakes:** Preheat oven to 450 degrees. In mixing bowl, mix together 3 eggs, 1 to 2 cups flour and 1/2 cup milk.

Grease a 9" pie pan by melting 2 tbsps. margarine or butter in pie pan. Pour mixture into pan. Bake 10-15 minutes. The pancake will climb the sides of the pan. Remove and fill with sliced bananas, raspberries, pineapple chunks, brown sugar, a dollop of sour cream, and a sprinkle of brown sugar.

● **Breakfast Parfait:** In a parfait glass layer in granola, yogurt, and fruit.

● **No-Milk Cereal** (good for people with milk allergies): Take a shredded wheat biscuit and cover with fruit and orange juice.

● **Painted Toast:** Add a few drops of food coloring to 1/4 cup milk. Paint designs on bread, then toast.

Make Ice Cream with Your Feet!

If you like unusual ways of preparing food, try this ice-cream recipe made without any special equipment—just your feet and tin cans! You can also try the next recipe for a sherbet mold that looks like a watermelon.

■ Kick-the-Can Ice Cream

3/4 cup whole milk
1 cup cream
1/3 cup sugar
1/2 tsp. vanilla
1 cold raw egg (optional)
Any flavoring you want (chocolate syrup, raspberry, etc.)
A 1-lb. and a 3-lb. coffee can and plastic lids (so one can fit inside the other)
Crushed ice
3/4 cup salt or rock salt

In a small can, combine milk, cream, sugar, vanilla, egg, and flavoring, then stir. Place plastic lid on can and put into 3-lb. coffee can. Pack with ice and rock salt; then put lid on can. Roll can back and forth to a friend for 10 minutes. After 10 to 15 minutes of rolling, take lid off and, with table knife, scrape the ice cream off sides and stir into mixture. If it needs more freezing, drain water out of large can. Place small can back into large can and pack with ice and rock salt, and roll 5 minutes more.

■ Sherbet Watermelon

2 qts. lime sherbet, softened
2 qts. raspberry sherbet, softened
Chocolate chips

Line a large round glass bowl with plastic wrap. Spoon softened lime sherbet around the sides and edges, 3/4" thick, and smooth. Let harden in refrigerator. Mix together raspberry sherbet and chocolate chips and place mixture inside lime sherbet "rind." Freeze for 1-1/2 hours. Unmold; remove plastic wrap, and slice like a watermelon.

Plastic Wrap

A $15,000 Beef Salad

This recipe recently won a $15,000 grand prize at the National Beef Cookoff—it is just fabulous! The recipe was created by Annette Erbeck.

■ Pacific Rim Beef Salad—Definitely a Winner for Salad Lovers

2 lbs. boneless beef top sirloin steak, cut 1-1/2 inches thick
3/4 cup soy sauce
3/4 cup sugar, divided (1/2 cup and 1/4 cup)
1 tbsp. plus 1-1/2 tsps. finely grated fresh ginger
3 large cloves garlic, minced
1/4 cup vegetable oil, divided
1 lb. fresh spinach, stems removed
4 oz. fresh bean sprouts
6 center-cut red onion slices, separated into rings
1/4 cup each catsup and rice wine vinegar
1/2 tsp. hot pepper sauce
2 tsps. Oriental dark-roasted sesame oil
1 tbsp. sesame seeds, toasted*
Fresh enoki mushrooms or button mushrooms
Cherry tomatoes

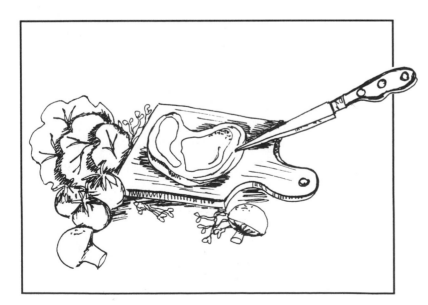

Trim excess fat from boneless beef top sirloin steak. Combine soy sauce, 1/2 cup sugar, ginger, and garlic, stirring well. Place steak and marinade in plastic bag. Turn to coat. Marinate in bag in refrigerator 2 to 4 hours, turning occasionally.

Remove steak from marinade; pat dry with paper towels. Reserve 2 tbsps. marinade. Heat 2 tbsps. vegetable oil in large heavy frying pan until hot. Add steak and sear 4 to 6 minutes, turning once. Continue cooking on medium heat 10 to 12 minutes or until steak is rare (140 degrees F.) to medium rare (150 degrees F.) or to desired doneness. Let steak stand 10 minutes before carving.

Meanwhile, combine spinach, bean sprouts, and onion in large bowl. Combine catsup, vinegar, pepper sauce, remaining 1/4 cup sugar, remaining 2 tbsps. vegetable oil, and reserved 2 tbsps. marinade in small saucepan. Carve steak into thin slices. Bring dressing to a boil over medium heat, stirring constantly. Remove from heat; stir in sesame oil. Pour hot dressing over spinach mixture and toss. Place spinach mixture on platter. Arrange beef strips on top of salad; sprinkle with sesame seeds. Garnish with mushrooms and cherry tomatoes. Serves six.

*To toast sesame seeds, heat sesame seeds in small pan over medium heat until golden, stirring constantly.

Dutch Oven Recipes

These are the winning recipes from a recent World Championship Dutch Oven cookoff. Winners were Craig Ruech and Dellis Hatch of Salt Lake City.

■ Marie's Fabulous French Rolls

1 1/2 cups water
2 tbsps. yeast
1 tbsp. sugar
1 tsp. salt
4 tbsps. margarine or butter, divided
4 cups flour
1 tsp. sesame seeds

Heat water in Dutch oven until lukewarm. Remove 1/2 cup water and mix with yeast and sugar in separate bowl to dissolve. Set aside and let activate. Add salt and 2 tbsps. butter to hot water. In large mixing bowl, combine hot water mixture and 2 cups flour, beating until well blended. Add yeast mixture and 1 cup flour; mix, and add another cup of flour. Punch down and form into 12 balls. Dip balls into 2 tbsps. melted butter and place in lightly buttered #12 Dutch oven. Sprinkle with sesame seeds. Cover and allow to rise until double in size. Place 8 briquets on the bottom and about 15 on the top. Bake for 20-30 minutes. Rotate Dutch oven 1/4 turn every 5 minutes. Butter the tops of rolls when golden brown and serve with butter, honey, or jam.

■ Blueberry Poppy Binge

2 cups flour
3/4 cup water
1/2 cup chopped pecans
1 1/2 tsps. baking powder
1/2 cup vegetable oil
1 1/2 cups sugar
1 tsp. almond flavoring
1 1/2 cans blueberry pie filling
4 eggs
2 tsps. vanilla
1 pkg. (3 1/2 oz.) French vanilla
    pudding mix
1 tsp. butter flavoring
1 tsp. salt
1 cup sour cream
1/4 cup poppy seeds

◆ Binge Icing

8 oz. softened cream cheese
2 tsps. vanilla
1/3 cup fresh lemon juice
14 oz. sweetened condensed milk

Combine all ingredients except blueberries in a bowl. Heat for 2 minutes. Scrape batter into a greased and floured #12 Dutch oven. Bake for 30-40 minutes with 6-8 briquets on the bottom and 10-12 on the top. Remove from heat when cake begins to pull away from the side of the oven and a toothpick inserted into the middle comes out clean. Let cool with lid off for 5-10 minutes, then invert cake onto a rack. Invert again onto the Dutch oven lid so that cake is right side up. Allow to cool for additional 1/2 hour. Split the cake in half horizontally. Set the top half to the side. For icing, combine all ingredients and whip until smooth. Spread half of the icing on the bottom half, then spread on half of the blueberry topping. Replace the top half. Repeat step with icing and blueberries on top. Cut into 12 wedges and serve.

A Whole Month of School Lunches

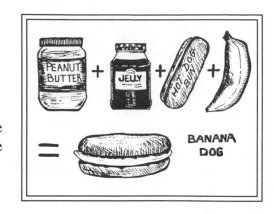

One hundred and eighty school lunches are packed before the end of the school year. Here are a few creative ideas to make the task easier.

■ Freeze a Whole Month of Sandwiches

● **Roll up sandwiches.** Cut crusts off bread; roll bread with rolling pin; spread with desired filling; and roll up. Tip: Meat fillings freeze best. Do not freeze mayonnaise.

● **Canoe sandwich.** Scoop out center of French roll or hoagie bun to make "canoe." Butter both sides and add a filling—such as chicken. Cut roll in half for lunches for smaller children.

● **Pear spread.** Mix mashed pears, cinnamon, and peanut butter; spread on bread.

◆ *Freezer Wrapping Tips:*

Double bag everything to keep air out.

Put each sandwich in a small resealable plastic bag.

Fill a one-gallon self-sealing plastic bag with the same kinds of sandwiches and label it.

◆ *Thawing Instructions:*

Place frozen sandwich directly into lunch box.

Add a frozen box of juice to keep entire lunch cool.

By lunchtime, sandwich (and juice) will have thawed.

For faster thawing, microwave sandwich for ten seconds.

■ Banana Dog (this isn't frozen, but it's fun)

● Open a hot dog bun and spread one side with peanut butter, the other with jelly. Wrap it and put it in the lunch bag.

● Pack a whole banana in a bag.

● At lunchtime, your child peels the banana and puts in bun like a hot dog!

173

■ And for Dessert (you can play with it and eat it)

■ Nutty Putty

3 1/2 cups peanut butter
4 cups powdered sugar
3 1/2 cups honey
4 cups dried milk powder

Mix ingredients together. Divide into 10 to 15 portions. Store
extra portions in plastic bags in refrigerator or freezer. This treat can serve as fun dough. With clean
hands, children can mold and shape into animals, flowers, and other objects while they eat it.

■ Inside-Out Cakes

This solves the problem of frosting sticking to the plastic wrap. Take a square of cake with frosting
on top. Slice cake through the middle horizontally. Turn top half upside down so frosting is in the
middle. Wrap in plastic wrap and you won't lose any frosting.

■ Finally, a Great Idea for Chili Hot Dogs Served Piping Hot:

● Put well-heated chili in a thermos.

● Tie a length of dental floss around a cooked hot dog; put in thermos with the
floss hanging out.

● In a lunch bag, put a spoon and bun.

● When it's time for lunch, your child can pull out the hot dog, remove
the floss for use after lunch, and spoon chili on the bun with the hot dog.

174

A Winter Picnic in the Snow

You probably know what an appetite you can build up when sledding, skating, skiing, or playing outside in the snow. Here are some good ideas for a picnic. Be sure you take along a poncho to lay over the snow. Cardboard boxes for sitting can later be used for sledding.

The hot food has to be kept in a hot box. Choose a box 3-4 inches larger than your food container. Place a 1" stack of newspapers on the bottom of the box. Line each side of the box with an additional 1"-thick pad of newspapers.

Make sure the food and its container are very hot! A thick aluminum pot or a heavy cast-iron kettle with a good lid will help food hold heat the best. Place the container of hot food in the newspaper-lined box. If the newspapers do not fit snugly around the container, stuff in additional newspapers so that the container nests tightly and cannot move. Place at least one inch of newspapers over the top of the container, then close the box flaps or lid tightly over the newspaper. This insulated box will help keep food hot at least three hours.

■ Chili in Bread Bowls

Heat your favorite chili until very hot. Bake or buy 3-to-4 inch hard rolls. Slice off the top quarter of each roll. Carefully hollow out the center of each roll, leaving a 1/2" crust to form each bowl. Place in an airtight container or plastic bag. When you are ready to serve, spoon chili into the edible bowls. Stew and thick hearty soups also taste delicious served in bread bowls.

■ Snowman in Hot Chocolate

Turn two large marshmallows into a snowman to float on your hot chocolate. For each snowman, dip the tip of a toothpick in blue food coloring. Use it to dot eyes and a nose on one marshmallow, and a vertical row of buttons on a second. Use another toothpick dipped in red food coloring to paint the mouth of the snowman. Pack the marshmallows in self-sealing bags or airtight plastic containers. Heat chocolate drink, then pour into thermos. To serve, pour hot chocolate in a cup, then float the two marshmallows together on the hot drink to form your snowman.

Cooking in Your Fireplace

You don't have to stand out in the cold and snow to barbecue in the middle of winter. Use your fireplace—after all, this is how people cooked before there were ovens.

First, get a good steady fire going that will burn down to enough coals for cooking. This will take 30 to 40 minutes of burning. Make sure you have enough kindling, wood, or coal on hand. Then put down four bricks and prop a cookie sheet or oven rack on top. By adding more bricks, you can lower the temperature for grilling, boiling, or frying. For baking, you'll need a Dutch oven. You might want to cover the hearth with extra-heavy foil to protect it from drips.

■ Enchilada Pie—A Super Supper

2 lbs. ground beef
2 tsp. salt
1 med. onion, chopped
1 10 3/4-oz. can condensed tomato soup
2 10-oz. cans mild enchilada sauce
1 cup water
9 8" flour tortillas
2 cups (8 oz.) shredded cheddar
or mozzarella cheese

Working over an open fire, brown ground beef with salt and onion in a Dutch oven. Drain off drippings. Add condensed soup, enchilada sauce, and water. Simmer 5 minutes. Spoon 3/4 of the mixture into a medium bowl.

Arrange 2 to 3 tortillas over mixture remaining in pan. Alternate meat, cheese, and tortillas in 3 layers. Replace lid on Dutch oven. Simmer 7 to 10 minutes or until cheese melts and tortillas soften. Serve pie with remaining tortillas as side bread. Serves 6 to 8.

■ Meatloaf in an Onion—An Unusual Family Treat

1 lb. lean ground beef
1 egg
1/4 cup tomato sauce
1/8 tsp. pepper
1/2 tsp. salt
1/2 tsp. dry mustard
3 medium onions

Cut six 12" x 14" rectangles of heavy-duty foil; set aside. In a medium bowl, mix ground beef, egg, tomato sauce, pepper, salt, and dry mustard. Set aside. Cut onions in half horizontally and remove centers, leaving 1/4" shell. Chop onion centers. Stir 2 tablespoons into meat mixture. Spoon meat mixture into 6 onion halves, rounding on top. Place remaining onion halves on top of filled onion halves. Place one filled onion on each piece of foil. Bring ends of foil up over onion. Fold foil down in small folds. Press sides of foil close to onion. Flatten ends and roll toward onion. Cook on coals 14 to 20 minutes on each side. Serves 6.

■ Banana Boat—A Delicious Dessert to Cook in Coals

4 bananas, unpeeled
1/2 cup milk chocolate pieces
1/2 cup miniature marshmallows

With knife starting at stem end, cut through top peel of the banana from one end to the other. Spread banana apart and fill with milk chocolate chips and miniature marshmallows. Wrap securely in heavy-duty foil. Heat 5 minutes over coals until chocolate and marshmallows melt. Serves 4.

176

Brrr! Camping Out in Winter

For all of you who think winter is not an ideal time to camp out, follow these ideas to find out how and why it is. The challenge is not the cold but being prepared for it.

● **To understand how to stay warm and comfortable in the cold,** it is important to understand how your body responds to cold. Your body's metabolic rate will increase so you will need to increase your intake of food and water to fuel this hotter furnace. Your body will restrict heat in the extremities to keep the core (brain and organs) warm. Your body can experience hypothermia if the "core" of your body becomes chilled.

● **Stopping body heat loss is as important as producing good body heat.** Clothing is the most vital shelter in the cold. Cotton, wool, down, or other natural materials will pick up and trap moisture. One special line, "Expedition Series Clothing System," was designed by Gil Phillips of Northern Outfitters, the result of 30 years of research on how to keep the body warm. This system uses a polyurethane foam which won't pick up or hold water. It allows moisture to escape and body heat to remain next to the skin, keeping you warm.

● **You can adapt your winter clothing by replacing the traditional lining with a 1" layer of polyurethane foam.** Figures 1, 2, and 3 below will give the basic layout and pattern to make a hat and a coat lining. All types of winter clothing can be adapted this way, including coats, pants, hats, boots, socks, gloves, etc.

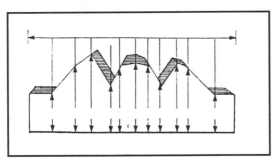

Fig. 1

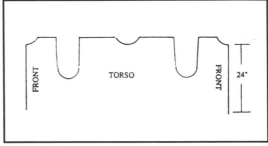

Fig. 2

Fig. 3

Start with a piece of foam 28" long and 8" wide. Draw the pattern on a piece of stiff paper, cut it out, lay it on the foam, and outline it with a felt-tip marker. Use scissors or a very sharp knife to cut the foam around the pattern. Fold until edges meet and glue them together with an adhesive such as 3-M Spray Cement. Known as "butt-gluing," this method of cementing two flat edges together is used in almost all foam gear construction. Insert the foam lining into your winter clothing.

Note: Figures 1, 2, and 3 are used with permission from the book *Without Fire or Shelter* by Jim Phillips of 1083 North State Street, Orem, Utah 84057.

● **Water is critical to cold weather nutrition.** Your body will dehydrate quickly. Drink a gallon or more of water each day. Eat food containing complete carbohydrates, fats, oils, and proteins such as whole grains, nuts, seeds, dried fruits, cheese, butter, meat, etc. This recipe for **Iron Man Mix** is a good example of high-fat, high-protein food which will help keep you warm and your energy level high. Mix together: 1 cup raisins, 1 cup nonprocessed cheese (cubed), 1 cup peanuts, and 1 cup beef jerky (diced).

■ Three Great Camping Ideas

● **To store camping equipment year round,** use plastic boxes, about 20" wide by 30" long by 18" high. Label each box accordingly:

<u>Staples</u>: aluminum foil, plastic wrap, paper towels, matches, toilet tissue, salt/pepper and other spices, syrup, coffee creamer, soup mixes, paper cups and plates, insect repellent, measuring cups, napkins, reusable plastic bags, garbage bags, hot cocoa mix, can opener, collapsible canteen, and tablecloth.

<u>Cooking Supplies</u>: Kitchen equipment to keep stored includes hot pads, steel wool pads, knives, spatula, tongs, silverware, cutting board, cookie racks, dish towels, frying pans, pots, and dish soap.

<u>Tools</u>: Camping necessities include a flashlight, lantern, saw, hatchet, shovel, pliers, screwdriver, batteries, rope, and first-aid kit.

Put all empty tubes, cans, paper towel cardboard, etc., in a large plastic bag when you run out and you'll then know what needs to be purchased. Replenish boxes immediately upon your return and store boxes in an easy-access spot in your garage or storage room.

● **An easy shortcut to cooking a great meal while camping** is to bake your meal in a muffin tin. Transport the following items in separate resealable plastic bags via your cooler: uncooked meatloaf, peeled and diced potatoes and carrots, and muffin mix. When you're ready to make dinner, line each opening with paper liners and fill a row (usually three or four openings across) with each item so you have a row of meatloaf, a row of diced potatoes, a row of carrots, and one row with muffin mix. Place paper liners upside down over muffin mix. Place an empty muffin tin upside down over muffin tin containing food and clamp together with large metal paper holders. Place in coals to cook and lay extra coals on top of muffin tin where meatloaf is cooking because it takes longer.

● **Use for sterilizing hands:** Fill an empty liquid detergent bottle with water, two tablespoons rubbing alcohol, and one tablespoon liquid dish soap. Wash hands before preparing food, or as needed.

A Cool Sport, Ice Fishing

For starters, you will need a fishing license. When you purchase it, ask for information on places to go as well as rules and regulations. Remember, regulations vary from state to state and from season to season.

▲ *You will need*: Proper clothing—wear several layers of warm clothing. You can remove or add layers as the weather changes. One-piece-type snowsuits are good. You'll also need waterproof boots (preferably insulated ones); several pairs of warm socks (you can purchase battery-powered warming socks at most camping stores); and at least two pairs of gloves (they're sure to get wet). Proper equipment—an ax or ice auger to make the hole; large scoop or strainer to remove ice chips from the hole; fishing pole—a regular pole will work, but there are ones made especially for ice fishing; hooks, #2 up to #14, single or treble; weights, small lead weight sinkers; lures, any type; bait, salmon eggs, angle worms, or plastic worms; knife for cleaning the fish; and something to sit on. You could get by with a bucket turned upside down, but even better, take along a lawn chair and a thick quilt or sleeping bag for padding and warmth and a small hibachi grill or portable propane grill to provide warmth as well as a place to keep coffee or hot chocolate warm. It is also a good idea to set up a regular camping tent for protection from the weather.

◆ *Hint*: When you have all of your equipment together, tie it to a sled for easy transportation across snow and ice.

When you reach your destination, it is very easy to find out if the ice is thick enough. Simply ask people in the area. If there isn't anyone to ask, drill a test hole. The ice should be a minimum of 6" deep. Drill a hole and enjoy the catch. Note: Ice fishing on rivers can be very dangerous and is not for beginners.

■ Basic Recipes for Cooking Fish

● Baked Fish
Thoroughly clean the fish and remove head and tail. Place the fish on a large piece of aluminum foil. Place slices of onion, garlic (fresh), salt, and lemon pepper inside the fish. Wrap tightly in the foil and place on a cookie sheet. Bake at 350 degrees for 45 minutes.

● Fried Fish
Season the cleaned fish as above. Roll the fish in cornmeal or flour. Fry in oil or butter until lightly crisped on the underside. Gently turn over and fry the second side.

● Poached or Broiled Fish
Place two or three cleaned fish (depending on the size) in a large, deep frying pan. Place two or more fish crosswise on top of them. Add 1/2" to 1" of water. Cover and boil about 10 minutes. Remove the fish and let cool slightly. Remove the fins. With a fork, gently open the fish, allowing the bones to separate from the meat. With the fish open, remove the entire skeleton. Garnish the opened fish with lemon slices and add seasoning. Place the fish under the broiler for a few minutes until slightly crisp.

Snow Igloos

Are you tired of the same old winter activities? Would you like to try something different and exciting with your family? Then it's time for winter camping in snow shelters. With the help of Jim Phillips, a leading expert on outdoor shelters, it's easy to make a snow igloo right in your own backyard.

▲ *To make, you'll need:* 30 sticks or dowels 10 inches long, painted black on one end; a sturdy shovel; and some patience.

▼ *Directions:* 1. Begin making the igloo by shoveling up a mound of snow about 6 feet high and 10 to 12 feet in diameter at the base. If you have a snow blower, this can be done very quickly. Simply start walking in a large circle, gradually blowing all the snow to the center. Once the snow is all piled up, push all the sticks (painted first) into it at about 18" intervals, pointing toward the center. Let the mound set for at least 2 hours, though overnight would be better. This will allow the snow to settle and consolidate. 2. As close to the ground as possible, cut a 2' high entrance with your shovel in the mound. Start hollowing out the mound, piling the snow at the side of the entrance as a wind barrier. Continue digging until you see the ends of the sticks. You should now have a roomy, peaceful shelter.

A second type of shelter that you can build is the snow cave. It is built on the same principles as the snow igloo, except that it is built in deep drifts or steep, stable snow slopes. If you decide to build this type, however, please be aware of extreme avalanche danger. Begin by digging a tunnel in the drift, angling it upward several feet. Excavate a dome-shaped room at the top of the tunnel following the same techniques as for the snow igloo, using sticks pushed in the drift to indicate the thickness. Smooth the curved roof to remove sharp edges that may cause moisture to drip onto you.

◆ *Helpful Hints*: 1. Wear appropriate, waterproof clothing. Dress in layers. As much as possible, keep the snow brushed off your clothing. Colorful outer clothing will make you more visible in case of an emergency. 2. It is easy to lose equipment in the snow. Keep everything stored on your sled or in your pack or pockets. You could even tie brightly colored ribbon to small pieces of gear so that they can be easily seen. 3. As much as possible, keep the entrance to your snow shelter lower than the floor (rising warm air won't escape through it and heavier cold air can't come in). It can be as much as 30 degrees warmer inside a snow shelter than outside. 4. Be sure to have a plastic ground cloth or mat to sit on so that you will stay dry. ‹

Before you sleep in your snow dome, there are some very important safety precautions you should take: 1. For ventilation, punch out a few holes at a 45-degree angle to the floor with a ski pole or long stick. Occasionally check to make sure these holes are still open and that drifting or blowing snow has not blocked them. 2. Never burn a stove or lantern inside as they may give off poisonous carbon monoxide gas. Do all of your cooking outside. 3. You may use candles inside your shelter for light and warmth.

Camping with Kids Can Be Fun If You Plan Ahead

No need to have any private disquieting moments if the family is going on a camping trip. Plan ahead, anticipate problems, and find solutions—and it'll be fun and rewarding for the whole family.

● Teach your children about dangers, such as poisonous plants, by showing them pictures. Reinforce their knowledge by having them draw their own pictures.

● Children will be happy campers if they are comfortable and protected from bugs and weather. To keep crawling bugs and prickly weeds off children's legs, elasticize the ankles of their pants. To do this, you will need to sew a casing, using wide bias tape, on the inside bottom of each pant leg and insert elastic. Just be sure you don't make the elastic too tight for feet to go through.

To protect your child from flying insects, all you need is a favorite cap, some mosquito netting (available at most camping supply stores), scissors, needle, and thread. First, measure the distance from the top of the child's head to just below the shoulder area. Second, measure from the top of the arm, across the front of the body to the top of the other arm, and around the back, returning to the starting point. Add 1" to 2" to each of these measurements for seams and ease of movement, then cut the rectangle from the netting. Sew the side seam. Sew a gathering stitch around the top edge of the rectangle, pull it tight, and attach to the top of the hat. Roll the netting onto the brim of the hat; then when insects become a bother, simply pull the netting down over the face for protection.

● To prevent neck and shoulder sunburn when hiking, take a cap (baseball type works very well), a piece of material, and some Velcro. You will need two measurements: the distance from the cap edge to just below the shoulder areas plus 2" to 3", and the distance around the back of the cap (be sure to allow for any stretch or cap adjustment). Cut a square of fabric to these measurements. Narrowly hem all edges, then sew one side of the Velcro to the top edge. Sew the other side of the Velcro to the cap edge. Stick them together whenever protection is needed.

● The weather can change quickly when you're hiking or camping. Some cotton webbing and a sewing machine will ensure that each child has his or her jacket at all times. Measure the diagonal distance from the center back neck edge of the jacket to the side seam just below the arm hole and add 3". Cut two pieces of webbing to this measurement. Sew the ends at the neck and side below the sleeve seam. Slip your child's arms through the webbing and wear the jacket just like a backpack.

● It is important when camping with small children to make your campsite a safe and recognizable place. Make a family flag or banner from brightly colored material and put it on top of your tent or hang it from a nearby tree to make it easy for your child to identify your campsite. Or, tie a noisy bell to the zipper or opening flap of your tent. If a child tries to leave the tent in the middle of the night, the bell will immediately alert you. For more information on camping, refer to *Roughing It Easy* by Dian Thomas.

Cooking Out While Camping Out

Whether your camping trip is for a week or just an overnighter, here are a few creative ways to put more fun into camping.

■ Tackle Box

A small tackle box placed near the grill can hold spatulas, knives, peelers, etc., in the bottom and seasonings in the trays. Look for a tackle box that will fit your needs.

■ Carpenter's Apron

Fill a carpenter's apron with cooking necessities, such as hot pad mitt, spatula, tongs, spices, etc. Stitch pockets to fit utensils.

■ Vertical Spit Cooking

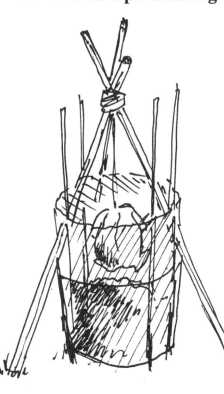

Cook chicken using this method, which is like an uncovered oven, by driving four 3'-long metal stakes into the ground 12-14" apart, forming a square. Cut four pieces of 1" mesh chicken wire 2' long and nine holes wide (leave nine holes and cut tenth in half). Fasten the two long sides of each roll together, making long, tube-like cages. Slip each wire cage vertically down over each metal stake and fill cages with briquets (one row of briquets from ground to top of cage). Light briquets. When hot, wrap heavy-duty foil around outside of four stakes to hold in heat. Make a tripod out of three sticks or lengths of metal about 4' long, tying together at top with rope or picture wire. Place tripod over four stakes so that tripod is centered over them. Tie wings of a chicken (fryer) to its body. Tie a long enough length of heavy string or picture wire to legs of chicken so that when the other end of string or wire is tied to the top of the tripod the chicken will dangle about 3-4" above the ground. Roasting time: 1-1/2 hours. If you baste the chicken with barbecue sauce, do it the last 15 minutes or the sauce will burn.

■ Cardboard Box Oven

Cut the top and bottom from a cardboard box that measures approximately 12" square and 13-14" deep. Wrap either whole box or just bottom edges (which will be near the coals) with heavy-duty foil to protect it from burning. Place a pile of about 24 briquets on ground and light. After 40 minutes when coals are hot, push a backpacker's rack into ground until top part of rack is 3" from briquets (you can get these at camping supply stores).

Put cookie cooling rack inside box about halfway between top and bottom of box. Poke holes on sides of box with nail or other sharp object at corners of cooling rack. Poke two holes for each corner and insert one end of twist tie through top hole, secure around cooking rack, and push back out through bottom hole. Twist tie until cooling rack is held firmly in place. Repeat process for all corners. Place box on backpacker's rack over briquets. Place the item to be baked on center of cooling rack. Cover box with see-through oven cooking bag (turkey size). Hook rubber bands together until they form a circle slightly smaller than circumference of box. Put elastic band around box to hold oven cooking bag firmly in place.

The oven can be lifted on and off coals as needed. Optional: A portable oven thermometer can be hung on the upper inside of the box to determine heat of oven. To lower heat, raise the rack. To raise heat, add briquets or lower rack.

■ Rock Cooking

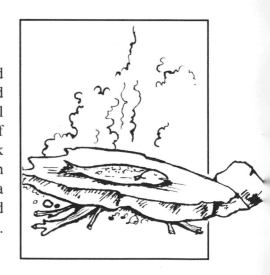

A fun alternative to using a campstove or grill is a rock. Heat is conducted through rock from coal or fire below. Find a flat rock under 2" thick. Avoid rocks that have recently been in water or that retain moisture, such as shell and limestone, because they may explode. Heat rock slowly and evenly. If one side heats too fast and expands more quickly than the other side, the rock may break. When rock is hot, place directly over coals and use as grill. When upper surface cools, turn rock over, brush it off, and cook on hot side. If a rock is thin enough, the heat will be conducted through and it will not need to be turned. You can cook directly on a clean rock or cover rock with foil.

■ Dirt Dessert

2 small packages vanilla instant pudding mix
4 cups cold milk
1 large container frozen whipped topping, thawed
1 6-ounce package miniature chocolate chips
1 large package Oreo® cookies, crushed to crumb
  consistency
Gummi worms
1 child's sand bucket and shovel, cleaned thoroughly

Mix pudding according to package directions. Allow to set for a few minutes; fold in whipped topping and chocolate chips. Put half of pudding mixture in bottom of sand bucket. Top with half of the cookie crumbs. Layer with rest of pudding and then the rest of the cookie crumbs. Top with Gummi worms; chill. Use shovel to serve. Variation: To make individual servings, layer pudding mixture and cookie crumbs in plastic cups. Use pipe cleaners for the handles and plastic spoons for the shovels.

■ Tin Can Newspaper Stove

The tall can stove is a quick method for cooking meats with only a small amount of fat.

▲ *To make, you'll need*: Square 5-gallon can, heavy-duty can opener, wire rack that fits on the can (such as cookie cooling rack), newspapers, and water spray bottle.

◆ *Note*: Do not use refrigerator racks because they give off toxic fumes and they may melt in the heat. Do not use newspapers with colored ink. They produce toxic fumes when burned.

▼ *Directions*:

Remove the top from can with can opener. Cut one 2 1/2" vent on side of can about 3" from bottom. Place cooling rack over top of can for the grill. The fuel for this method of cooking is rolled-up newspapers. Four or five sheets of newspaper are loosely twisted and crushed lightly into small "logs," then placed in stove bottom. A single sheet of newspaper wadded up and set on top of logs is lit first. Dripping meat fats will keep the log papers burning. If the flames become too high, spray with water.

■ ■

A New Dessert for Cook-Outs

It doesn't take too long into the barbecue/cook-out season before you're muttering, "What can I make that's different?" Here's the answer—apple pie on a stick.

■ Apple Pie on a Stick

Purchase some prerolled pie crusts, some medium-sized dowels (cut to about 24" lengths), and some Jonathan or Rome apples. (Delicious apples can be used, but they are not as good for cooking. Their skins remain tough and do not pop open as the peel of the Jonathan and/or Rome does.)

The pies on sticks can be cooked over the hot coals of a barbecue or on the rotisserie in the kitchen. To begin, place a washed apple on a length of dowel and rotate it over the heat until the peel bubbles and pops. Remove from the source of heat and carefully peel away the skin. The fruit will be quite warm, so children should be supervised at this point by an adult.

Roll the peeled apple, still on the dowel, in cinnamon sugar, or, if you are using the rotisserie, put the cinnamon sugar in a salt shaker and sprinkle on the apple. If you want to eat the apple without a pastry covering, return it to the heat and turn and roast it until the sugar mixture melts or caramelizes and turns brown.

To make a crust for your "pie," roll out the prerolled pastry more thinly than it is when you purchase it from the market. Then press the pastry around the apple that has been covered with the cinnamon and sugar mixture. It takes about 1/3 to 1/2 of a rolled pastry per apple. As the pastry is rolled around the apple, leave some of the apple showing at one end so that the steam can vent as the fruit cooks.

Next, wrap the entire "pie" with a piece of aluminum foil. Leave some of the foil open on one end so that the pastry will brown.

The apple needs about 15-20 minutes on medium high to be completely cooked. Outdoor cooking often requires more patience and a longer cooking time than indoor cooking. Watch the "pie" and rotate the stick for even cooking. It's fun to eat the "pies" from the stick, but they can also be placed in small dishes and served with half-and-half poured over the hot fruit.

● ●

Camping Tips

● To make sure your loaf of bread survives the trip and doesn't get smashed, simply pack the whole loaf in a shoe box, replace the lid, and hold it in place with a couple of elastics.

● One of the worst chores when camping is cleaning all those blackened pots and pans. Washing them can be a breeze if you just take a few minutes before cooking to spread a thin film of dishwashing detergent all over the bottoms and sides. The pans will still turn black when cooking over the campfire, but they will wash clean with just a little water and no scrubbing.

● Damp matches can be a real frustration when camping. Just a little effort before leaving home can prevent that problem. All you need is a piece of corrugated cardboard about 2" x 10" and some clear fingernail polish. Fold the cardboard in half so that it will stand with the holes facing up. Dip the matches in the polish and then insert them in the holes to dry. A second method for waterproofing matches requires paraffin wax, a double boiler (use a regular pan filled with water and an old coffee can to hold the wax as the second pot), and a piece of corrugated cardboard 2" wide and slightly less than the diameter of the can when folded in half. Melt the wax using the "double boiler." Insert a row of matches in the holes in the cardboard, then dip them in the wax. Allow to dry for a few seconds and then dip a second time.

Campfire Ragout/ Hot Box

For this ragout, use a cast-iron pot, preferably one with legs so that the briquets or coals can be put underneath.

■ Campfire Ragout

1/3 to 1/2 lb. bacon
2 lbs. round steak, cut into strips
3 onions, sliced
6-8 carrots, sliced
6-8 potatoes, sliced
1 cup water
Salt and pepper

Layer bottom of pot with bacon. Add layer of round steak strips and salt and pepper. Add layer of onions and layer of sliced carrots and salt and pepper; add layer of sliced potatoes and salt and pepper. Add water, cover, and cook slowly (about one hour on stove, longer on campfire). To serve, cut through layers and dish onto plates.

■ Hot Box

If your family is going to want to eat right away when you arrive at the campsite, here's an easy way to start cooking at home and let the dish finish in the car with a hot box. At home, cook the ragout until it's about two-thirds done. While it's in the oven, make a hot box by lining a cardboard box with 1 inch of newspaper on all sides. Take pot directly from oven and place in lined box, add more newspapers, and cover box so that pot fits snugly. Close box. The food will continue to cook and stay warm. A cast iron or heavy aluminum pan will work the best.

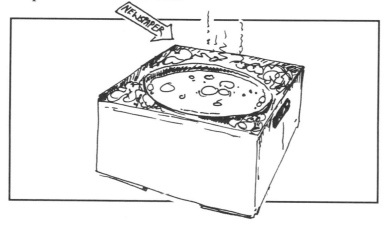

Camping in Your Own Backyard

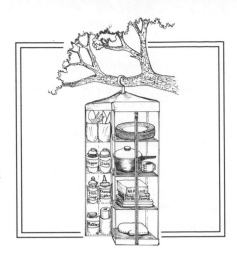

Camping season usually begins with Memorial Day. These tips are good for the big outdoors or your own backyard.

■ Hanging Equipment Bag

Organize cooking equipment so that it stays clean and convenient for cooking by using a hanging shoe/purse storage bag with see-through compartments. Put in paper plates, napkins, and utensils for cooking and eating. Hang from a handy tree limb near your food preparation area.

■ Improvised Barbecues

You can improvise a barbecue for cooking your favorite outdoor dishes by using anything from a garbage can lid to a child's wagon. You need a container impervious to heat, some dirt or gravel, heavy-duty foil, briquets, and a cooking rack. *Child's wagon barbecue*: You can wheel this where it will be most convenient for cooking. Line wagon with heavy foil. Shovel 2-3" of dirt or gravel into wagon. Place more foil over dirt or gravel so that coals do not nest and cut off air circulation necessary for proper burning. Place briquets on foil and light as directed on package. Prop a grill (oven or cookie cooling rack—not a refrigerator rack because some are coated with a substance noxious when burned) on rocks or bricks far enough from coals for proper cooking.

● **Ironing-Board Buffet**—Change your ironing board into a portable serving table. Keep it from tipping by placing sandbags over the bar or putting bricks against the legs. Cover it with a decorative tablecloth. Arrange plates, cups and flatware so people can pick them up as they go through the buffet line.

To make a spit for roasting a chicken, place a stack of three bricks (use bricks with three holes) on both sides of the wheelbarrow. Insert 1/2" dowels into the two outside holes in each stack of bricks. Push dowels through bricks into the dirt. Drill three holes 3" apart through the center of 1" dowel. Push dowel through chicken cavity. Secure chicken to dowel using heavy string, making sure string passes through the holes and around the chicken. This will insure that the chicken will turn as the stick is turned. The wheelbarrow can be placed on any flat area in the yard. In the evening the family can gather around the wheelbarrow "campfire" to enjoy a roasted chicken, roasted marshmallows, or hot dogs cooked on a stick.

■ Bleach Bottle Hand Wash

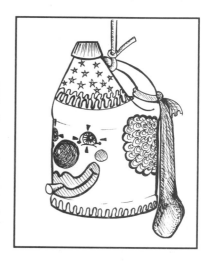

To keep water handy for washing hands and faces, you need an empty, thoroughly cleaned bleach bottle, golf tee, a length of rope, bar of soap, and an old clean pair of pantyhose. Puncture a small hole near bottom of bottle on side opposite handle. Plug hole with golf tee. Tie rope to handle of bottle. Place soap in the toe of pantyhose, then knot hose to handle of bottle. Fill bottle with water, capping the top securely. Tie free end of rope to a tree branch near the edge of camp at appropriate height. To use handwash, uncap bottle and remove tee. The water comes out in a small stream just right for washing up. Stop water by replacing bottle's lid.

● **Laundry Basket Ice Chest**—Take a laundry basket and line with a heavy-duty garbage bag or plastic. Fill with crushed ice and place pop cans and bottles down in ice to keep cool. If basket is too large, fill bottom half with crushed newspaper, then place plastic or garbage bag on top of newspaper.

● **Wheelbarrow Party-Server**—Line wheelbarrow with plastic and fill with ice. It is ideal for serving salads and canned pop. Wheelbarrow can be rolled to a convenient, shady spot for serving. Ice will keep drinks and salads cool.

188

Outdoor Cooking Magic

These tempting ideas will make you want to pack up your camping gear or just wander off to the nearest woods to try out this outdoor cooking magic. Imagine being able to say, "We're going on a dingle fan roast!"

■ Pineapple Upside-Down Cake

1 can pineapple slices
8-10 maraschino cherry halves
1/2 cup brown sugar
2-3 tbsps. pineapple juice
1 white or yellow cake mix, adjusted for altitude

Line a 10" Dutch oven with heavy-duty foil, turning it down at top edge of oven. Grease the foil on bottom and up sides with oil or butter. Line the bottom of the pan with pineapple slices and place half a maraschino cherry in middle of each pineapple slice. Sprinkle with brown sugar and pineapple juice. Prepare cake mix and pour over pineapple. Cover with lid and place in hot coals. Baking time can vary from 25-45 minutes, depending on how hot the coals are. Just check about every 5 minutes after the first 25.

■ Reflector Oven

Equipment needed: Cardboard box, aluminum foil, wire coat hanger, and large rocks.

Instructions: Cut the cardboard box in half diagonally and cover the inside of the box with aluminum foil, shiny side out, to reflect the heat. Place two or three wires from side to side in the middle of the box to make a shelf and then cover the shelf with foil. Place two large rocks under the back of the box to hold it up and brace it in front of the fire.

■ Dingle Fan Roaster

You can make a dingle fan roaster by resting a long pole on a large rock with one end of the pole anchored to the ground by another heavy rock. The free end of the pole will rise into the air near the fire. To this end of the pole, attach a length of chain about six inches long, then tie a heavy piece of string to the end of the chain. Tie a loop for a hook at the end of the string.

Using a wire or a green switch, make a loop about nine inches in diameter and cover it with a bandanna (by placing the bandanna over the loop and tying the four ends of the bandanna with a string and drawing them together) to form the dingle fan. Tie the handle of the loop (two to three inches away from the fan) to the string just below the chain and attach to the end of the handle (opposite the bandanna fan) a chunk of wood or stone to counterbalance the fan. Tie the roast or chicken with wire or heavy string, placing one hook at the top and another at the bottom of the meat so it can be rotated. Place a foil pan under the meat to catch the drippings. Baste the meat occasionally until it is well done. Be sure to keep the fire burning; the hot air will keep the fan turning.

The Right, Smart Way to Backpack

When you go backpacking, you are literally taking your home on your back. You'll need three basic essentials: shelter to keep out the elements, a warm bed, and food that is nourishing and easy to prepare at a reasonable price. Most important, you need to pack these items so that your pack weighs as little as possible. You also want to evenly distribute the weight in your pack to make it balanced and easier to carry.

● **You Will Need:** Pack, tent or tarp for a roof overhead, lightweight sleeping bag, air mattress (one that is self-inflating), cooking utensils (lightweight nesting pans to save space and a backpacker's stove, dishes, plates, cups, and cutlery), and food. Clothing: slacks or jeans; long-sleeved cotton shirt; lightweight jacket or parka; two pairs of socks, one lightweight and one wool; underwear; and raincoat or poncho. In addition, you'll also need a flashlight with extra batteries and bulb, first-aid kit, bug dope, map of backpacking trails in your area, suntan lotion, dark glasses, rope (nylon cord), and toilet tissue.

● **Travel Light:** Experienced backpackers pride themselves on traveling light. Here's a list of easy ways to cut down on the weight—even down to the ounce. ▲ Take small tubes of toothpaste that have only a little toothpaste left in them. ▲ Remove the cardboard tube from the roll of toilet tissue. ▲ Measure out the exact amount of food needed and pack it in resealable plastic bags—then use the bags to mix food and as serving dishes. ▲ Cut off the bottom three-fourths of a pair of jeans; stitch Velcro on the inside of the top portion of the jeans and on the outside of the bottom portion of the jeans. This way you avoid taking a pair of long pants and a pair of shorts. Simply remove bottom portion when you're hot and replace as it cools down. ▲ Carry scouring pads with built-in soap.

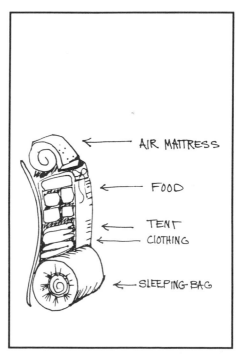

● **Packing a Pack:** Most people try to get by with lower weights: 30 pounds for a woman (maximum 40 pounds) and 40 to 50 pounds for an adult male. It all depends, however, upon the physical condition and experience of the individual, the terrain to be covered, the length of the trip, and the time of year. You might use the following plan to pack your backpack (see illustration): Put water bottle, first-aid supplies, jacket, and lunch in side pockets. ▲ To pack food: Although dehydrated food has progressed a long way, both in taste and variety, it is also expensive. Instead, use regular grocery items such as instant rice, instant potatoes, instant puddings, and other foods which call for water. Transfer each food item to a resealable plastic bag and either cut off instructions from box and tape inside bag or write instructions on bag with a waterproof pen. ▲ Pack staples in food tubes— such as peanut butter and jelly combined in one, or ketchup and mustard in another, etc. These can be purchased at any sporting goods store.

◆ *Put water bottle, first-aid supplies, jacket, and lunch in side pockets.*

Delegating Household Responsibilities

If you need ideas for delegating chores from the youngest child on up without complaints, try these tricks that will help get them done.

■ Task Chart for Tots

Preschool children can understand simple line charts with the name of a task and picture to remind the child what to do. Bedmaking line on chart might show picture of a bed. Cleaning-up-the-bedroom line might show picture of room with toys placed neatly on shelves. Draw series of empty squares after each picture. As child completes task, put foil star or colorful sticker in corresponding square.

Another method is to make a permanent chart with children's names, jobs, and a line of hooks on a board. On each hook hang disk with picture of tasks to be accomplished. As child completes task, turn disk over to reveal smiling face on the other side.

■ Cupcake Delegation

A novel way to assign household chores is to bake assignments into cupcakes or muffins. Write tasks on small slips of paper. Roll or fold papers in foil and place in bottom of cupcake liners in muffin tin. Fill liners with cupcake batter and bake. As you hand out cupcakes, you're delegating weekly chores! Assignments can even be placed in cupcake after baking. Variation: Place papers in bottom of flat ice-cream cones. Fill cones 2/3 full with cake batter. Place on baking sheet and bake.

■ Encouraging Proper Table Setting

Here's a way to teach children to set the table properly. Buy a plain-colored vinyl placemat for each family member and Contact paper to complement kitchen or dining room colors. Turn plate, glass, and flatware upside down on back on Contact paper. Trace silhouette and cut out. Remove backing from Contact paper and place silhouettes on placemats in appropriate spots. Children match flatware, plate, and glass to corresponding silhouettes to set table perfectly every time.

■ Early Bird Gets the Easiest Chore

To get the family up and going, list chores for the day or a special dinner on a blackboard. Assignments are chosen on a first-come, first-choice basis by each family member. For those who fail to follow through and complete tasks, it's cleanup and dish duty.

Spruce Up Your Garage

■ Storage

Since most of us use the garage for storage, begin by deciding what you want to store things in. You might purchase cardboard boxes with lids at a local stock box company (check your yellow pages). They measure 15 1/2" long, 12 1/2" wide, and 10 1/2" deep. Color code and label them according to specific needs. Example: Holidays—orange for Halloween, red for Christmas, etc. The size of the storage shelves is determined by the box measurements. If you want to store two boxes per shelf, have shelves built and painted to accommodate them. But be sure to determine what your personal needs are before you begin.

To store outdoor sports equipment such as basketballs, soccer balls, nets, toys, etc., you might hang a hammock from the ceiling on one side of the garage high enough to walk under.

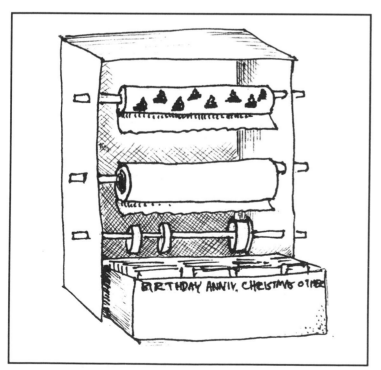

■ Gift Wrap Center

In one corner of the garage, you might want to build a gift wrap center. Wooden dowels are used to hold rolls of gift wrap and ribbon, with shelves above and a worktable below to store boxes and party supplies. Keep greeting cards on hand, filing them in manila folders under each occasion. The manila folders are stored in a box and placed on a shelf beneath the worktable.

Gifts can be purchased ahead and stored in a metal cabinet near the gift wrap center. They are wrapped and the contents of the package are noted on removable paper.

■ Garage Floor

To make a fun play surface on your garage floor, first clean bare cement with a mixture of water and muratic acid (check for this at your local paint store). Brush clean with an old broom, then let dry for a day.

After floor is completely dry, paint base coat of high gloss enamel paint using a roller and extension. Let dry thoroughly. Apply second coat and let dry.

Before painting roads, houses, etc., on floor, you may want to pencil in where you want to paint. Begin stenciling road by dipping a small square sponge into yellow enamel paint. Continue until road is complete. Let dry. For houses, trees, etc., you can purchase stencils at a crafts store. With masking tape, secure stencils to floor, dip sponge in paint, and dab paint until stencil is filled in. Carefully remove stencil. Repeat process until your creation is finished. This is a fun project to include your children in. Let them use their imaginations! (If you have a crack in the cement floor, try painting it like a river!)

■ Hopscotch Mat

▲ *To make, you'll need*: 7'10" x 3' piece of rubber-backed indoor/outdoor carpet, 5" number stencils 1-10 (purchase at office supply store), 1"-wide and 2"-wide rolls of masking tape, carpet knife, spray paint, piece of string, and black permanent marker.

▼ *Directions*: 1. To make semicircle at top of hopscotch mat: on rubber-backed side of carpet, measure 18" to center of carpet, then measure 19" down from top of carpet piece and mark with "X" (see Fig. 1). Tie a 24" length of string to black marker. Hold string on "X." Extend marker toward edge of carpet piece and draw half circle, holding marker and string taut. Cut with carpet knife. 2. Turn carpet over (to right side) and make markings with tape as illustrated in Fig. 1. 3. Place 1"-wide masking tape where indicated on Fig. 2. Place 2"-wide masking tape on both sides of 1"-wide masking tape. Remove 1"- wide masking tape. This is where you spray the paint to give your line markings. Tape numbered stencils to mat where indicated on Fig. 2. Spray paint; let dry. Remove stencils and tape, and your mat is finished.

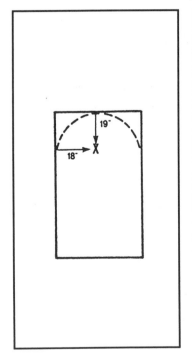

Fig. 1   *Fig. 2*

How to Hold a Successful Garage Sale

These days, it seems like everyone is having a yard sale. Some work, some don't. The ones that do work show a little creativity.

■ Advertise

1. There's usually no charge for placing an ad in neighborhood papers, so be creative when you write up your sale. A catch-phrase if you're going in with other friends is "multifamily sale." Remember to list items.
2. Make a sandwich board with creative drawings and descriptions and place on top of car roof. Park the car in a strategically visible spot.
3. Make a scarecrow out of two pieces of crossed wood; dress it in sale clothing with glued-on face and a sign on the front with sale information.

■ Lay It Out

1. Set up a homey refreshment stand—coffee, lemonade—free or at a nominal charge. It keeps them browsing.
2. Keep your electrical appliances near an outlet so they can be tested.
3. String up a clothesline to hang clothes. Make sure they're washed and ironed. A neat item sells faster.
4. Set up a changing room by hanging an umbrella upside down from a tree and hanging an old shower curtain hook on the tips.
5. Put hats on empty cartons and bottles of different sizes for an attractive display.

■ How Much Is It?

1. Antiques: Get a quote from a dealer. If items don't sell, you can always fall back on the dealer.
2. Collectibles: Do some research first, so you don't give things away. Comics, baseball cards, etc., are worth money these days.
3. Records: Oldies but goodies go for 50 cents to $1.
4. Paperbacks: 10 cents to 25 cents; hardbacks: $1-2.
5. Brick-a-brac and household: Try to keep under $1.
6. Appliances and electronics: Check in local newspaper, generally one-half to one-third retail price if in decent shape.

■ Freebies

The "free box" is a nifty idea, one for adults and one for children. Put in items you know you won't sell; limit one to a person. It gets people into the sale, and sometimes works on their "guilt factor" of feeling obligated to buy something after getting something for free.

■ Multifamily Garage Sales

To keep track of who sold what, color code your items and have matching cash boxes at the desk.

Store Stuff Step-by-Step

Think you've run out of storage space? Think there's not one square inch left in your home to organize what is politely called "stuff?" There is lots of extra space under the basement or attic steps—not under the bottom, but under the tread of each step—and it doesn't matter whether your stairs have risers or not. How's that for creating space?

▲ *For each stair tread unit, you'll need*: Two plastic dish pans (make sure they have a lip on them and are no deeper than your stair is high), three strips of pine wood 1 1/2" x 1" x 12", one strip of 1/4" x 2 1/2" x 12" plywood, two strips of 1/4" x 2" x 12" plywood, six wood screws about 1 3/4" long, screwdriver, and pencil.

▼ *Directions*: 1. Begin by making runners for the pans to slide in and out on. Layer one strip of pine with one strip of the 2"-wide plywood, long sides even. This piece will be put under the stair tread and as far to one side as possible (see illustration). Screw into place at the front and back of the tread. (You may need to predrill the screw holes.) 2. Slide the lip of the pan along the edge of the plywood and hold it in place. With a pencil, mark the placement of the other side of the pan on the stair tread. 3. Center the second piece of pine on the 2 1/2" piece of plywood, leaving a 1/2" edge on either side. Line the pine up with the mark on the tread and screw into place. (You may want to place this runner just slightly wider than your mark to make sliding the pan out easier.) 4. Repeat the procedure with the last pieces of wood to make the outside runner for the second pan. Label each pan and slide it into place. You can put storage under every stair tread if you like. One very important safety precaution must be taken if using this type of storage on a stair with no riser—the pan must always be pushed back into place—never left open for someone to trip on!

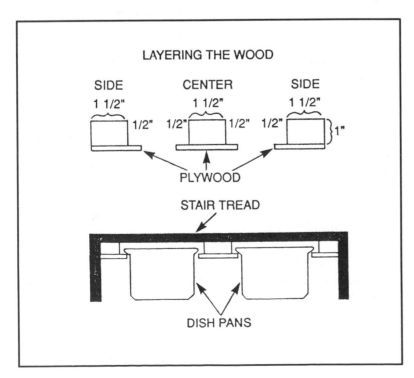

LAYERING THE WOOD

SIDE 1 1/2"   CENTER 1 1/2"   SIDE 1 1/2"

1/2"   1/2"   1/2"   1/2"   1"

PLYWOOD

STAIR TREAD

DISH PANS

◆ *Variations*: This same technique can be used for larger bins attached to the ceiling in a basement or storage room. Additional storage hints: Remember that hammock you had to make room to store last fall? Instead of letting it take up space, let it help you store other seasonal items. Just hang it up high in the corner of the basement or garage and store balls, cushions, etc., in it. If you have an unfinished ceiling in a basement, the space between the floor joists can be used to store long items such as skis. Simply screw pine strips, spacing them two or three feet apart, across two joists, allowing the skis to rest on the strips between the joists.

Take the Eye of a Potato . . .

If you can see seeds from lemons and eyes from a potato, you can see trees. Follow these directions and don't throw any kitchen scraps away. All you need in order to succeed is a supply of good quality commercial potting soil, a small pot or container, and clear plastic bags.

■ To Plant Seeds

As you use lemons, oranges, or other citrus fruits, take out the seeds or pits, rinse them off, and place them in a small dish of water. Allow them to soak for about 24 hours to soften the outside covering. For seeds that have a hard outer shell, remove or peel off the outer layer. Plant the soaked seeds about 1/2" deep in damp potting soil. Cover the entire pot by slipping it inside a plastic bag and zipping or tying the bag shut. Moisture will condense from the damp soil onto the bag and "rain" back onto the soil to water the seed. Do not place the bagged and potted seed in direct sunlight, or it will bake and not germinate.

Watch for a tiny white or green shoot. When you see the shoot, remove the plastic covering and place the pot in a warm (65-70 degrees), well-lighted place. Keep the soil damp, not wet. As pairs of leaves form, plants can be replanted into larger pots.

■ To Plant Avocado Pits

Remove pit and wash it off. Stick a toothpick into each of the four sides of the pit at equal distances from the ends of the pit. Then suspend toothpicks on top of a clear glass or jar and you can watch roots form on the new plant. Be sure that the flat end of the pit is in the water and keep the water over that end of the pit. After roots have formed, plant the pit in a 6" pot and place the pot in a warm, light place. Keep the soil damp. Transplant as the new avocado plant grows.

■ To Plant Sweet Potato

Use toothpicks placed around the center of the sweet potato to suspend the end in water (same procedure as for the avocado pit). When the roots and shoots start to grow, transplant into a container of potting soil.

■ To Plant Pineapple

Carefully twist the top from a fresh pineapple. Pull off four or five leaves from the bottom of the "crown" and place in a dry, shady place for a couple of weeks. This allows the bottom of the "crown" to dry to prevent rotting, and it allows the plant to become acclimatized to your house. After several weeks, plant the crown in potting soil in an 8" pot. A red clay pot with good drainage is best for pineapple. Keep the soil damp. Transplant as the pineapple grows.

Fun at Home with Dian Thomas

INDEX

NESTING, COCOONING, BURROWING...

It's what America is doing in the '90s—
And Dian Thomas shows how to make it easy and fun!

Americans are finding their greatest pleasures at home. Enjoying their families. Entertaining their friends. And they're looking for ways to do it that are cheaper and easier—and more fun.

Dian Thomas has been showing America how to do just that on major television shows. She's a regular on ABC's *Home* show and has appeared on NBC's Today and The Tonight Show. She has delighted audiences with her innovative–and sometimes zany–ideas.

Now you can get in on the excitement. Choose from Dian's complete assortment of books, videos and craft kits and mail in the order form. Or to order toll free, call 1-800-8-HOME-55.

And let the fun begin!

FUN AT HOME WITH DIAN THOMAS

Dian's latest! This all-new collection of creative ideas demonstrated on ABC's Home show has something for everyone. Dian shows you how to to keep the kids busy on a rainy day. Organize a Superbowl or Oscar-night party. Make Kick-the-Can ice cream or craft attractive holiday decorations. Don't miss it! Contains 203 pages with over 500 illustrations. **$14.95 each**

ROUGHING IT EASY

Even the camp cooks have fun when they're Roughing It Easy. This New York Times best-seller is chock full of recipes and great ideas that make outdoor cooking an adventure, such as cooking eggs and bacon in a paper bag or boiling water in a paper cup. Includes equipment lists, campsite information and first aid hints. Great for backyard fun and family gatherings, too. 203 pages.
~~**$12.95 each**~~
14.99

TODAY'S TIPS FOR EASY LIVING

Contains 400 terrific ideas for today's time-strapped families. Features recipes for handy breakfasts, bag lunches and quick-prep meals, plus party/special occasion ideas. Also includes instructions for homemade toys, rainy-day activities, kids' costumes and more. 160 pages with 265 photographs.
$12.95 each

"U-Can-Do . . ." VIDEOS ▲

Discover for yourself that U-Can-Do it! Dian gives you step-by-step instructions for holiday decorations and party ideas. Patterns included. Please order by title. **$9.95 each**

Let's Party
Quick and Easy Holiday Ideas
Creating Fun & Easy Toy Projects

"Can-Do" Crafts for Adults I
"Can-Do" Crafts for Kids I

CREATIVE PACKETS ▶

Create your own fun by making up one of Dian's creative packets. Please order by title.
$4.95 each

Pet Purses
Tomato Cage Dolls
Kiddy Packs

▲ NEW!
THE DIAN THOMAS HOME LIBRARY

Brings together Dian's most popular products in a handsome plastic case. Includes Today's Tips for Easy Living, Roughing It Easy and Fun at Home with Dian Thomas, plus the exciting all-new audio cassette *Developing Your Creative Spirit*.
$59.95 each

- - - - - - - - - - - - - - CUT ON DOTTED LINE - - - - - - - - - - - - - -

ORDER BY MAIL OR CALL TOLL FREE 1-800-8-HOME-55

Complete form below, detach and send with payment or credit card information to:
The Dian Thomas Company, P.O. Box 171107, Holladay, UT 84117
(To keep this sheet, send photocopy or hand-written order.)

Name _____

Address _____

City/State/ZIP _____

Telephone (   ) _____

____Check/Money Order (please, no currency)
    Make checks payable to: **The Dian Thomas Co.**

____VISA ____MasterCard

____Discover

CARD ACCOUNT NUMBER (PLEASE LIST ALL NUMBERS ON CARD)

Expiration Date_____Customer Signature _____

DESCRIPTION	QTY	UNIT PRICE	TOTAL

*Add $2.50 shipping/handling for first item, $1.00 for each additional item.

Subtotal $_____

Shipping and handling* $_____

Utah residents add 6.25% sales tax $_____

TOTAL $_____

● Canadian residents add 20% to price and postage.

Dear Friends,

Thank you for all your incredible support through the years. Creativity is my spice to life and I love sharing it with you on T.V., in books, and with friends.

May these ideas open your mind and heart to the wide world of fun through creativity. Love,

Dian